Listening & Speaking 2

A Revised Edition of
Get It? Got It!

....

Mary McVey Gill

Pamela Hartmann

THOMSON

HEINLE

United States • Australia • Canada • Mexico • Singapore • Spain • United Kingdom

To our mothers, Bea Hartmann and Mary Elizabeth McVey

THOMSON

HEINLE

Developmental Editors: Jennifer Monaghan, Jill Korey O'Sullivan
Sr. Production Coordinator: Maryellen E. Killeen
Market Development Director: Charlotte Sturdy
Sr. Manufacturing Coordinator: Mary Beth Hennebury
Interior Design: Julia Gecha
Illustrations: Pre-Press Company, Inc., Len Shalansky
Photo Research: Martha Friedman

Cover Design: Ha Nguyen Design
Cover Images: PhotoDisc®
Composition/Production: Pre-Press Company, Inc.
Freelance Production Editor: Janet McCartney
Copyeditor: Donald Pharr
Printer/Binder: Bawden

For permission to use material from this text, contact us:
web   www.thomsonrights.com
fax   1-800-730-2215
phone   1-800-730-2214

For photo credits, see page 245.
For international contact
information, see inside
back cover.

Heinle
25 Thomson Place
Boston, MA 02210

Library of Congress Cataloging-in-Publication Data
Gill, Mary McVey.
   Tapestry listening & speaking 2 / Mary McVey Gill, Pamela Hartmann.
      p. cm.
   ISBN 0-8384-0016-7 (alk. paper)
   1. English language—Textbooks for foreign speakers. 2. English language—Spoken
English—Problems, exercises, etc. 3. Listening—Problems, exercises, etc. I. Title:
Tapestry listening and speaking two. II. Hartmann, Pamela. III. Title.

PE1128 .G524 2000
428.3'4—dc21   99-057629

 This book is printed on acid-free recycled paper.

Printed in the United States of America.
   4 5 6 7 8 9 04 03 02

A VERY SPECIAL THANK YOU

The publisher and authors would like to thank the following coordinators and instructors who have offered many helpful insights and suggestions for change throughout the development of the new *Tapestry*.

Alicia Aguirre, *Cañada College*
Fred Allen, *Mission College*
Maya Alvarez-Galvan, *University of Southern California*
Geraldine Arbach, *Collège de l'Outaouais, Canada*
Dolores Avila, *Pasadena City College*
Sarah Bain, *Eastern Washington University*
Kate Baldus, *San Francisco State University*
Fe Baran, *Chabot College*
Gail Barta, *West Valley College*
Karen Bauman, *Biola University*
Liza Becker, *Mt. San Antonio College*
Leslie Biaggi, *Miami-Dade Community College*
Andrzej Bojarczak, *Pasadena City College*
Nancy Boyer, *Golden West College*
Glenda Bro, *Mt. San Antonio College*
Brooke Brummitt, *Palomar College*
Linda Caputo, *California State University, Fresno*
Alyce Campbell, *Mt. San Antonio College*
Barbara Campbell, *State University of New York, Buffalo*
Robin Carlson, *Cañada College*
Ellen Clegg, *Chapman College*
Karin Cintron, *Aspect ILS*
Diane Colvin, *Orange Coast College*
Martha Compton, *University of California, Irvine*
Nora Dawkins, *Miami-Dade Community College*
Beth Erickson, *University of California, Davis*
Charles Estus, *Eastern Michigan University*
Gail Feinstein Forman, *San Diego City College*
Jeffra Flaitz, *University of South Florida*
Kathleen Flynn, *Glendale Community College*
Ann Fontanella, *City College of San Francisco*
Sally Gearhart, *Santa Rosa Junior College*
Alice Gosak, *San José City College*
Kristina Grey, *Northern Virginia Community College*
Tammy Guy, *University of Washington*
Gail Hamilton, *Hunter College*
Patty Heiser, *University of Washington*
Virginia Heringer, *Pasadena City College*
Catherine Hirsch, *Mt. San Antonio College*

Helen Huntley, *West Virginia University*
Nina Ito, *California State University, Long Beach*
Patricia Jody, *University of South Florida*
Diana Jones, *Angloamericano, Mexico*
Loretta Joseph, *Irvine Valley College*
Christine Kawamura, *California State University, Long Beach*
Gregory Keech, *City College of San Francisco*
Kathleen Keesler, *Orange Coast College*
Daryl Kinney, *Los Angeles City College*
Maria Lerma, *Orange Coast College*
Mary March, *San José State University*
Heather McIntosh, *University of British Columbia, Canada*
Myra Medina, *Miami-Dade Community College*
Elizabeth Mejia, *Washington State University*
Cristi Mitchell, *Miami-Dade Community College*
Sylvette Morin, *Orange Coast College*
Blanca Moss, *El Paso Community College*
Karen O'Neill, *San José State University*
Bjarne Nielsen, *Central Piedmont Community College*
Katy Ordon, *Mission College*
Luis Quesada, *Miami-Dade Community College*
Gustavo Ramírez Toledo, *Colegio Cristóbol Colón, Mexico*
Nuha Salibi, *Orange Coast College*
Alice Savage, *North Harris College*
Dawn Schmid, *California State University, San Marcos*
Mary Kay Seales, *University of Washington*
Denise Selleck, *City College of San Francisco*
Gail Slater, *Brooklyn and Staten Island Superintendency*
Susanne Spangler, *East Los Angeles College*
Karen Stanley, *Central Piedmont Community College*
Sara Storm, *Orange Coast College*
Margaret Teske, *ELS Language Centers*
Maria Vargas-O'Neel, *Miami-Dade Community College*
James Wilson, *Mt. San Antonio College and Pasadena City College*
Karen Yoshihara, *Foothill College*

ACKNOWLEDGMENTS

Thanks to Erik Gundersen, the acquiring editor, for his expertise in shaping the new *Tapestry;* to Jennifer Monaghan for her editorial guidance; and to Jill Kinkade for her support and assistance. A special thank you to William Logan for his recording of "Sometimes I Feel Like a Motherless Child" and an affectionate thanks to Bea Hartmann, Mary Elizabeth and Richard McVey, and John Gill for their help in finding materials and for their constant support.

CHAPTER	LISTENING & SPEAKING SKILLS FOCUS	LANGUAGE LEARNING STRATEGIES
1 The Whole World Is Your Classroom Page 2	Practicing English with native speakers Beginning a conversation Making small talk Introducing someone Apologizing Expressing thanks Ending a conversation	When you listen to a teacher's lecture, pay special attention whenever the teacher emphasizes or repeats points. Pay attention to a speaker's intonation.
2 Change and Choice Page 22	Asking for, understanding, and giving directions Communicating when using public transportation Speaking to landlords about a problem	Get information by taking a poll. Be aware of tone of voice.
3 This Is Who I Am Page 44	Understanding speech reductions Asking questions when you don't understand something Using gerunds Expressing encouragement when someone is telling a story	Organize your ideas before telling a story. Listen for stressed words when people speak.
4 Health: Getting the Most Out of Life Page 66	Ordering food in restaurants Giving advice about health	Brainstorm to explore your ideas. Be aware that not all accents in English are the same.
5 When Cultures Meet Page 90	Avoiding forming stereotypes Using modals of suggestion	Take notes when you listen to a lecture. Learn to distinguish between the main idea and supporting details when listening to a speaker.

![] ACADEMIC POWER STRATEGIES	![CNN] CNN VIDEO CLIPS	PRONUNCIATION: THE SOUND OF IT	![] LISTENING OPPORTUNITIES
Seek out native speakers as conversation partners and make small talk with them.	"Singlish" This CNN segment introduces a new dictionary of English words and idioms that are used specifically in Singapore—in other words, a dictionary of Singlish.	Understanding intonation in tag questions	Listening 1: a lecture given by a teacher about effective ways to learn English Listening 2: four conversations between people making small talk Listening 3: Four conversations between people in specific situations (introducing someone new, excusing yourself, apologizing, and expressing thanks)
Keep a journal.	"Moving Day" An interview with an American family on a day when they are moving to another city; they talk about how they feel about the move, the changes in their lives, special difficulties for the children, and so on.	Understanding reductions	Listening 1: a conversation between neighbors about how to find things in the neighborhood Listening 2: two conversations between a passenger and two different bus drivers Listening 3: a conversation between an apartment renter and her landlord Listening 4: an immigrant to California gives her opinion about the American lifestyle and the mobility of Americans
Make realistic goals for yourself in order to start working towards your academic and professional dreams.	"Frank McCourt" The best-selling author Frank McCourt survived a childhood of poverty and hunger, but he is able to find humor shining through the tragedy.	Understanding intonation in questions with *or* Understanding reductions	Listening 1: six people talk about their interests Listening 2: a person talks about her job Listening 3: four people talk about their goals and their plans to reach these goals
Work in groups to help improve your English.	"Healthy Aging" This segment explores healthy aging from an international perspective. It describes things that you can do at any age (young or old) to be healthy in the future.	Listening for stressed words— *can* or *can't?*	Listening 1: two conversations that take place in a restaurant Listening 2: five people talk about what they do to get exercise Listening 3: four people talk about how stress affects their health habits Listening 4: an interview with a health expert Listening 5: a television show about older people
Avoid making stereotypes	"Britain's Changing Society" The British people are famous for their belief in a class system and for not showing emotion. However, this CNN segment suggests that things might be changing.	Understanding reductions	Listening 1: a lecture about culture shock Listening 2: three people talk about their experience with culture shock Listening 3: two people tell about experiences that they had when they first arrived in a country new to them

CHAPTER	LISTENING & SPEAKING SKILLS FOCUS	LANGUAGE LEARNING STRATEGIES
6 **What Do You Mean? Thought and Communication** Page 110	Recognizing differences between men's and women's communication styles Making an appointment	Pay attention to people's intonation, not just their words. Learn how to respond to a negative question—or more specifically, a negative statement with intonation that goes up at the end.
7 **Making Friends and Finding Love** Page 134	Making invitations and suggestions Recognizing the difference between general and specific invitations Accepting and declining invitations Sharing ideas and working together with your classmates Asking personal questions in a polite way Understanding meaning from intonation Organizing and giving a short report	Pay attention to a speaker's choice of words when the person is making an invitation. Make inferences in English, as in your first language, by paying attention to the entire context.
8 **Tell Me What I Want: Advertising . . . and Shopping** Page 152	Understanding messages on message machines Finding opportunities to practice English outside the classroom Making a purchase Returning something to a store Expressing agreement and disagreement	Think ahead and predict what people will say. Learn to understand incomplete sentences.
9 **What's in the News?** Page 176	Understanding weather reports Describing the weather Understanding news headlines and stories Expressing agreement and disagreement	Summarize what you hear or read. Improve your language skills by watching the news on television on an English channel.
10 **Planethood** Page 196	Using ecology-related vocabulary Working with other students to think of solutions to environmental problems	Use new words as soon—and as often—as possible. Notice and understand parts of words as a way to determine meaning.

Listening Transcripts   Page 214

Skills Index   Page 241

ACADEMIC POWER STRATEGIES	CNN VIDEO CLIPS	PRONUNCIATION: THE SOUND OF IT	LISTENING OPPORTUNITIES
Become aware of your stereotypes and *be open-minded* about changing them.	"Workplace Communication" Some problems in the workplace are the result of the different communication styles of women and men. The CNN segment explores one possible solution.	Understanding reductions	Listening 1: a talk given by an expert on language and an expert on human culture Listening 2: statements indicating the speakers' level of enthusiasm Listening 3: three telephone conversations in response to notices on a college bulletin board
Share ideas and work together with your classmates.	"Romance Survey in Japan" This segment gives the result of a survey about romance. It answers this question: What do Japanese men and women think about each other's ability to be romantic?	Listening for stressed words	Listening 1: a famous American storyteller, Garrison Keillor, tells about an experience on a New York street Listening 2: four conversations in which one person invites the other person to do something Listening 3: an author, Robert Rand, talks about affectionate nicknames that his parents used for each other and ones that he and his wife use for each other Listening 4: an advertisement for a pasta company illustrating the importance of intonation
Find opportunities to practice English outside the classroom.	"Jeans for Everyone" Commercials for relaxed-fit (larger) jeans are the topic here. A psychologist talks about image and how not all people look like the models in the commercials. There may be room for all of us (slim or not) in today's advertising.	Understanding incomplete sentences	Listening 1: radio advertisements Listening 2: the message on the answering machine in a bicycle store Listening 3: a conversation between a customer and a salesclerk in a computer store Listening 4: an advertisement for a telecommunications company Listening 5: an advertisement for a television network
Use today's technology to find out about the news and practice your English at the same time.	"Violence in the Media" This segment examines a possible relationship between violence in real life (for instance, murders at high schools) and violence on television.	Understanding numbers	Listening 1: four short weather reports from the morning news Listening 2: five news stories Listening 3: an advertisement for a television news show
Be careful to choose the correct definition when you use a dictionary.	"Ecotourism in Brazil" Ecotourism is becoming more popular in Brazil. This segment presents two benefits and one drawback of this trend.	Pronouncing the *t* in the middle of words	Listening 1: six people talk about what they do to help the environment Listening 2: a radio report about plastic and its effects on the environment Listening 3: a radio report about a city in Brazil that is solving environmental problems

Welcome to TAPESTRY!

Empower your students with the **Tapestry Listening & Speaking** series!

Language learning can be seen as an ever-developing tapestry woven with many threads and colors. The elements of the tapestry are related to different language skills such as listening and speaking, reading, and writing; the characteristics of the teachers; the desires, needs, and backgrounds of the students; and the general second language development process. When all of these elements are working together harmoniously, the result is a colorful, continuously growing tapestry of language competence of which the student and the teacher can be proud.

Tapestry is built upon a framework of concepts that helps students become proficient in English and prepared for the academic and social challenges in college and beyond. The following principles underlie the instruction provided in all of the components of the **Tapestry** program:

◈ Empowering students to be responsible for their learning

◈ Using Language Learning Strategies and Academic Power Strategies to enhance one's learning, both in and out of the classroom

◈ Offering motivating activities that recognize a variety of learning styles

◈ Providing authentic and meaningful input to heighten learning and communication

◈ Learning to understand and value different cultures

◈ Integrating language skills to increase communicative competence

◈ Providing goals and ongoing self-assessment to monitor progress

Guide to **Tapestry Listening & Speaking**

Setting Goals focuses students' attention on the learning they will do in each chapter.

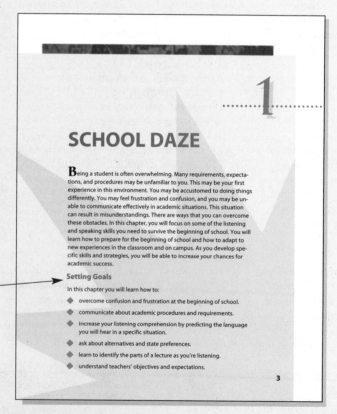

1

SCHOOL DAZE

Being a student is often overwhelming. Many requirements, expectations, and procedures may be unfamiliar to you. This may be your first experience in this environment. You may be accustomed to doing things differently. You may feel frustration and confusion, and you may be unable to communicate effectively in academic situations. This situation can result in misunderstandings. There are ways that you can overcome these obstacles. In this chapter, you will focus on some of the listening and speaking skills you need to survive the beginning of school. You will learn how to prepare for the beginning of school and how to adapt to new experiences in the classroom and on campus. As you develop specific skills and strategies, you will be able to increase your chances for academic success.

Setting Goals

In this chapter you will learn how to:

◈ overcome confusion and frustration at the beginning of school.

◈ communicate about academic procedures and requirements.

◈ increase your listening comprehension by predicting the language you will hear in a specific situation.

◈ ask about alternatives and state preferences.

◈ learn to identify the parts of a lecture as you're listening.

◈ understand teachers' objectives and expectations.

3

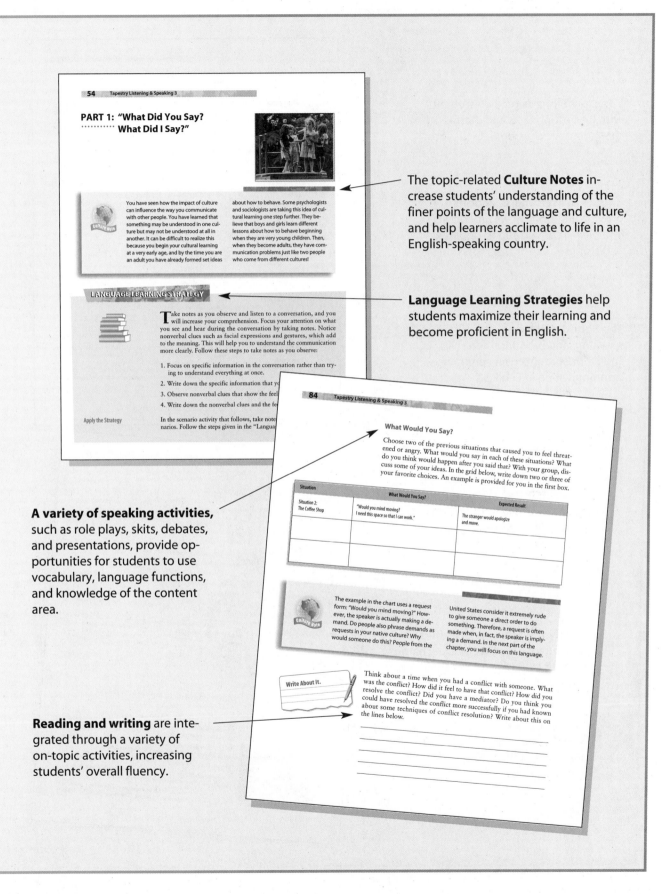

PART 1: "What Did You Say? What Did I Say?"

You have seen how the impact of culture can influence the way you communicate with other people. You have learned that something may be understood in one culture but may not be understood at all in another. It can be difficult to realize this because you begin your cultural learning at a very early age, and by the time you are an adult you have already formed set ideas about how to behave. Some psychologists and sociologists are taking this idea of cultural learning one step further. They believe that boys and girls learn different lessons about how to behave beginning when they are very young children. Then, when they become adults, they have communication problems just like two people who come from different cultures!

LANGUAGE LEARNING STRATEGY

Take notes as you observe and listen to a conversation, and you will increase your comprehension. Focus your attention on what you see and hear during the conversation by taking notes. Notice nonverbal clues such as facial expressions and gestures, which add to the meaning. This will help you to understand the communication more clearly. Follow these steps to take notes as you observe:

1. Focus on specific information in the conversation rather than trying to understand everything at once.

2. Write down the specific information that yo...

3. Observe nonverbal clues that show the feel...

4. Write down the nonverbal clues and the fee...

Apply the Strategy

In the scenario activity that follows, take note... narios. Follow the steps given in the "Langua...

The topic-related **Culture Notes** increase students' understanding of the finer points of the language and culture, and help learners acclimate to life in an English-speaking country.

Language Learning Strategies help students maximize their learning and become proficient in English.

What Would You Say?

Choose two of the previous situations that caused you to feel threatened or angry. What would you say in each of these situations? What do you think would happen after you said that? With your group, discuss some of your ideas. In the grid below, write down two or three of your favorite choices. An example is provided for you in the first box.

Situation	What Would You Say?	
Situation 2: The Coffee Shop	"Would you mind moving? I need this space so that I can work."	Expected Result — The stranger would apologize and move.

The example in the chart uses a request form: "Would you mind moving?" However, the speaker is actually making a demand. Do people also phrase demands as requests in your native culture? Why would someone do this? People from the United States consider it extremely rude to give someone a direct order to do something. Therefore, a request is often made when, in fact, the speaker is implying a demand. In the next part of the chapter, you will focus on this language.

Write About It.

Think about a time when you had a conflict with someone. What was the conflict? How did it feel to have that conflict? How did you resolve the conflict? Did you have a mediator? Do you think you could have resolved the conflict more successfully if you had known about some techniques of conflict resolution? Write about this on the lines below.

_____

_____

_____

_____

A variety of speaking activities, such as role plays, skits, debates, and presentations, provide opportunities for students to use vocabulary, language functions, and knowledge of the content area.

Reading and writing are integrated through a variety of on-topic activities, increasing students' overall fluency.

Tapestry Threads provide students with interesting facts and quotes that jumpstart classroom discussions.

Engaging listening selections provide authentic news broadcasts, interviews, conversations, debates, and stories.

The Sound of It refines listening, speaking, and pronunciation skills, and helps students gain confidence communicating in English.

Academic Power Strategies give students the knowledge and skills to become successful, independent learners.

Apply the Strategy activities encourage students to take charge of their learning and use their new skills and strategies.

CNN® video clips provide authentic input and further develop listening and speaking skills.

REAL PEOPLE/REAL VOICES

◆ **Getting Ready to Listen**

> The world is so fast that there are days when the person who says it can't be done is interrupted by the person who is doing it.
>
> —ANONYMOUS

You are going to hear two people talking about the stress in their lives. Andrew is a student who has just finished his first semester at college. Henry is a working man with children. For each of them, make one prediction about what causes them stress. Write down your prediction on the line.

Andrew—college student

I think _____ causes Andrew stress.

Henry—working parent

I think _____ causes Henry stress.

◆ **Listen**

Listening 1: Andrew's and Henry's Experiences

Write A if the statement is true about Andrew and H if the statement is true about Henry.

1. _____ Worries give him the most stress.
2. _____ He has a frantic schedule.
3. _____ Academic pressure makes him nervous.
4. _____ He worries about his kids.
5. _____ Sport helps him to deal with stress.
6. _____ Solving one problem at a time helps him to deal with stress.

◆ **After You Listen**

For each of the two speakers you heard on the tape, give a suggestion for how he can deal with his stress.

Andrew: _____

Henry: _____

◆ **The Sound of It: "Filler" Sounds and Words**

In spoken language, a *filler* is a sound or word that fills in the space and gives the speaker time to think before continuing. In spoken English, "um" is the most common filler. It's important to recognize this sound so that you don't confuse it with part of another word. Listen to the tape again, and count the number of times each speaker uses the filler "um."

Andrew: _____

Henry: _____

ACADEMIC POWER STRATEGY

Contribute your ideas in group activities. Actively participating in group activities helps you remember your ideas and gives your teacher a chance to see you working hard to succeed in class. There are some easy things you can do to practice speaking in group discussions:

1. Ask questions. Ask your teacher. Ask other students. Show that you are interested and want to learn.
2. Use your notes to help prepare ideas you can share.
3. Paraphrase—repeat in your own words an idea from a lecture, discussion, or activity.
4. If you have something to say but it's not a good time, make a note to yourself and save your good idea to share later in the discussion.

Apply the Strategy

In small groups, discuss your observation of each simulation based on your notes in the grid. Be sure that everyone in the group contributes ideas. Compare your responses to other members of your group. Do you agree or disagree on the problem, the reason, and the perception?

TUNING IN: "The Bilingual Storyteller"

You will see a CNN video clip about a man who tries to help children be proud of their cultural identities. Before you watch the clip, talk with a partner and answer these questions.

Do you think it is easier for children or adults to adapt to a culture that is different from the culture of their families?

Why do you think this?

What are some of the things parents and other adults can do to help children become comfortable in a new culture?

Antonio is a teacher. He tells stories to children. He tells the stories in a mix of English and Spanish. The stories help the children

Test-Taking Tips offer students practical steps for improving their test results.

Check Your Progress helps students monitor their own progress.

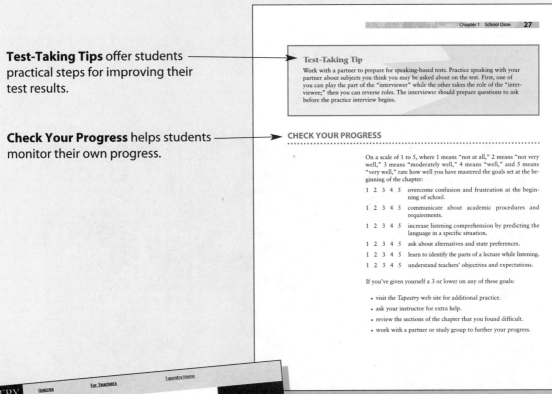

Test-Taking Tip

Work with a partner to prepare for speaking-based tests. Practice speaking with your partner about subjects you think you may be asked about on the test. First, one of you can play the part of the "interviewer" while the other takes the role of the "interviewee;" then you can reverse roles. The interviewer should prepare questions to ask before the practice interview begins.

CHECK YOUR PROGRESS

On a scale of 1 to 5, where 1 means "not at all," 2 means "not very well," 3 means "moderately well," 4 means "well," and 5 means "very well," rate how well you have mastered the goals set at the beginning of the chapter:

1 2 3 4 5   overcome confusion and frustration at the beginning of school.

1 2 3 4 5   communicate about academic procedures and requirements.

1 2 3 4 5   increase listening comprehension by predicting the language in a specific situation.

1 2 3 4 5   ask about alternatives and state preferences.

1 2 3 4 5   learn to identify the parts of a lecture while listening.

1 2 3 4 5   understand teachers' objectives and expectations.

If you've given yourself a 3 or lower on any of these goals:

- visit the *Tapestry* web site for additional practice.
- ask your instructor for extra help.
- review the sections of the chapter that you found difficult.
- work with a partner or study group to further your progress.

Expand your classroom at Tapestry Online
www.tapestry.heinle.com

- Online Quizzes
- Instructor's Manuals
- Opportunities to use and expand the Academic Power Strategies
- More!

For a well-integrated curriculum, try the **Tapestry Reading** series and the **Tapestry Writing** series, also from Heinle & Heinle.

To learn more about the **Tapestry** principles, read *The Tapestry of Language Learning,* by Rebecca L. Oxford and Robin C. Scarcella, also from Heinle & Heinle Publishers. ISBN 0-8384-2359-0.

What language do these students probably use in most of their classes? What language(s) might they speak with their friends and family? What are some ways in which they can learn another language?

THE WHOLE WORLD IS YOUR CLASSROOM

Many students need years to learn a new language. They might spend several hours a day in the classroom and more time, after class, on homework. But most people find that they can learn a lot even when they aren't in a language class. In this chapter, you'll find out how to improve your English outside the classroom, and you'll practice starting conversations, making small talk, and ending conversations. You'll also see a CNN segment about the use of language in Singapore.

Setting Goals

In this chapter you will learn:

◈ some good things to do to learn a language.

◈ to pay attention to emphasis and repetition in lectures.

◈ how to practice English with native speakers.

◈ how to begin a conversation.

◈ how to make small talk.

◈ how to understand intonation in tag questions.

◈ to pay attention to a speaker's intonation.

◈ how to introduce someone.

◈ how to apologize.

◈ how to express thanks.

◈ how to end a conversation.

Getting Started

Here are some quotations about language. What does each one mean? Discuss them in a small group.

Language is a steed [horse] that carries one into a far country.
—Arab proverb

The strength of one is the tongue, and speech is mightier [more powerful] than all fighting.
—Ptahhotep (Egypt, 3400 B.C.)

A person who speaks two languages is worth two people.
—Spanish proverb

Just as birds have wings, man has language.
—George Henry Lewes

Getting Ready to Read

Making Predictions Look at the picture on page 5 and answer these questions:

1. What time of day is it?

2. Who are the people in the picture?

3. What might be their nationality?

4. What are they talking about?

5. What might be important to these people?

Vocabulary Building

The following words are taken from the reading on pages 5–6. Match the definition with the word on the left. If necessary, use a dictionary or ask your teacher for help.

1. _____ dirt-poor   a. breathe in

2. _____ recall   b. without any money at all

3. _____ clattering   c. a book of maps

4. _____ dialect   d. noisy

5. _____ inhale   e. variety of a language

6. _____ atlas   f. remember

7. _____ conducted   g. a book or set of books with information on many subjects

8. _____ encyclopedia   h. led

Read

Read this excerpt from a book by psychologist/author Leo Buscaglia. When you finish reading, put any words that are important to you in a Vocabulary Log. A vocabulary log is a thin notebook or a section of your binder. In this, each day, you will put new words that you want to remember. For each new word, include the following information:

- the word and its part of speech (Is it a noun? Verb? Adjective?)
- a sentence with the word in it (find a sentence in the reading or in a dictionary)
- the meaning of the word

Our Dinner Table University

1   When Papa was growing up at the turn of the century in a village in northern Italy, education was for the rich. Papa was the son of a **dirt-poor** farmer. He used to tell us that he couldn't **recall** a single day when he wasn't working. He was taken from school in the fifth grade and went to work in a factory.

2   The world became his school. He was interested in everything. He read all the books, magazines, and newspapers he could lay his hands on. He loved to listen to the town elders and learn about the world beyond this tiny region that was home to generations of Buscaglias before him.

3   Papa insisted that we learn at least one new thing each day. And dinner seemed the perfect time for sharing what we had learned that day. Naturally, as children, we thought this was crazy.

4   When my brother and sisters and I got together in the bathroom to clean up for dinner, the question was: "What did *you* learn today?" If the answer was "Nothing," we did not dare sit at the table without first finding a fact in our much-used **encyclopedia.** "The population of Nepal is . . ."

5   Now, with our fact, we were ready for dinner. I can still see the table, with mountains of pasta so large that I was often unable to see my sister sitting across the table from me.

6   Dinner was a noisy time of **clattering** dishes and conversations, **conducted** in an Italian **dialect** since Mama didn't speak English.

7   Then came the time to share the day's new learning. Papa, at the head of the table, would push back his chair, pour a glass of red wine, light up a cigar, and **inhale** deeply.

8   Finally, his attention would settle on one of us. "Felice," he'd say, "tell me what you learned today."

9   "I learned the population of Nepal is . . ."

10   Silence.

11   First, Papa would think about it. "The population of Nepal. Hmmm. Well."

12   He would then look down the table at Mama, fixing her favorite fruit in a bit of leftover wine. "Mama, did you know that?"

13   "Nepal?" she'd say. "I don't even know where in God's world it is!"

14   "Felice," Papa would say, "Get the **atlas** so we can show Mama where Nepal is." And the whole family went on a search for Nepal.

15   This same experience was repeated until each family member had a turn. No dinner ended without at least half a dozen such facts.

16   Papa's technique has served me well all my life. Now before my head hits the pillow each night, I hear Papa's voice: "Felice, what did you learn today?"

—Adapted from *Papa, My Father,* by Leo Buscaglia, Ph.D. Copyright 1989, by Leo F. Buscaglia, Inc. Published by Slack, Inc.

> **Education is discipline for the adventure of life.**
>
> **—ALFRED NORTH WHITEHEAD**

◆ After You Read

Checking Your Understanding Look in the reading for the answers to these questions. Underline the answers when you find them.

1. When did Leo ("Felice") Buscaglia's father leave school? Where did he get his education?

2. What language did the family speak at the dinner table? Why?

3. What did each Buscaglia child need to do at the dinner table every night?

4. What does Leo Buscaglia think about each night before he goes to sleep?

Discussion With a partner, answer these questions:

1. When you were a child, what did you usually talk about at dinnertime?

2. What was something useful that you learned from your family when you were a child—something that you appreciate now?

PART 1: Learning a New Language

◆ **Getting Ready to Listen**

> **You're never too old to learn.**
>
> —ANONYMOUS

Making Categories: Good or Bad?

What can you do to learn English more quickly? Which activities are important for you to do? This exercise will help you to decide.

Read this list of activities. Which do you think are good? Put a check mark (✔) on the lines. Which are bad? Put an X on the lines.

_____ Come to class every day.

_____ Ask the teacher when you don't understand something.

_____ Read a lot.

_____ When you read, look up every new word (in a dictionary) and translate it.

_____ Make friends with people who don't speak your language.

_____ Watch the news on TV every night.

_____ Speak English with native speakers whenever possible.

_____ When you read, _don't_ look up every new word. Try to guess the meaning instead.

_____ Go to English-language movies.

_____ Keep a list of new words that you want to learn.

_____ Talk with other students in English during class breaks.

_____ Take a class (in English) in something that interests you.

_____ Don't say anything in English if the grammar isn't correct.

_____ Don't be afraid to make mistakes.

_____ Other: _____

Compare your list with another student's list. Are your ideas similar or different? Which activities did you say were not helpful in language learning? Ask your teacher for his or her ideas. Which activities does your teacher say are not helpful in language learning?

◆ **Vocabulary Building**

Guessing Meaning from Context

Before you listen, guess the meaning of the underlined words and phrases in the sentences on the following page.

1. We didn't talk about anything important. We just <u>made small talk</u> about the weather.

2. We need some fresh fruit and vegetables, so I'll go over to the <u>produce</u> section while you get the bread.

3. He looks so happy! He's <u>grinning from ear to ear</u>. I've never seen such a big smile on his face before!

4. She's been planning this trip for a long time. Now she's found out that she can't go. She's very <u>disappointed</u>. She really wanted to go.

Listen

Listening 1: Learning a New Language

You are going to hear a teacher talk about learning English. Use this Language Learning Strategy to get the most out of the lecture.

LANGUAGE LEARNING STRATEGY

When you listen to a teacher's lecture, pay special attention whenever the teacher emphasizes or repeats points. These are probably the main ideas or important details.

Apply the Strategy

In the following lecture, you will hear a teacher talk about how to learn English more quickly. Listen once to each section. Pay special attention if the teacher emphasizes or repeats a point. After you listen to the section, stop and answer the question about it. Then listen to the next section.

Section 1

Who is the best teacher, according to the speaker?

_____ 1. a strict teacher who gives a lot of homework and does all of the talking

_____ 2. a friendly teacher who lets the students talk a lot

_____ 3. you, the learner

Section 2

The teacher gives a lot of examples of where to practice English outside of class. What examples does she give? Listen once and check (✔) the answers.

_____ 1. supermarket   _____ 4. bus stop

_____ 2. movie theater   _____ 5. library

_____ 3. hospital   _____ 6. school

Section 3

The teacher talks about her friend Sara. What four things did Sara do to learn English? Listen once and check the answers.

_____ 1. talked with people everywhere

_____ 2. took a class in English as a second language

_____ 3. asked friends for help

_____ 4. listened carefully

_____ 5. wrote idioms in a notebook

Section 4

The teacher talks about her own experience. With whom did she practice a lot of Greek? Listen once and check the best answer.

_____ 1. her Greek teacher   _____ 3. friends

_____ 2. taxi drivers   _____ 4. neighbors

> **Personally, I'm always ready to learn, although I do not always like being taught.**
>
> **—WINSTON CHURCHILL**

◆ **After You Listen**

Discussion Work with a small group (three to four students). Answer the following questions:

1. According to the lecture, what is small talk?

2. Where can you make small talk in English in your city?

3. With whom can you speak English?

PART 2: Beginning a Conversation and Making Small Talk
• • • • • • • • • • •

◆ **Getting Ready to Listen**   **Identifying Photos**

_____

_____

Making Predictions The people in the photos on page 10 don't know each other. They're making small talk. What are they saying? (Make guesses.) With your partner, write a very short conversation (at least two sentences) under each photo.

Listen

Listening 2: Making Small Talk

Identifying Conversations You will hear four short conversations. Look at the photos on page 10. Which conversation goes with each photo? Listen and write the number (1, 2, 3, or 4) in the box next to the appropriate photo.

Choosing a Response Listen again to the first sentence of each conversation. Choose a response (answer). Write the number of the conversation (1, 2, 3, or 4) on the line.

Don't knock the weather; nine-tenths of the people couldn't start a conversation if it didn't change once in a while.

—KIN HUBBARD

_____ It was terrible! I don't think I did very well.

_____ Thanks. She's pretty happy most of the time.

_____ Yeah. And the music's wonderful.

_____ It sure seems to be. Honestly, this bus is late *so* often!

After You Listen

ACADEMIC POWER STRATEGY

Apply the Strategy

Seek out native speakers as conversation partners and make small talk with them. This is one good way to practice your English. In many countries, there are certain situations in which it is possible to have a very short conversation with a stranger—in other words, to make small talk. This is usually as short as two or three sentences and is usually about something unimportant, like the weather.

A. How do people *politely* begin a conversation with a stranger? Does it depend on their culture? Ask students from different countries how acceptable it is in their native country to begin conversations with the sentences in the chart on the following page. Then ask your teacher about the United States and Canada. Put checks (✓) for sentences that people say are polite. Put Xs for sentences that are impolite.

(continued on next page)

Situation	First Sentence in a Conversation with a Stranger	Country #1: _____	Country #2: _____	Country #3: _____	Country #4: _____	Country #5: The U.S.
at the bus stop	It's hot today, isn't it?					
at the post office	This line is really slow, isn't it?					
at a party	You have beautiful eyes. Are you married?					
in a supermarket	These tomatoes look terrible, don't they?					
on a bus	You're a foreigner, aren't you?					
anywhere	I want to practice English with you.					
in a museum	This is a wonderful painting, isn't it?					

B. Work in small groups. Discuss the answers on your chart. What countries or cultures have the same customs for beginning a conversation? Which ones have different customs? Are there customs in some countries that are not appropriate in the United States?

C. Work with a partner. Pretend you are in the situations below. Make polite small talk.

It's fairly common for many people in the United States to make small talk with strangers. They see it as a small moment of human contact. However, these short conversations with strangers seem to be more common in small towns than in big cities. And people everywhere are careful to speak with strangers only in a "safe" situation—in a public place with other people nearby.

Write About It.

In a journal (a separate notebook or section in your three-ring binder), write your ideas about small talk. Do people in your native culture make small talk with strangers? If so, in what situations? Do you feel comfortable making small talk?

The Sound of It: Understanding Intonation in Tag Questions

We often begin a conversation with a sentence that includes a tag question. We add a "tag" to a sentence, and it becomes a question. Our voice goes up on the tag if we aren't sure about the answer; it becomes a real question. Our voice goes down on the tag if we already know the answer and are making small talk.

Examples: We haven't met before, have we?
(Voice goes up—the speaker isn't sure of the answer.)

We haven't met before, have we?
(Voice goes down—the speaker knows the answer already.)

A. Listen to the conversation Where does it take place? Check the answer.

_____ 1. in a supermarket

_____ 2. in a school cafeteria

_____ 3. in a health-food store

B. Listen and repeat.

Unsure of the Answer	Sure of the Answer
1. The food is awful, isn't it?	The food is awful, isn't it?
2. You don't see any fresh fruit, do you?	You don't see any fresh fruit, do you?
3. There isn't any yogurt, is there?	There isn't any yogurt, is there?
4. There's lots of sugar, isn't there?	There's lots of sugar, isn't there?
5. You haven't seen a good health-food place, have you?	You haven't seen a good health-food place, have you?

LANGUAGE LEARNING STRATEGY

Pay attention to a speaker's intonation. As you've seen, intonation in a tag question carries meaning. If the voice goes up, the person is unsure of the answer and is asking a real question. If the voice goes down, the person already knows the answer and is just making small talk. Paying attention to intonation will help you better understand a speaker's meaning.

Apply the Strategy

Listen to these sentences. Are the speakers unsure or sure of the answers? Put check marks on the lines. You will hear each sentence two times.

	REAL QUESTIONS (UNSURE OF THE ANSWER)	SMALL TALK (SURE OF THE ANSWER)
1.	_____	_____
2.	_____	_____
3.	_____	_____
4.	_____	_____
5.	_____	_____
6.	_____	_____
7.	_____	_____
8.	_____	_____

LANGUAGE YOU CAN USE:
ASKING TAG QUESTIONS

Notice the grammar in tag questions: if the verb in the main clause is affirmative, the verb in the "tag" (last two words) is negative. If the verb in the main clause is negative, the verb in the "tag" (last two words) is affirmative.

Examples: It's warm today, isn't it?

It isn't very windy today, is it?

USING NEW LANGUAGE

Work with a partner. Have a very short conversation for each situation. One person begins with a tag question (with the voice going *down* at the end). The other person answers. Use the cue words.

Example:

SITUATION	CUE WORDS
Two people are at a bus stop.	A: bus/late again B: yes

Student A: The bus is late again, isn't it?

Student B: Yes, it is.

SITUATIONS	CUE WORDS
1. Two people are in the produce section of a market.	A: tomatoes/not very ripe B: no
2. Two people are in line at a supermarket.	A: line/really long B: yes
3. Two people are at a party.	A: the music/loud B: yes
4. Two students are walking out of class.	A: class/really hard B: yes
5. Two neighbors are walking out of their apartment building.	A: it/really cold B: yes
6. Two students are in line to register for classes.	A: line/not moving B: no

PART 3: Useful Expressions

◆ Getting Ready to Listen

Making Predictions Work with a partner. Decide what you can say in the following situations. (There are many possible answers.)

SITUATIONS	WHAT YOU CAN SAY
1. _____ By mistake, you have just stepped on someone's foot.	_____
2. _____ You are introducing a friend to your parents.	_____
3. _____ You're talking with a friend at school, but you need to leave because you have a class.	_____
4. _____ Someone gives you a present. You weren't expecting it.	_____

Listen   **Listening 3: Identifying Conversations**

You will hear four short conversations—one for each situation in Making Predictions on page 15. Listen for common expressions. Match each conversation with the situation. Listen and write the letter (a, b, c, or d) on the short line next to the appropriate situation.

LANGUAGE YOU CAN USE:
COMMON EXPRESSIONS IN CONVERSATION

After You Listen   Here are some common expressions you can use in conversations:

Introducing Someone	Responses
I'd like you to meet . . . This is . . . a friend of mine (my sister, etc.). Have you met . . .?	Nice (Glad, Pleased) to meet you.
Ending a Conversation	
Well, I've got to run. Good-bye. So long. See you later (Friday, etc.). Have a good day. Have a good weekend.	I have to go now, but I'll see (call) you . . . It's been good seeing you (talking to you). Talk to you soon. Keep in touch.
Expressing Thanks	**Responses**
Thanks. Thank you very much (so much). That was very kind of you. How thoughtful! I appreciate it. I'm very grateful.	You're welcome. Don't mention it.
Giving an Apology	**Responses**
I'm very sorry. Excuse me. Forgive me. It was my fault.	No problem. That's OK. That's all right. Don't worry about it.

USING NEW LANGUAGE

Work with a partner. Have a short conversation for each of the following situations. In each one, use some of the expressions in the box on page 16. Your teacher may ask you to put your conversations on tape or perform one of them for the class.

Situation 1: You are walking with a friend at school. You meet another friend. Introduce your two friends. Then tell the friend you met where the two of you are going. Have a short conversation. Then say good-bye.

Situation 2: Someone comes up to you at a party. You don't remember the person, but the person knows your name and says that the two of you met before. Say that you are sorry and ask where you met. Tell the person that it was nice to talk to him or her again.

Situation 3: Telephone a friend who gave you a present. Say something about what the present was and express thanks. Then say good-bye.

Situation 4: You and your boyfriend (or girlfriend) had a fight. Telephone to say that you're sorry. Your boyfriend (or girlfriend) is also sorry and thanks you for calling. You say good-bye.

PART 4: Singlish

Learning English requires a mind that is open and flexible! If you use the English language in travel abroad, you'll probably find some words that are used differently from country to country. The back space of a car, for example, is a *trunk* in the United States but a *boot* in England. The CNN video that you are going to see is about the use of language in Singapore.

Thinking Ahead In a small group, discuss the answers to these questions:

1. Where is Singapore? What languages are spoken there? Do you know anything about Singapore culture? If so, tell your group.

2. The title of this video segment is "Singlish." What language do you think Singlish is?

3. In American English, people would say that the woman in the photo is using a *cell phone—a cellular phone*. What do you call it in your native language?

In American English, you'll sometimes hear the expression "Two's company; three's a crowd." This refers to a situation in which there are three people together—maybe a boyfriend, girlfriend, and the girlfriend's little sister. The boyfriend and girlfriend would prefer to be alone with each other. Do you have an expression for this in your native language?

Vocabulary Building

The words on this list are from the video segment. If necessary, use a dictionary to help you complete each of the following sentences with one of these words.

unique	notion	data	version	slang
shortcuts	competitive	database	trio	look down on

1. Researchers are collecting _____ for their study of changing language in Singapore.

2. There are some words that are _____ to Singapore. You can't find these words in any other country.

3. In some societies, people _____ those who don't use the language well.

4. It's usually fine to use _____ when you're talking with friends, but it's not usually a good idea to use such language in a formal situation.

5. An unhappy _____ sat at the table next to ours in the restaurant: a young man, a young woman, and a very noisy little boy.

6. That's an interesting _____. Let's discuss this idea at our meeting next week.

7. An American might say, "We started the project together, but then John left me holding the bag." (This means that I had to take responsibility for finishing the project.) The British _____ of the same idiom is "holding the *baby*."

8. A group of friends sometimes has _____ to communication. They can express some big ideas in just a few words.

9. They added their information to the large _____ in the university computer.

10. He's a very _____ person. He works extra hard because he wants to be the most successful person at the company.

TUNING IN: "Singlish"

Getting Main Ideas As you watch the video the first time, listen for the answer to this question: What is Singlish, and why is it in the news?

Understanding Details Watch the video again. Find the answers to these questions:

1. What do these Singlish terms mean in American English?
   - hawker center
   - void deck

2. What does the most common Singlish word mean (in American English)?

3. What does someone mean if he says, "You're a lamppost"?

4. What new Singlish product is now available in Singapore?

5. Why are university students pleased with the new Singlish product?

6. Why do some people object to the use of Singlish?

Discussion Talk about your answers to these questions:

1. The video segment mentioned the words *airphone* and *handphone*. What do you think these mean?

2. In your native country, are there new slang words that don't exist in other countries?

3. In your native language, are there words that came from English? If so, what are some of them?

PUTTING IT ALL TOGETHER

Choose *one* of these projects:

Project 1

Interview five native speakers of English. Ask them these questions. Make notes on their answers. Then report on their answers to a small group of students.

Project 2

Interview five people who are not native speakers of English (but not students in your class). Ask them these questions. Make notes on their answers. Then report on their answers to a small group of students.

Questions

1. Do you sometimes make small talk with strangers? If so, where? What do you say?

2. Do you speak a language besides your native language? If so, how did you learn it? In your opinion, what were some activities that helped you (or are helping you) to learn it?

3. Can you think of words from other languages that people use in your native language? If so, what are some of them?

Test-Taking Tip

Use technology to help you practice for an upcoming speaking test. Prepare a few possible test questions. Then, giving yourself the same amount of time you will be given for the test, record yourself answering the questions with a tape recorder or, if possible, a video camera. This will allow you to evaluate your style of presentation, the clarity and accuracy of your speech, and the content and organization of your answers.

CHECK YOUR PROGRESS

On a scale of 1 to 5, where 1 means "not at all," 2 means "not very well," 3 means "moderately well," 4 means "well," and 5 means "very well," rate how well you have mastered the goals set at the beginning of the chapter:

1 2 3 4 5   know some good things to do to learn a language.

1 2 3 4 5   pay attention to emphasis and repetition in lectures.

1 2 3 4 5   practice English with native speakers.

1 2 3 4 5   begin a conversation.

1 2 3 4 5   make small talk.

1 2 3 4 5   understand the intonation in tag questions.

1 2 3 4 5   pay attention to a speaker's intonation.

1 2 3 4 5   introduce someone.

1 2 3 4 5   apologize.

1 2 3 4 5   express thanks.

1 2 3 4 5   end a conversation.

If you've given yourself a 3 or lower on any of these goals:

- visit the *Tapestry* web site for additional practice.
- ask your instructor for extra help.
- review the sections of the chapter that you found difficult.
- work with a partner or study group to further your progress.

Millions of immigrants passed through Ellis Island, near New York City, on their way to a new life. Says writer Jonathan Raban, "On the way from Europe, they'd lost their names, families, occupations, uniforms, languages." When they arrived in America, he says, they had a new choice: Who did they want to become?   —Jonathan Raban, *Hunting Mr. Heartbreak* (London: Collins Harvill, 1990), p. 61.

How can moving to a new place affect your life? What kinds of things must you adjust to in a new place? What kinds of things must you learn?

CHANGE AND CHOICE

In this chapter you'll explore ideas about moving, learn some practical things about living in a new place where you need to speak English, and have the opportunity to view a CNN segment about moving in North America.

Setting Goals

In this chapter you will learn:

- ◈ to ask for, understand, and give directions.
- ◈ to get information by taking a poll.
- ◈ to be aware of tone of voice.
- ◈ to communicate when using public transportation.
- ◈ to speak to landlords about a problem.
- ◈ to understand speech reductions.
- ◈ to keep a journal.

Getting Started

Here are some proverbs about moving and change. Do you agree with them or not? Discuss them in a small group.

> The rolling stone gathers no moss.
>
> —English proverb

(Moss is the green plant that grows on stones or trees. This proverb means that it's not good to stay in one place too long. The group "The Rolling Stones" probably took their name from this saying.)

> The grass is always greener on the other side of the fence.
>
> —English proverb

> You can't get away from the cross of your parish.
>
> —Spanish proverb

(A parish is a local area. The cross is a symbol of responsibility. You can't get away from responsbilities or things you should do for others in the area that you are from.)

> The fallen leaf goes back to the root.
>
> —Chinese proverb

(Used to mean that older people usually go back to their villages or home towns.)

Every year, about 16 percent of Americans relocate.

Getting Ready to Read

Vocabulary Building

The following words and phrases are from the reading. Check the ones you already know. Add new words you learn to your Vocabulary Log.

_____ adventure   _____ mobile   _____ residence

_____ census   _____ population   _____ suburbs

Find the word above that matches each synonym or definition below.

1. group of people   _____

2. area surrounding a city   _____

3. moving or able to move   _____

4. the place or house where one lives   _____

5. trip or experience, usually exciting   _____

6. official count of how many people there are in a certain region   _____

Read

1 The truck in the photo belongs to the U-Haul company. For many years this company had a saying, "Make Moving an **Adventure**." According to the U.S. **Census** Bureau, in 1997, 42 million Americans moved—16 percent of the **population.** Many young people ages 20–29 moved; the probability is over 30 percent that a person 20–29 will change **residence.** As people grow older, the chance that they will move becomes smaller. In 1997, 1.3 million people moved to the United States, and 92 percent of these immigrants went to cities. Many people moved to the South of the United States from other areas, usually from colder places to warmer places. Also, there were about 3 million fewer people in the central cities and 2.8 million more people in the **suburbs.** According to writer Patricia Skalka,

> The United States has one of the most **mobile** populations in the world. The average American moves more than ten times during his life. This year more than 40 million of us— roughly one in six—will change addresses, and it will cost us more than $5 billion.
> —Patricia Skalka, "Reader's Digest Guide to Moving" (*Reader's Digest*, March 1989), p. M1.

2 People move for many reasons. For some people, moving *does* mean adventure. As writer Charles Kuralt said,

> My family moved from one town to another in eastern North Carolina, and I loved every move. . . . I am still on the move. . . . I keep thinking I'll find something wonderful just around the next bend. And I always do.
> —Charles Kuralt, "What I Learned on the Road," from *A Life on the Road* (*Reader's Digest*, March 1991), p. 99.

◆ **After You Read**

Discussion

More than half of all Americans who move to new states move to Florida, California, Arizona, and Texas.

1. How many times does the average American move in his or her life?

2. About how many Americans will move this year? Do more younger people or older people move?

3. Where do most immigrants to the United States move—to cities or to suburbs?

4. According to Jonathan Raban, Americans can move to any state or country—and still speak English, watch the TV shows they watched at home, and eat at Burger King restaurants. This is true all over the United States, he says, and all over the world. Is it easier for a person from your native country to live in the United States or Canada or for an American or Canadian to live in your native country? Why?

5. Yakov Smirnoff, a comedian, came to the United States from Russia and is now an American citizen. He says, "You can go to England, but you can't become an Englishman. You can go to France, but you can't become a Frenchman. But you can come to America and become an American." Do you agree? Can you come to America and *become an American?* Give examples to show your point of view.

PART 1: Asking for, Understanding, and Giving Directions

◆ **Getting Ready to Listen**

Reading a Map Susan Evans is one of over 40 million Americans who has moved during the past year. She moved to be closer to the school where she is a student. Her neighbor, Takeshi Matsui, is a very nice student at the same college. Susan asks him questions about where to find things in the neighborhood. Look at the map on the next page.

   Here are some things Takeshi tells her.

1. The post office is **across the street** from the bank.

2. The bakery is **down the street from** the post office.

3. The laundromat is **next to (beside)** the grocery store.

4. The drugstore is **around the corner from** the laundromat.

5. There's a bus stop **in front of** the library.

6. There's a parking lot **behind (in back of)** the department store.

 Listen   **Listening 1: Understanding Directions**

Identifying Takeshi tells Susan where to find things that she needs. Look at the map again. Listen and complete the sentences. Check the correct answers.

1. _____ a. bookstore

   _____ b. park

   _____ c. laundromat

2. _____ a. bookstore

   _____ b. park

   _____ c. drugstore

3. _____ a. bank

   _____ b. grocery store

   _____ c. Chinese restaurant

4. _____ a. post office

_____ b. laundromat

_____ c. bookstore

5. _____ a. department store

_____ b. park

_____ c. bakery

6. _____ a. library

_____ b. bakery

_____ c. drugstore

 **After You Listen**

Making a Map Work in groups and make a map. One person is the map maker. The others give directions. Make a simple map of the area around your school. Include stores, banks, and so on. Don't point to the map. *Tell* the map maker where to put each thing. Use these expressions: *across the street from, down the street from, next to, beside, around the corner from, in front of, in back of, behind.*

Examples: Kim's Market is in front of the school, on Main Street.

There's a Chinese restaurant around the corner from the school, on Fifth and Main.

LANGUAGE YOU CAN USE: GIVING DIRECTIONS

Here are some words and phrases you can use when giving directions:

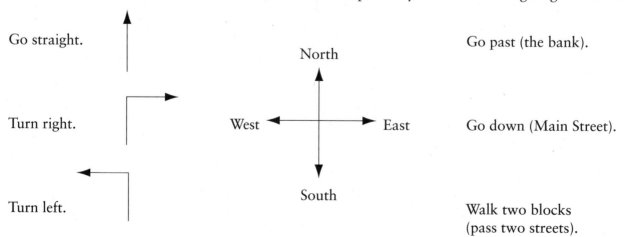

Go straight.

Turn right.

Turn left.

North

West ← → East

South

Go past (the bank).

Go down (Main Street).

Walk two blocks (pass two streets).

USING NEW LANGUAGE

Play a guessing game. Look at the map your group made of the area around your school. One person in the group chooses a place but doesn't tell anyone. He or she gives directions from the school to that place. The others try to guess the name of the place.

Example: Student A: Go out of the school onto First Street and turn left. Walk two blocks. Turn right. Pass the library. It's on your left.

Student B: Lincoln Park?

Student A: Yes!

LANGUAGE YOU CAN USE: ASKING FOR DIRECTIONS

Here are some phrases you can use when asking for directions:

How do you get to . . .?

Could you tell me where . . . is?

Is . . . far from here?

I'm looking for . . .

I'm trying to find . . .

In what direction is . . .?

USING NEW LANGUAGE

Work with a partner. Student A looks at Map A of San Francisco on page 30. Student B looks at Map B of San Francisco on page 31. Under each map is a list of places. Ask your partner how to get to each place on the list under your map. Your partner will give you directions. Begin each time from Market and Powell, where the cable car line starts. Listen to your partner and write the name of the place by one of the question marks on your map. Then your partner will ask you how to get to one of the places in the list under his or her map. Find the place on your map and give your partner directions. Remember to start from Market and Powell. Take turns.

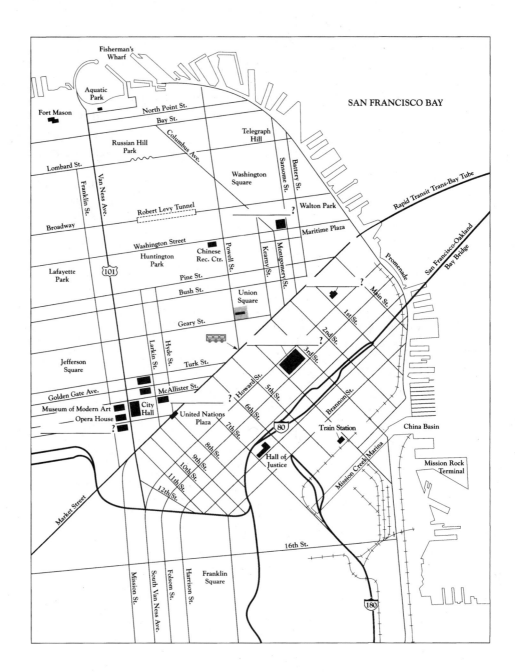

How can I get to . . . ?

1. Moscone Center
2. the library
3. Davies Symphony Hall
4. the immigration office
5. the bus station

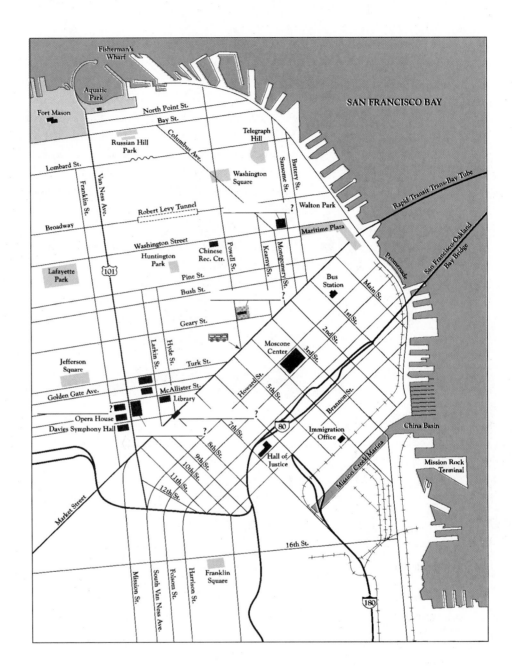

How can I get to . . . ?

1. City Hall

2. the United Nations Plaza

3. Union Square

4. the train station

5. the Museum of Modern Art

LANGUAGE LEARNING STRATEGY

G et information by taking a poll. Interviewing or talking to other people about a specific topic is called *taking a poll*. Taking a poll will give you new ideas and information. To get someone's attention to ask a question, try saying the following: "Excuse me. I'm taking a poll for my English class. May I ask you a quick question?"

Apply the Strategy

Talk to three classmates, people at your school, or people in your community. Ask them where to find each of these things. Complete the chart with their answers.

Example: Where can I find a good Chinese restaurant?

The Great Wall on Santa Cruz Avenue.

	Person 1	Person 2	Person 3
1. a good Chinese restaurant			
2. a good Mexican restaurant			
3. a good ———— (you fill in) restaurant			
4. a movie theater			
5. an inexpensive supermarket			
6. a good drugstore			
7. a nice park			
8. a great place to go on weekends			

PART 2: Using Public Transportation;
Asking for and Understanding Directions

 Getting Ready to Listen

Vocabulary Match

For each expression on the left, find the expression on the right with the same meaning. Write its letter on the line.

_b_	1. Excuse me.	a. paper money
_____	2. to transfer	b. Pardon me.
_____	3. dollar bills	c. correct amount of coins
_____	4. exact change	d. to change

 Listen

Listening 2: Understanding Tone of Voice

LANGUAGE LEARNING STRATEGY

Be aware of tone of voice. Tone of voice refers to how a voice sounds, not just the words a person uses. Understanding tone of voice can help you better understand what people mean. For instance, the tone of a message may be friendly even if the words are not friendly. It's helpful to listen to people's tone of voice because sometimes their voices tell more than their words.

Apply the Strategy

Susan has two conversations on her way to her friend's house, with two different bus drivers. Listen to Conversations 1 and 2. One of the drivers is friendly, and one is unfriendly. Which driver is friendly?

_____ the driver in Conversation 1

_____ the driver in Conversation 2

Culture Note

It's not very polite to call a woman *lady*. *Miss* is much more polite. *Ma'am* is for older women. You can call a man *sir*, but it's not polite to call a man *mister* without his last name.

Understanding Directions Listen to Conversations 1 and 2 again. Answer these questions. Check the correct answers. You may need to listen several times.

> There is nothing permanent except change.
>
> —HERACLITUS

Conversation 1

1. What buses does Susan need to take to Seventh and Lake Streets?

    _____ a. the 13 and the 30

    _____ b. the 30 and the 38

2. Where does she transfer?

    _____ a. at Geary Street

    _____ b. at Lake Street

Conversation 2

1. How much does it cost to take the bus?

    _____ a. 85 cents

    _____ b. one dollar and 85 cents

2. What does Susan need?

    _____ a. exact change

    _____ b. a dollar bill

◆After You Listen

Creating a Conversation Work with a partner. Student A wants to take the bus. Student B is a bus driver. Have a conversation. Follow this model:

A: Excuse me. Does this bus go to . . .?

B: No, . . . You need bus number . . . .

A: Where do I get . . .?

B: . . .

A: How much . . .?

B: . . .

A: Thanks.

After you finish, write your conversation. Your teacher may want you to present it to the class or put it on tape.

PART 3: Talking to Landlords or Apartment Managers; Making a Complaint

◀Getting Ready to Listen

Creating a Conversation When Susan found her apartment, she was very happy. With a partner, practice a conversation she had with the landlord, Mrs. West. You can choose words to create the conversation.

Susan: Oh, what a { big / sunny / lovely } apartment!

Mrs. West: Yes, it { is beautiful. / is large. / gets a lot of light. }

Susan: What a nice, clean kitchen! The { oven / stove / refrigerator } looks new.

Mrs. West: Right! And there's also a { lot of storage space. / garbage disposal. / dishwasher. }

Susan: Is there a { garage? / swimming pool? / security guard? }

Mrs. West: Yes, and there's { a tennis court / a recreation area / cable television } too.

Susan: Is there a { school / library / park } nearby?

Mrs. West: Of course, and there's a { bus stop / grocery store / hospital } right down the street.

Susan: I hope there's { a fireplace. / air conditioning. / a good view. }

Mrs. West: There is!

Susan: This is a { great / terrific / wonderful } apartment!

◀**Listen**

Listening 3: Reporting Problems

Identifying Problems After a few months, Susan has some trouble with her new apartment. She calls Mrs. West to complain. Listen to the conversation and check the problems she reports.

_____ 1. The garbage disposal is broken.

_____ 2. The roof is leaking.

_____ 3. The neighbors are too noisy.

_____ 4. The toilet doesn't work.

_____ 5. The food in the freezer is melting.

_____ 6. It's very hot, and the air conditioning doesn't seem to work.

◀**After You Listen**

Discussion

1. Do you have noisy neighbors? Are you a noisy neighbor sometimes? What's the best way to deal with this problem?

2. What problems have you had with apartments or rooms that you have rented? In groups, make a list. Did you find a solution on your own? Did you complain to the manager or landlord? What happened when you complained?

3. For each of the problems on your list, decide what is the best solution. Your teacher may give you advice. Report on one or two of the problems and solutions to the class.

◀**The Sound of It: Understanding Reductions**

A. In normal or fast speech, you will hear "reductions" of some words. For instance, *want to* may sound like *wanna*. Learning to understand reductions will help you become a better listener.

　　Listen to these examples of reductions from the conversations in this chapter. Can you hear the difference between the long forms and the short forms? Note: The short forms are not correct in writing.

LONG FORM	REDUCTION	SHORT FORM
Do you have any pets?	you → ya	Do ya have any pets?
What's your name?	what's your → whatcher	Whatcher name?
Does this bus go to Geary Street?	go to → goda	Does this bus goda Geary Street?
Do you want to see the kitchen?	want to → wanna	Do you wanna see the kitchen?
You have to have exact change.	have to → hafta	You hafta have exact change.

B. Listen to these sentences. Do you hear a reduction? Check *Long Form* or *Short Form* as you listen. You will hear each sentence two times.

	LONG FORM	SHORT FORM
Examples: a. You need bus number 3.	X	
b. You need bus number 3.		X
1. Are you Susan Evans?		
2. You can't use dollar bills.		
3. What's your phone number?		
4. What's your address?		
5. I need to go to the store.		
6. Do you go to Parkwood Avenue?		
7. Does he want to pay that much?		
8. I don't want to walk.		
9. Do you have to go?		
10. I have to buy some furniture.		

PART 4: Starting Again

Getting Ready to Listen

You are going to hear an opinion about the American lifestyle and the mobility of Americans. Pilar Hernández, an immigrant to California and a former teacher for an American school in her country, will answer these questions: "Do people in your country move often? How are things different in America?"

Vocabulary Match

Which definition on the right matches the word on the left? Write its letter on the line.

_____ 1. opportunities   a. admired

_____ 2. to look down   b. possibilities, chances
           on someone   to do something

_____ 3. respected   c. to think badly of someone

Listen

Listening 4: Starting Again

Getting Main Ideas Listen to Pilar and then tell whether these sentences are true or false:

_____ 1. Pilar worries because her mother is alone and lonely.

_____ 2. Pilar is not planning to go back to her country.

_____ 3. In Pilar's country, it is easy for a woman to leave a bad husband and move away and start a new life.

After You Listen

Expressing an Opinion Here is a quotation from Chilean writer Isabel Allende, who lives in California:

> In the United States, the fact that you can [move and] start again gives a lot of energy and strength and youth to this country. That is why it's so powerful in many ways, and so creative. However, it has the disadvantage of loneliness, of individuality carried to an extreme, where you don't belong to the group and where you can just do whatever you want and never think of other people. I think it's a great disadvantage—a moral and spiritual and ethical disadvantage.
>
> —Isabel Allende. From an interview by Bob Baldock and Dennis Bernstein for "Skirting the Brink: America's Leading Thinkers and Activists Confide Their Views of Our Predicament," a public radio project.

Work in pairs. List two advantages of being able to move easily. Then list two disadvantages of such mobility. Do you think that American mobility is mainly an advantage or a disadvantage?

Culture Note

The "average" person in the United States:

—has at least one pet (30 percent have a dog and 22 percent have a cat)

—lives in a household of three people

—spends one-third of his or her money on housing

—lives within 50 miles of a coastline

PART 5: Moving Day

◆Vocabulary Building

You are going to see a CNN video segment about moving in North America. First, complete each of the following sentences with one of these words from the video segment: *concerns, heavy, nightmare, pack, transition.*

1. The movers just left, but I have to _____ up these "odds and ends" and put them in the suitcases.

2. Wow! This suitcase is so _____ that I can't lift it.

3. Last night I had a terrible _____; I dreamed that I lost everything when I moved.

4. Moving can be a difficult _____, but you can make the change easier by following some simple steps.

5. The biggest _____ on my mind right now are settling into my new home and learning the "lay" of the land. I don't know where anything is!

TUNING IN: "Moving Day"

Making Predictions Watch the video the first time without sound. What topics do you think that the video will cover? The teacher will write your answers on the board.

Getting Information Watch the video again. How many of the topics on the board are in the video?

Which of the following ideas about making moving easier are in the video? Put a check by the suggestions that are in the video.

_____ 1. Have a positive attitude and believe that the move will provide new opportunities.

_____ 2. Make it a family experience, something that the family will go through together.

_____ 3. Look on the Internet for information about the new area.

_____ 4. Explore the house and neighborhood.

_____ 5. Get a new doctor ahead of time.

_____ 6. Help children make new friends.

© CNN

_____ 7. Learn the "lay" of the land, where things are around the area.

_____ 8. Call the local Chamber of Commerce for information about the new town or city.

Discussion What do you think of the Hollis's attitude toward moving? What effect will so many moves have on their children? For you, does moving mean an exciting adventure? Do people in your country move often? Why or why not?

Write a list of at least five recommendations for someone who is going to move. You may use ideas from the video or your own suggestions.

Write About It.

_____

_____

_____

_____

_____

_____

PUTTING IT ALL TOGETHER

Taking a Poll Interview five or six people from your class or school, including the teacher. Find out how often they and their families have moved. Record the results in the chart.

Name	TIMES THEY HAVE MOVED IN THEIR LIFETIME			TIMES THEIR PARENTS HAVE MOVED IN THEIR LIFETIME		
	1–3	4–6	7–10	1–3	4–6	7–10
_____	____	____	____	____	____	____
_____	____	____	____	____	____	____
_____	____	____	____	____	____	____
_____	____	____	____	____	____	____
_____	____	____	____	____	____	____
_____	____	____	____	____	____	____

Discussion

1. Do your classmates move often?

2. Do your classmates' parents move often? Who has moved more, your classmates or their parents?

3. The average American moves ten times in his or her lifetime. How do your classmates compare to the average American?

ACADEMIC POWER STRATEGY

Keep a journal. Writing your ideas in a notebook or on a computer can help you improve your English and learn about yourself at the same time. The more you write in English, the better your English will become. You can write your thoughts, feelings, goals, and the plans you have to reach your goals. You can read back over your journal and look for patterns in your life. For instance, you may become aware of a problem because you see that it comes up (appears) several times in your journal. Just becoming aware of a problem is an important step toward solving it.

If you have trouble beginning a journal, just try to write for five minutes without stopping. Keep your hand moving and write anything that you think of. You can use your journal to make notes about things or people in your life, to record your feelings during the day, or to write a letter to someone (even if you don't plan to send it). A journal can help you decide what is important to you and what your goals are; you can learn about yourself while you learn English.

Apply the Strategy

Start a journal if you do not have one. (If you have one, open it to a new page.) Write an entry about the last time you moved. Answer these questions: Was it difficult to move? Were you sad at first? How do you feel now about the place that you moved to? In what ways did the move give you new choices or opportunities?

◈ Just for Fun

Songs can tell a lot about a culture. Listening to music can help you understand another culture, even if you don't understand all the words to the song.

Listen to the song "Oh, California," about the people who went to California looking for gold in 1849. It is similar to the famous song "Oh, Susanna" by Stephen Foster and makes fun of people who thought they would get rich in California. (Most people did not find gold there.)

> It is not the strongest of the species that survives, nor the most intelligent; it is the one that is most adaptable to change.
>
> —CHARLES ROBERT DARWIN

Oh, California
....

I sailed from Salem City with my washbowl on my knee.
I'm going to California, the gold dust for to see.
It rained all night the day I left, the weather it was dry;
The sun so hot I froze to death, oh brothers don't you cry.
Oh, California, that's the land for me.
I'm going to San Francisco with my washbowl on my knee.
I soon shall be in Frisco, and there I'll look around.
And when I find the gold lumps there, I'll pick them off the ground.
I'll scrape the mountains clean, my boys, I'll drain the rivers dry;
A pocketful of rocks bring home, oh brothers don't you cry.
Oh, California, that's the land for me.
I'm going to San Francisco with my washbowl on my knee.

© WEM Records, Kent McNeil, "Moving West"

Test-Taking Tip

Pay attention to your appearance on the day of a speaking test. Appearance can have an effect on your instructor's overall impression of your preparedness and presentation. Wear appropriate clothes that are clean, neat, and unwrinkled. During the test, hold yourself in a way that shows confidence: maintain eye contact and stand straight.

CHECK YOUR PROGRESS

On a scale of 1 to 5, rate how well you have mastered the goals set at the beginning of the chapter:

1 2 3 4 5   ask for, understand, and give directions.

1 2 3 4 5   get information by taking a poll.

1 2 3 4 5   be aware of tone of voice.

1 2 3 4 5   communicate when using public transportation.

1 2 3 4 5   speak to landlords about a problem.

1 2 3 4 5   understand speech reductions.

1 2 3 4 5   keep a journal.

If you've given yourself a 3 or lower on any of these goals:

- visit the *Tapestry* web site for additional practice.
- ask your instructor for extra help.
- review the sections of the chapter that you found difficult.
- work with a partner or study group to further your progress.

Frank McCourt, English teacher and author of the well-known book about his childhood, *Angela's Ashes*, says: "Everyone has a story to tell. Write about what you know, . . . from the heart. Find your own voice and dance your own dance!"

What stories can you tell about your life? What people, events, and experiences have made you who you are?

3

THIS IS WHO I AM

In this chapter, you'll listen to people talking about their lives, and you'll tell others about your own life. You'll tell a story about something that happened in your past, discuss your interests, and make plans for your future. You'll also view a CNN segment about the life of writer Frank McCourt.

Setting Goals

In this chapter you will learn to:

◈ use gerunds.

◈ ask questions when you don't understand something.

◈ understand intonation in questions with *or*.

◈ organize your ideas before telling a story.

◈ express encouragement when someone is telling a story.

◈ listen for stressed words when people speak.

◈ make realistic goals for yourself.

◈ understand speech reductions.

◇ Getting Started

Here are some quotations about youth and aging. Do you agree with them or not? Discuss them in a small group.

> There is always one moment in childhood when the door opens and lets the future in.
> —Graham Greene, *The Power and the Glory*

> It is only an illusion that youth is happy, an illusion of those who have lost it.
> —W. Somerset Maugham, *Of Human Bondage*

> To be seventy years young is sometimes far more cheerful and hopeful than to be forty years old.
> —Oliver Wendell Holmes

> I like the dreams of the future better than the history of the past.
> —Thomas Jefferson, letter to John Adams, 1816

> One is as young as one's illusions and as old as one's memories.
> —Spanish proverb

◇ Getting Ready to Read

Making Predictions

Look at the photos of the three people on page 47 and answer these questions:

1. Do you know why these people are famous?

2. Do you know anything about their lives?

Vocabulary Building

Work with a partner to guess a word for each definition. Some of these words appear in the following reading.

Definition	Word
1. the period of life or state of being a child	childhood
2. the period of life or state of being an adult	_____
3. the state of being an orphan (a child without parents)	_____
4. the state of being a parent	_____
5. the state of being a widow (a woman whose husband has died)	_____
6. the state of being a mother	_____
7. the state of being a father	_____

◆Read

Read these quotations from three well-known people.

Brad Pitt

Brad Pitt grew up in Missouri. He sang in the church choir, was a member of the high school student council, and went on to the University of Missouri. Nothing in school excited him the way that movies excited him as a child. He liked going to movies by himself. He says, "I remember going to an Ape-athon—all five *Planet of the Apes* movies, all day long. My mom packed me a lunch. My peanut-butter-and-jelly sandwich got smashed against the seat back. I had some Hot Tamales. It was a great day."

—Brad Pitt, quoted by
C. Spines in "Lost Horizon,"
http://tlgrooms.simplenet.com/horizon.htm

Yelena Bonner

Yelena Bonner describes her early life: "I'm 63, and I've never had a house. . . . I started out like everyone else: a normal **childhood,** but then came a strange **orphanhood**—father and mother arrested and no one knowing whether they were alive or not. Later, after the war, we had a room in a communal apartment—there were 48 people in one apartment and one toilet."

—Yelena Bonner, quoted in
Newsweek (June 2, 1986)

Gerard Depardieu

Gerard Depardieu was the third of six in a family that he describes as "poorer than poor." He says, "It's good for an actor to be raised in poverty. The poor dream more."

—Gerard Depardieu,
quoted in *People Magazine*
(February 4, 1991)

◆After You Read

Checking Your Understanding Look at the quotations for the answers to these questions:

1. Which person grew up without parents for some time?

2. Why does Depardieu believe that it's good for an actor to grow up poor?

3. Which person seemed to have had a happy childhood?

Discussion With a partner, answer these questions:

1. How might childhood experiences have influenced these three people in their adulthood?

2. Do you know anything about the childhood of any other famous people? If so, how did their childhood influence their adulthood?

3. What is one especially good memory that you have of your childhood (such as Pitt's "great day" at a movie marathon)?

PART 1: This Is What I Like

> **Getting Ready to Listen**

Thinking Ahead What do people do for fun in their free time? Write as many activities as you can think of on the lines below.

PHYSICAL ACTIVITIES	MENTAL ACTIVITIES	OTHER ACTIVITIES
roller-blading	reading	sailing

Share your ideas with a partner. Add any new activities to your list. Then share your ideas with the whole class.

> **Listen**

Listening 1: Interests and Hobbies

You'll hear six people talk about their interests. They all answer the question "What do you do in your free time?" Listen for the important words—the speakers' interests—and write only these words on the lines below. Use gerunds (words that end in *-ing*) or nouns. Listen two or three times.

Person 1: _____

Person 2: _____

Person 3: a. _____ b. _____
           c. _____

Person 4: a. _____ b. _____
           c. _____ d. _____

Person 5: a. _____ b. _____
           c. _____ d. _____
           e. _____

Person 6: a. _____ b. _____
           c. _____ d. _____
           e. _____

◁**After You Listen**

Verbs Followed by Nouns, Gerunds, or Infinitives After some verbs (such as *enjoy*), use a noun or a gerund (a word that ends in *-ing*).

Examples: I enjoy sports. (noun)

              I enjoy exercising. (gerund)

After other verbs (such as *like*), use a noun, a gerund, or an infinitive (*to + verb*).

Examples: I like sports.

              I like exercising.

              I like to exercise.

Talk with your classmates, teacher, people at your school, and people in your community. Ask them the question "What do you do in your free time?" Complete the chart on the following page with their answers. (Note: When a classmate asks *you* this question, answer with the verb *enjoy* or *like*.)

LANGUAGE YOU CAN USE: ASKING FOR CLARIFICATION
• •

If you don't understand someone, it's important to ask a question for clarification. Here are some questions that you can ask:

- Excuse me?
- Could you repeat that?

- What was that again?
- How do you spell that?

USING NEW LANGUAGE

When you listen to people's answers during the next activity, ask them for clarification if you don't understand something.

Person's Name	Interests/Activities

Discussion In a small group, discuss your charts. Which activities seem to be most popular? Which are most active? Which are most unusual?

_____

_____

_____

_____

The Sound of It: Understanding Intonation in Questions with *Or*

There are two kinds of questions with the word *or*: *yes/no* questions and *either/or* questions:

1. In *yes/no* questions, the answer is "Yes" or "No." The speaker's voice goes up two times.

Example: Question: Would you like coffee or tea?
Answer: Yes, please.

2. In *either/or* questions, the answer is one of the two items from the question. The speaker's voice goes up on the first item and down on the second item.

Example: Question: Would you like coffee or tea?
Answer: Tea, please.

A. Listen to these questions and repeat them. Notice the intonation.

Yes/No Questions	Either/Or Questions
1. Do you like TV or movies?	Do you like TV or movies?
2. Does she enjoy ice skating or roller-blading?	Does she enjoy ice skating or roller-blading?
3. Does he swim at the gym or at home?	Does he swim at the gym or at home?
4. Is he an actor or a musician?	Is he an actor or a musician?
5. Did she work during the summer or after school?	Did she work during the summer or after school?

B. Listen to the intonation in each question. Is it a *yes/no* question or an *either/or* question? For each *yes/no* question, write *yes* on the line. For each *either/or* question, write one of the two items from the question. You will hear each question two times.

1. _____   6. _____
2. _____   7. _____
3. _____   8. _____
4. _____   9. _____
5. _____   10. _____

> **May you live every day of your life.**
>
> —JONATHAN SWIFT

C. Which of the following questions are *yes/no* questions? Which are *either/or* questions? Work with a partner and decide on the intonation for each question. Then practice saying it.

1. Question: Do they enjoy water skiing or snow skiing?
   Answer: Snow skiing.

2. Question: Do you like classical music or jazz?
   Answer: Jazz.

3. Question: Does she travel on weekends or during the summer?
   Answer: Yes.

4. Question: Does he spend much time with his friends or family?
   Answer: No.

5. Question: Do they eat at good restaurants or fast-food places?
   Answer: Usually at fast-food places.

D. Take turns with your partner asking and answering these questions. When you *ask*, choose which intonation you want: *yes/no* or *either/or*. When you *answer*, be sure to listen carefully to your partner's intonation so that you can use correct intonation in the answer.

1. Do they go dancing on Fridays or Saturdays?

2. Does he like swimming or surfing?

3. Do you live with your family or a friend?

4. On weekends, does he play baseball or basketball?

5. Do you like Chinese food or Italian food?

6. Do you enjoy walking or jogging?

PART 2: This Is Where I've Been

Getting Ready to Listen

Thinking Ahead In a small group, discuss this question: In your culture, do high school or college students sometimes have jobs? If so, what are typical jobs?

Vocabulary Building

Guessing Meaning from Context You're going to hear one person tell a story about her first job. Before you listen, guess the meanings of the underlined words in the sentences below. These are words from the story.

1. The <u>store detectives</u> arrested the thief for trying to steal a jacket. They caught him at the exit before he could leave.

2. She's a <u>shoplifter</u>. She steals things from stores and puts them in her purse or under her coat.

3. He's a terrible <u>racist</u>. He doesn't like anyone who isn't the same race as he is.

4. I don't <u>trust</u> him. I simply don't believe he's telling the truth.

5. The child <u>burst into tears</u>. He suddenly started crying when he thought he was lost.

6. He's such a <u>vain</u> person. He's always looking at himself in the mirror and worrying about his appearance.

Listen

Work is a necessity for man. Man invented the alarm clock.

—PABLO PICASSO

Listening 2: Telling a Story

Read these sentences. Then listen to the speaker. Why didn't she like her job in the department store? Check the answers. (There are several answers.)

_____ 1. The job was boring.

_____ 2. Her boss was a racist.

_____ 3. Her salary was low.

_____ 4. She spent all her money at the store.

_____ 5. She wasn't good at her job.

Making Inferences The speaker didn't enjoy her job as a store detective. How do you think she feels about the experience now? Why do you think that? Discuss your answer with one other student.

After You Listen

Discussion

1. Have you ever had a job, or do you have one now?

2. If so, did/do you enjoy it?

LANGUAGE LEARNING STRATEGY

Organize your ideas before telling a story, and you'll feel more confident as you speak. To prepare to tell a story, follow these steps:

1. Decide on the main point of the story.

2. Think about each part of the story, in order of time.

3. Write down notes—not complete sentences.

4. Cross out any elements that seem off the track—not important to the point of the story.

5. Look up any words that you'll need when you tell the story.

(continued on next page)

Apply the Strategy

Think of one experience from your past. For homework, organize your ideas about it and make notes. What happened? How did you feel about the experience? How do you feel about it now? Did you learn something from this experience? Then, during the next class, tell this experience to a small group of students. Choose *one* of these topics:

- an experience from your childhood
- a memory of a family member (mother, grandfather, cousin, etc.)
- something unusual that your family used to do
- your first day of school *or* your first date *or* your first job
- a memory of a teacher from elementary school
- an experience that changed your life

LANGUAGE YOU CAN USE: EXPRESSING ENCOURAGEMENT

Express encouragement to someone who is telling a story to let the person know that you're interested in what he or she is saying. Here are some possible expressions:

Right.	And?	Wow.
OK.	Well?	Gosh.
Really?	And then?	
Yeah?	And so?	

USING NEW LANGUAGE

In your group, be sure to listen carefully when other students speak. Use the words and phrases above to express encouragement.

In all cultures, there are questions that are common to ask a new acquaintance and other questions that people consider impolite.

People in the U.S. usually *don't* ask:

- How old are you?
- Are you married?
- How much money do you make?

People in the U.S. frequently ask:

- What do you do?
  (What kind of work?)
- Where are you from?

LANGUAGE LEARNING STRATEGY

Listen especially for stressed words when people speak. In English, people stress (emphasize) the important words in a sentence. If you understand the stressed words, you can usually understand the important information.

How do you know which words are stressed? They are *higher* (the voice goes up), *louder,* and *clearer* than the other words. Listen for the "mountains" in speech—not the "valleys." The meaning of a sentence can change if the stress changes.

Examples: I *LIKED* Anna (but I don't like her now).

I liked *ANNA* (but I didn't like her brother).

I liked Anna (but other people didn't).

Apply the Strategy

A. Listen for important words in these sentences and repeat each sentence:

1. It was a TERRIBLE day.

2. WE'LL take those.

3. I was SUPPOSED to catch shoplifters.

4. They're going to TAKE something.

5. I couldn't SEE anything.

(continued on next page)

B. Listen to the important (stressed) words in these sentences. Underline them. You will hear each sentence two times.

1. That was my boss.

2. That was my boss.

3. I don't remember.

4. I don't remember.

5. George used to work there.

6. George used to work there.

7. What do you do?

8. What do you do?

9. She said she didn't take it.

10. She said she didn't take it.

11. She said she didn't take it.

C. Work with a partner. Figure out which word needs to be stressed in each answer below. Underline the word. When you finish all six, listen to the tape to see if you were right. Then practice saying the questions and answers.

1. Question: What's your favorite SPORT?
   Answer: I really like skiing.

2. Question: What's HER favorite sport?
   Answer: I think she likes skiing, too.

3. Question: Where do they COME from?
   Answer: They come from Brazil.

4. Question: Where does HE come from?
   Answer: He comes from Hong Kong.

5. Question: What are you going to TAKE?
   Answer: I'm going to take economics.

6. Question: What are THEY going to take?
   Answer: They have no idea.

D. With your partner, figure out which word(s) you need to stress in each question and answer below. Underline it (or them). Then listen to the tape to check your answers. Repeat each question and answer after the speaker.

1. Question: Where did your brother find a job?
   Answer: He found a job in Chicago.

2. Question: Whose brother found a job?
   Answer: My brother found a job.

3. Question: What did your brother do?
   Answer: He found a job in Chicago.

PART 3: This Is Where I'm Going

Getting Ready to Listen

One Person's Dream Read this selection by Yelena Bonner, widow of Andrei Sakharov. Then answer the questions.

A Quirky Farewell to America

1 Americans do not want war. What Americans want is a house. The house is a symbol of independence.

2   I also want a house in addition to my usual wants that everyone be together and healthy and that there be no war. With enough land around it, and no more, for me to plant flowers. . . . I don't need a lot of bedrooms, just one for us and one for Mother, a guest room, and one more so that I'm always ready for our grandchildren.

3   My dream, my own house, is unattainable for my husband and myself, as unattainable as heaven on earth. But I want a house. If not for me, then for my son and his family in America.

1. What is Bonner's dream?

2. In her opinion, why is a house important to Americans?

3. Does she think that her dream can come true? In other words, is her dream attainable?

Thinking Ahead You're going to hear four people talk about their goals and dreams. People's goals usually change as they get older. In groups, discuss these questions:

1. What are some possible goals and dreams of teenagers in high school?

2. When young adults (in their twenties) think about the future, what might some of their goals and dreams be?

3. What are some possible goals and dreams of middle-aged people (in their forties and fifties)?

4. When older people (in their sixties and seventies) think about the future, what might some of their goals and dreams be?

Listen

Listening 3: Taking About Goals

You will hear speakers talk about their goals and their plans to reach these goals. Take notes about each person; do not write complete sentences. Also, make an inference about the age of each person and write it on the line. (Which person is probably a teenager? A young adult? Middle-aged? Older?)

Listen as many times as you need to. The first one has been done as an example.

Person 1: <u>young adult</u>

Goal:

<u>to give daughter a good life</u>

Plans to reach this goal:

<u>buy a house with a garden</u>

<u>change work times</u>

<u>save money for her college education</u>

Person 2: _____

Goal:

_____

Plans to reach this goal:

_____

_____

_____

> **My interest is in the future because I am going to spend the rest of my life there.**
>
> **—CHARLES F. KETTERING**

Person 3: _____

Goal:

_____

Plans to reach this goal:

_____

_____

_____

Person 4: _____

Goal:

_____

Plans to reach this goal:

_____

_____

_____

> **Learn from yesterday, live for today, hope for tomorrow.**
>
> **—ANONYMOUS**

After You Listen

Discussion

1. Which person seems to have the most practical goal?
2. Which person seems to be a dreamer?

LANGUAGE YOU CAN USE: TALKING ABOUT FUTURE PLANS

When you talk about future plans and intentions, use *be going to* + verb.

Examples: I'm going to go to college.

He's going to become a lawyer.

When you talk about future predictions, use *be going to* + verb or *will* + verb.

Examples: She's going to work with animals.

They'll live here for a few years.

I won't retire for another twenty years.

USING NEW LANGUAGE

In small groups, make predictions and talk about your own plans for the future. Use *be going to* and/or *will*. Choose two of these topics:

- relationships with other people
- education
- money

- where to live
- work
- travel

ACADEMIC POWER STRATEGY

Make realistic goals for yourself in order to start working toward your academic and professional dreams. Most students have dreams about their future. They can make these dreams come true by developing realistic goals. To do this, it's a good idea to begin by thinking of your major goals in life—two or three "big" goals— and then considering each step necessary to attain those goals.

Apply the Strategy

On the lines below, write two major goals and steps you can take to reach these goals. These goals should relate to your education or future profession. Just write notes; don't write sentences.

1. Goal: _____

    Steps to reach this goal: _____

    _____

    _____

2. Goal: _____

    Steps to reach this goal: _____

    _____

    _____

With another student, discuss your goals and the steps to reach them. When your classmate is speaking, express encouragement. Ask for clarification if necessary.

Write About It.

Choose *one* of your two goals. Write one paragraph about this goal and your steps to reach it. Use your notes from the Academic Power Strategy to help you.

The Sound of It: Understanding Reductions

A. In normal or fast speech, you will hear "reductions" of some words. Listen to these examples. Can you hear the difference between the long forms and the short forms? (Note: The short forms are not correct in writing.)

Long Form	Reduction	Short Form
What do you do?	what do you → whadaya	Whadaya do?
What are you doing?	what are you → whatcha	Whatcha doing?
What kind of childhood was it?	kind of → kinda	What kinda childhood was it?
What did you do?	did you → didja	What didja do?
What did he do?	did he → didee	What didee do?
They used to live here.	used to → yoosta	They yoosta live here.
I'm going to buy a house.	going to → gonna	I'm gonna buy a house.

B. Listen to these sentences. Do you hear a reduction? Check *Long Form* or *Short Form* as you listen. You will hear each sentence two times.

	LONG FORM	SHORT FORM
Examples:		
a. <u>What are you</u> looking at?		X
b. <u>What are you</u> looking at?	X	
1. <u>Did you</u> enjoy school?		
2. I'm <u>going to</u> study history.		
3. What <u>kind of</u> sports do you like?		
4. He <u>used to</u> live with his grandmother.		

	LONG FORM	SHORT FORM
5. Where <u>did he</u> go to school?	_____	_____
6. <u>What do you</u> think about it?	_____	_____
7. I'm <u>kind of</u> tired.	_____	_____
8. How are you <u>going to</u> do it?	_____	_____
9. Why <u>did you</u> do that?	_____	_____
10. <u>What do you</u> want to do?	_____	_____

C. Listen to these conversations. You'll hear reduced (short) forms. Write the long forms. You will hear each conversation two times.

1. A: _____ see that movie on TV last night?

   B: Yeah, I thought it was _____ be funny, but it was really sad.

2. A: What _____ sports do you like?

   B: Oh, tennis, swimming, basketball. I _____ play tennis in high school.

3. A: _____ planning to do on the weekend?

   B: Bob and I are _____ look for a new car. _____ tell you about the accident with the old car?

   A: Yeah. That's too bad.

PART 4: The Childhood of Frank McCourt

In recent years, some of the most popular and best-selling books have been memoirs. A memoir is a book about personal memories and experiences—an autobiography. One of the most famous of these memoirs is *Angela's Ashes*, a book by a New York teacher, Frank McCourt. A best-selling book for many months, it is about his childhood in Ireland. As we learn in this CNN video clip, his childhood was a miserable one, full of poverty and hunger. But humor was a saving grace—in other words, a quality that made a bad situation better.

Vocabulary Building

If necessary, use a dictionary to help you match the words or expressions with their definitions. Write the letters on the lines.

_____ 1. pious

_____ 2. youngster

_____ 3. omnipresent

_____ 4. monotony

_____ 5. envy

_____ 6. chum

_____ 7. obscurity

_____ 8. sequel

_____ 9. slum

_____ 10. to hang on

a. a situation in which a person is not well-known, not famous

b. religious

c. a very poor neighborhood

d. the feeling of wanting something that another person has

e. to wait; to not give up

f. sameness; unchanging, boring time

g. a book or movie that continues a story from a previous book or movie

h. friend

i. always present

j. child

A *funeral* is a ritual ceremony for a person who has died. In some cultures, there is also a *wake*—a time when friends and relatives come to the house and watch over the dead body. In Irish culture, the wake includes food and drink and sometimes music. An Irish wake might seem almost like a party.

TUNING IN: "Frank McCourt"

Getting the "Big Picture" As you watch the video the first time, listen for the answer to this question: What were two reasons that Frank McCourt and his chums enjoyed wakes during their childhood in Ireland?

Understanding Details True or false? Watch the video again. Mark *T* if the sentence is true or *F* if it is false.

_____ 1. McCourt feels guilty that he wasn't kinder to his mother.

_____ 2. McCourt's mother gave birth to six children, three of whom died.

© CNN

_____ 3. McCourt was born in Brooklyn, New York, and later moved to Ireland.

_____ 4. To help one friend, McCourt went to church and prayed that his friend's sister would get well.

_____ 5. There might be a movie version of this book.

_____ 6. McCourt isn't writing any more memoirs.

Discussion In small groups, discuss these questions:

1. Do you agree that humor is a "saving grace" for someone who is living through a terrible time, or is humor not appropriate in such a situation?

2. Describe a typical funeral in your culture. Are there wakes in your culture, also? If so, what are they like?

PUTTING IT ALL TOGETHER

Truth or Bluff In this game, you say some things that are true and other things that are not true. People try to guess when you are telling the truth and when you are bluffing (lying). Follow these steps:

1. Write three sentences about yourself, but don't show them to anyone. One or two of these should be true; the others should be bluffs. Include the following:

   • one sentence about your childhood

   • one sentence about your interests

   • one sentence about your plans for the future

2. In a small group, read your sentences out loud.

3. For each sentence, the group members will decide if you're telling the truth or bluffing. Afterward, tell them if they are right or not. Each time they aren't right, you win one point.

4. Move on to the next student.

Example: A: When I was a kid, my father was a rock musician.

B: You're bluffing!

C: Yeah. I agree. That's not true.

D: I agree. That's a bluff.

A: Well, it's actually true! For about two years, my father was in a rock group. This was when I was still a baby.

B: Wow! That's amazing. One point for you. OK, give us another.

Test-Taking Tip

At the start of a test, listen closely to the verbal instructions your teacher gives you. Then read the directions on the test slowly and carefully. If there is anything you do not understand, ask your teacher for help with the directions before you begin the test.

CHECK YOUR PROGRESS

On a scale of 1 to 5, rate how well you have mastered the goals set at the beginning of the chapter:

1 2 3 4 5   use gerunds.

1 2 3 4 5   ask questions when you don't understand something.

1 2 3 4 5   understand intonation in questions with *or*.

1 2 3 4 5   organize your ideas before telling a story.

1 2 3 4 5   express encouragement when someone is telling a story.

1 2 3 4 5   listen for stressed words when people speak.

1 2 3 4 5   make realistic goals for yourself.

1 2 3 4 5   understand speech reductions.

If you've given yourself a 3 or lower on any of these goals:

- visit the *Tapestry* web site for additional practice.
- ask your instructor for extra help.
- review the sections of the chapter that you found difficult.
- work with a partner or study group to further your progress.

An important part of staying healthy is keeping a positive mental attitude, being hopeful and cheerful. Do you usually "look on the bright side"—that is, look at things from a positive point of view? Do you feel that your health is good, overall? What do you do to keep yourself healthy?

4

HEALTH: GETTING THE MOST OUT OF LIFE

In this chapter, you'll find out some things about how to feel your best, some practical things about ordering food in English, and some advice from older people about health. You'll also have the opportunity to view a CNN segment on how to stay healthy.

Setting Goals

In this chapter you will learn to:

◈ get information and order food in restaurants.

◈ brainstorm.

◈ work in groups to improve your English.

◈ give advice about health, including foods, exercise, and relaxation.

◈ hear the difference between *can* and *can't*.

Getting Started

Decide if the following statements are true or false.

_____ I have no trouble ordering food in English.

_____ I understand restaurant customs in English-speaking places.

_____ I eat good, healthful food most of the time.

_____ I have a good exercise plan.

_____ There's not much I can do now to prepare for a healthy old age.

Getting Ready to Read

Vocabulary Check

The following words and phrases are from the reading. Check the ones you already know. Add new words you learn to your Vocabulary Log.

_____ aerobics

_____ beneficial

_____ calories

_____ to consume

_____ fat

_____ fiber

_____ grains

_____ heart disease

_____ industrialized

_____ muscles

_____ overweight

_____ researchers

_____ rural

_____ stress

Vocabulary Building

Guessing Meaning from Context Guess the meanings of the underlined words in the sentences that follow.

1. One study of the diet of Chinese people living in <u>rural</u> areas showed that they eat much more fruit, vegetables, and <u>grains</u> (such as rice and wheat) than most people in <u>industrialized</u> countries like the United States or Canada.

2. They also <u>consume</u> three times as much <u>fiber</u> (the bulky or "tough" part of plants).

3. <u>Researchers</u> are studying the <u>beneficial</u> effects of eating a lot of fresh fruit and vegetables to find out why these foods are good for you.

4. Exercise helps control weight and relieve tension, or <u>stress</u>.

Choosing the Right Word

Choose the best word in parentheses to complete each sentence.

1. Doctors say that (fats/vegetables) are bad for one's health.

2. It's important to exercise, to strengthen (calories/muscles).

3. If you are (overweight/nervous), you should go on a diet.

4. (Aerobics/Heart disease) is a major cause of death in North America.

5. The energy we get from food comes from (calories/attitude).

 Read

1   Many aspects of our lives affect our health. One of these is how we eat, a subject that scientists are now studying. One study of the diet of Chinese people living in **rural** areas showed that they eat much more fruit, vegetables, and **grains** than most people in **industrialized** countries like the United States or Canada. They also consume three times as much **fiber.** These people get fewer **calories** from **fat** and eat meat only about once a week. The result? The rate of **heart disease** and certain cancers is very low.

2   Another aspect of our lives that affects health is exercise. While the Chinese people in the study **consume** more calories daily, they are not **overweight.** Why? They do more physical work, and since most of them do not have cars, they walk or ride bicycles. Doctors everywhere now recommend exercise for people of all ages. Exercise helps control weight and relieve tension and **stress.**

3   A positive mental attitude also seems to have a lot to do with health. Studies show that people with a good attitude about life seem to get sick less often than other people. Dr. William Fry, Jr., a Stanford University **researcher,** has studied the **beneficial** effects of laughter for many years. He says:

© General Foods Corporation. Bran cereal has a lot of fiber, which scientists say is healthful.

When we laugh, **muscles** are activated. When we stop laughing, these muscles relax. . . . Many people with arthritis, rheumatism and other painful conditions benefit greatly from a healthy dose of laughter. Many headache sufferers feel the same relief. [Nancy and Dean Hoch, "Take Time to Laugh," *Reader's Digest,* (February, 1988), pp. 59–64.]

4   Some people think that Americans worry too much about their health and about how to stay young. As writer Jane Walmsley says:

The single most important thing to know about Americans is that Americans think that death is optional [a choice]. They may not admit it, but it's a state of mind that colors everything they do. . . . This explains the common preoccupation with health, **aerobics,** plastic surgery, and education. . . .

Your life is in your own hands . . . and the quality of that life also. You owe it to yourself to be beautiful, clever, thin, successful, and healthy. If you fail, it's because you're not trying hard enough . . . (you didn't run regularly, you should've eaten more bran). Death becomes your fault. [Adapted from Jane Walmsley, *Britthink/Ameri-think: A Transatlantic Survival Guide* (New York: Penguin Books, 1987), pp. 2–3.]

◆ **After You Read**

Discussion

1. What did scientists find out about the diet of rural Chinese people? Do these people get more calories or fewer calories a day than most people in industrialized countries? Do they get more exercise or less exercise?

2. What do studies show about a positive mental attitude?

3. What happens when we laugh, according to Dr. William Fry? Do you "take time to laugh"? When do you laugh most?

4. According to Jane Walmsley, what do Americans think about death? About staying young?

PART 1: Eating Well at Home or in a Restaurant

◆ **Getting Ready to Listen**

Identifying Foods Work with a partner. Look at the part of the chart with the heading "...And 6 Foods That Kill." Match the names of the foods to the pictures. Draw lines matching them. What other pictures of foods in the chart do you recognize?

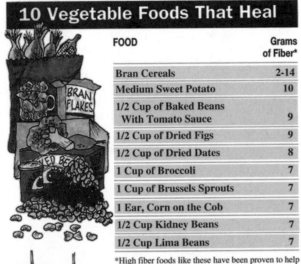

10 Vegetable Foods That Heal

FOOD	Grams of Fiber*
Bran Cereals	2-14
Medium Sweet Potato	10
1/2 Cup of Baked Beans With Tomato Sauce	9
1/2 Cup of Dried Figs	9
1/2 Cup of Dried Dates	8
1 Cup of Broccoli	7
1 Cup of Brussels Sprouts	7
1 Ear, Corn on the Cob	7
1/2 Cup Kidney Beans	7
1/2 Cup Lima Beans	7

*High fiber foods like these have been proven to help prevent colon cancer and reverse heart disease.

Three Meats That Heal

FOOD	Calories Per Serving	Grams of Fat	% Calories From Fat
Cod	89	.7	7%
Sole/Flounder	99	1.3	12%
Canned Tuna in Water	116	2.1	16%

High in Omega-3 fatty acids, proven to reverse heart disease

...And 6 Foods That Kill

The following foods are proven to increase your risk of heart disease, stroke, high blood pressure, colon cancer and other diseases:

- PRIME RIB ■ FRIED CHICKEN
- BISCUITS & GRAVY
- FRIED EGG ■ CHEESE
- EXCESSIVE ALCOHOL

© Phillips Publishing, Inc. From *Wellness Today*, February 1992, p. 12.

Understanding a Chart Read the notes under the pictures and answer these questions:

1. Which foods are high in *fiber*?

2. What diseases do foods with fiber help prevent?

3. What do "Omega-3 fatty acids" help prevent? What foods have these acids?

4. Which fish has more calories per serving?

    _____ a. cod

    _____ b. sole or flounder

    _____ c. canned tuna

5. What do you think *excessive* alcohol means?

    _____ a. too much

    _____ b. too little

6. What do prime rib, fried chicken, biscuits and gravy (meat sauce with milk or water and flour), fried eggs, and cheese have in common?

    _____ a. They have a lot of sugar.

    _____ b. They are very good for you.

    _____ c. They have a lot of fat.

Listen

Listening 1: Ordering a Meal

Making Inferences

You will hear two conversations that take place in a restaurant. In Conversation 1, a woman is ordering a meal, and in Conversation 2, a man is ordering a meal. Listen to both conversations and answer this question: Who cares more about health, the man or the woman?

Understanding Details

Read the following list of foods and drinks. Then listen to the conversations again. Write *M* next to the foods or drinks that the man orders. Write *W* next to the foods or drinks that the woman orders. You may have to listen several times.

MAIN DISHES	SIDE DISHES	DESSERTS	BEVERAGES
_____ prime rib	_____ rice	_____ lemon cake	_____ coffee
_____ steak	_____ potatoes (mashed, baked, or french fries)	_____ strawberries	_____ tea
_____ pork chops	_____ corn on the cob	_____ apple pie	_____ milk
_____ fried chicken	_____ sweet potatoes	_____ ice cream	_____ water
_____ sole	_____ baked beans	_____ fruit salad	
_____ cod	_____ biscuits and gravy	_____ chocolate pie	
	_____ green salad		
	_____ vegetable beef soup		

In most restaurants in the United States, customers leave a 15% tip for the waiter or waitress—a little more if the service was excellent and a little less for poor service. You can ask for separate checks if you and a friend are paying separately. That way it's easier to know how much each person should pay. If you are in a large group, the waiter or waitress may not want to do separate checks, however.

LANGUAGE YOU CAN USE:
ORDERING FOOD IN A RESTAURANT

Below are phrases you can use when ordering food in a restaurant.

Waiter	Customer
May I take your order?	What do you recommend?
What would you like?	What's the special today?
Would you like . . . with that?	How much is that?
How is everything here?	What's the soup of the day?
May I take your plate?	I'll have . . . /I'd like . . .
Would you like coffee or dessert?	May I have the check, please?

USING NEW LANGUAGE

Work with a partner. Look at the menu from Lyon's Restaurant on page 74 or at a menu from a local restaurant that your teacher brings to class. One person is the waiter or waitress, and one person is the customer. Have a conversation. Your teacher may ask you to present it to the class or put it on tape. Don't forget to include:

1. finding out and telling about the "specials" (what they are and how much they cost)

2. asking and answering questions about foods on the menu

3. getting the check

Write the conversation from your role-play.

Salads

Fresh Fruit Salad 6.95
A combination of luscious seasonal fresh fruit, served on a bed of mixed greens. Your choice of cottage cheese, frozen yogurt or sherbet.

SPECIAL SALADS
Fresh and delicious with mixed greens, seasonal vegetables and your choice of dressings: Ranch, Non-fat Italian, Bleu Cheese or 1000 Island. Roll and butter included.
NEW! **Try Our Honey Mustard Dressing.**

NEW! **Oriental Chicken Salad 6.95**
Strips of chicken breast atop a mixture of salad greens, tossed with honey ginger sesame dressing, almonds and mandarin oranges.

Cobb Salad 6.95
Breast of turkey, crumbled bleu cheese, bacon, tomato, egg and avocado, on a bed of mixed greens with your choice of dressing.

Shrimp Louie 7.25
A generous portion of succulent bay shrimp.

Chicken Fajita Salad 6.95
Breast of chicken pieces, lightly spiced and grilled with mushrooms, onions, and red and green bell peppers. Served warm.

Tuna Neptune 6.25
Dolphin-safe, all white albacore tuna salad.

Entrées

POPULAR COMBOS

Steak and Shrimp . . . 9.55
USDA choice top sirloin steak with a Lyon's share of golden fried shrimp.

Steak and Chicken 9.25
Grilled breast of chicken served teriyaki or lemon style with a broiled top sirloin steak.

Chicken and Shrimp 8.95
Grilled breast of chicken served teriyaki or lemon style with lots of golden fried shrimp.

BEEF

New York Steak 10.25
Broiled USDA choice 10 oz. New York.

Teriyaki Steak 9.45
Grilled USDA choice 8 oz. sirloin steak.

Liver 'n Onions 7.85
With bacon, add 85 cents.

Prime Rib Special
It's prime time daily!! From 4 p.m.-10 p.m. Try our thick, juicy cut of tender prime rib, served au jus with horseradish sauce.
New Lower Price! . . . 8.95
Extra Thick Cut: add $1.50

LYON'S SPECIALTIES

Baby Back Ribs 9.95
A full rack of meaty, tender pork ribs in zesty barbecue sauce.

Lyon's Chicken 7.95
Grilled boneless breast of chicken served teriyaki, lemon or barbecue style.

NEW! **Southern Fried Chicken 7.95**
Four pieces of tender, golden fried chicken with mashed potatoes and country gravy.

CHICKEN AND SEAFOOD

Chicken Cashew Stir Fry* 7.95
In teriyaki sauce with fresh mushrooms and Chinese vegetables. Served on rice.

Chicken Pasta Supreme* 7.85
Grilled chicken, mushrooms and fresh vegetables in Alfredo sauce on fettucine. With garlic bread.

English Style Fish and Chips 7.95
Hand-dipped in beer batter and deep fried.

Shrimps Galore 8.95
A platter of golden fried breaded shrimp.

FRESH FISH
We offer two or more fresh fish daily. Ask your server about today's fresh catches. Served grilled, or most fish can be broiled, if you prefer.
Priced daily ... from 7.95 to 9.65

Desserts

PIES ...
Fresh Daily

Hot Apple Pie with Cinnamon Sauce . . . 1.95
A la mode add **.75**

Chocolate Cream Pie 2.25
Our own special recipe. Rich chocolate whipped with thick, sweet cream and piled high in a tender, flaky crust. Topped with real whipped cream and chocolate sprinkles.

Specialty Pies
Ask your server for today's featured pies.

TAKE THE CAKE

Heavenly Chocolate Cake 2.15
Four-layer double chocolate cake made with a mixture of Dutch and semi-sweet chocolate with a rich fudge icing.

Three-Layer Carrot Cake 2.15
Our moist, luscious carrot cake with rich cream cheese frosting.

Cheesecake Supreme 2.35
Topped with hot fudge, blueberry or strawberry topping and chopped nuts.

Creamy Cheesecake 2.15
Dairy fresh, rich and velvety on a graham cracker crust.

© Lyon's Restaurants

Cultural Observation Go to a restaurant where people speak English and then answer these questions.

1. How did people get the waiter's attention? (How do you get the waiter's attention in your native culture?)

2. What specials did the restaurant have? How much did they cost?

3. Sometimes you pay at the table—the waiter or waitress takes your money—and sometimes at the cash register. (Often the check says, "Please pay at the register.") How did you get the check? How did you pay? Did you leave a tip?

In some restaurants, no one brings you your food because the restaurant is self-service or buffet style. This means that you get your own plate and serve yourself. In these restaurants, you don't have to leave a 15 percent tip. You can leave a smaller tip if you like.

PART 2: Increasing Your Energy

◇ Getting Ready to Listen   Understanding a Chart

Exercise is one way to increase your energy level. Exercise also helps the brain produce natural tranquilizers and fight stress, or tension. Read "The Fitness Plan," a guide to weekly exercise, on page 76. Each week, do three to four exercises from Column A, two from Column C, and two from Column E. The activities in Columns A, B, C, and E burn (use) 100 calories each; the activities in D burn 200 calories each. Healthy people try to burn 1,400 calories a week. You can do different kinds of activities to make your exercise plan more fun. You can use a box like the one in the chart to record your exercise workouts each day. Your teacher may act out some of the activities from the chart. Look at the chart and tell what activity he or she is doing.

Using a Chart Look at the chart on page 76. Work with a partner and answer these questions.

1. How long do you have to work in the garden to burn 100 calories? How long do you have to play a musical instrument to burn 100 calories? Sweep the floor? Rake leaves?

2. If you ride an exercise bike (a machine) indoors for 15 minutes, you burn 100 calories. How far do you have to ride a bicycle outdoors to burn 100 calories? How long do you have to walk in order to burn 100 calories? Swim? Jump rope?

3. Which burns more calories—rowing a boat for 30 minutes or vacuuming the floor for 40 minutes?

4. Do you do some of the activities in the chart? If so, which ones? How many calories do these activities burn?

THE FITNESS PLAN				
Column A: Aerobic exercise	Column B: Everyday exercise	Column C: Strength training	Column D: Fun and games	Column E: Flexibility and stress reduction

walk 20 minutes
swim 12 minutes
run 1 mile
ride a bike (outside)
  3 miles
aerobic dance
  15 minutes
ride exercise bike
  15 minutes
jump rope 10 minutes
stair-climb (machine)
  15 minutes
	garden 20 minutes
	play an instrument
	  25 minutes
	scrub a floor 16 minutes
	chop wood 16 minutes
	sweep 30 minutes
	vacuum 40 minutes
	paint house 22 minutes
	rake leaves 32 minutes
	mow lawn
	  (hand mower)
	  15 minutes
	shovel snow
	  15 minutes
		free weights 20 minutes
		gymnastics 30 minutes
		calisthenics (push-ups,
		  sit-ups) 20 minutes
		body-sculpting class
			row 30 minutes
			play baseball 1 hour
			play tennis 1 hour
			box 30 minutes
			bowl 1 hour
			dance (hip-hop)
			  30 minutes
			dance (ballroom) 1 hour
			ski (downhill) 30 minutes
			ski (cross-country)
			  30 minutes
			horseback ride 1 hour
			roller- or ice-skate
			  30 minutes
			hike 30 minutes
			sail 1 hour
			do karate 30 minutes
			play golf 40 minutes
			  (no cart)
			play soccer 30 minutes
				yoga class or 30-minute
				  at-home session
				stretching class or 30-minute
				  at-home session
				T'ai chi ch'uan class or 30-minute
				  at-home session
				self-defense class

Daily fitness allowances (two per day)				
Workout A B C D E Total calories burned				

© *Self*, April 1992, pp. 145–146

 Listen

Listening 2: Talking about Fitness

Identifying Activities You will hear five people answer the question "What do you do to get exercise?" On the chart above ("The Fitness Plan"), check the activities you hear. One of the activities is not on the chart.

Listen for Detail Listen again. Did you hear an activity that is not on the chart? What is it?

After You Listen

Taking a Poll Ask four people the question "What do you do to get exercise?" Write their answers below.

Exercise Activities	
Person 1:	
Person 2:	
Person 3:	
Person 4:	

PART 3: Stress and Your Health

Getting Ready to Listen

LANGUAGE LEARNING STRATEGY

Brainstorm to explore your ideas. Brainstorming is the process of rapidly discussing and listing ideas. Normally, these ideas are related to a main topic. Brainstorming helps you make mental connections.

Apply the Strategy

Work in groups and answer this question: In what situations do you feel tension, or stress? List as many ideas as you can, using ideas from everyone in your group.

Examples: in traffic, at the dentist's office

_____

_____

_____

_____

Listen

Listening 3: Stress and Your Health

Taking Notes You are going to hear four people answer the question "How does stress affect your health habits?" Write the answers, but do not write everything that they say. Write only the important information. The first one is an example.

Person 1: <u>can't sleep</u>

Person 2: _____

Person 3: _____

Person 4: _____

After You Listen

Discussion How does stress affect your health habits? Most people have a change in health habits when they feel stress; this is normal. Do you do any of the following things when you feel stress?

1. Eat more food? If yes, what type of food?

2. Eat less food?

3. Drink more alcohol?

4. Smoke more cigarettes?

5. Sleep more?

6. Sleep less? Wake up during the night?

In groups, write five sentences about how stress affects your health.

Comparing Amounts

as much as	Do you eat as much (meat, food) as I do?
as many as	Can you eat as many (hamburgers, crackers) as she did?
more	He eats more (sweets, fruit) than his sister does.
less	He eats less (fruit, food) than she does.
fewer	I eat fewer eggs than I used to.

Use *less* and *as much as* for noncount nouns (*butter, cereal*, etc.).
Use *fewer* and *as many as* for count nouns (*apples, oranges*, etc.).

Examples: Monica eats more fast food, like hamburgers, and drinks more soft drinks, like Coca-Cola.

> Getting enough sleep is important, but studies show that most Americans do not get as much sleep as they need. Not getting enough sleep can be dangerous. Many accidents (including 100,000 automobile accidents a year in the United States) happen because people do not get enough sleep.

Midori eats less.

Tak sleeps fewer hours.

Jesús drinks more coffee.

Write About It.

Write about a time when you felt a lot of tension, or stress. What happened? How did you feel? How did it affect your health habits?

_____

_____

_____

_____

_____

_____

ACADEMIC POWER STRATEGY

Work in groups to help improve your English. Many people get energy from others and think better when they share their ideas and their work. When you are in class, you will often work in groups, but you can also form a study group of your own outside of class. If you are shy, you can simply pass a piece of paper around your classroom and ask people who are interested to sign up. Or you can choose people from the class that you think would share your goals. Five or six people is a good number. Have a regular time to meet and study; you are more likely to study if other people are counting on you to come to a group and participate. Many people find that study groups are an enjoyable and effective way to learn.

Apply the Strategy

While you are working in groups in class, think about forming a study group. Which people would you work best with? Check the most important things to look for in a member of your group:

_____ people who are easy to work with

_____ people who pay attention in class and take good notes

(continued on next page)

_____ people who are organized and who bring everything they need to class

_____ people who do not speak your language and need to communicate with you in English

_____ other

What other qualities are important? _____

_____

LANGUAGE YOU CAN USE: GIVING ADVICE

Here are some phrases you can use when giving advice:

- You should (shouldn't) . . .
- You ought (not) to . . .
- You had better (not) . . .

- I advise you (not) to . . .
- I recommend that you (not) . . .

USING NEW LANGUAGE

Alcohol slows the body's ability to burn fat. That's why many beer drinkers develop a large stomach. In fact, in American English we call this a "beer belly."

Work in groups. Look at the list below of how to eat right when you feel stress or tension. Have a conversation. One person tells about a situation that causes stress in his or her life. (It doesn't have to be real.) The other people give advice. Use *should*, *shouldn't*, or *ought to*. Note: *wanes* = decreases; *avoid* = stay away from.

VitaList
How to Eat Right When You're Stressed

• Drink plenty of water.	• If you're overeating, pay attention.
• Eat high-fiber foods.	• Eat less if your appetite wanes.
• Don't skip meals.	• Avoid alcohol.
• Focus on variety.	• Cut back on caffeine.
• If you're ill, think nutrition.	• Avoid sugary snacks.

© *Vitality Digest*, November 1991, p. 21.

Example: My boyfriend (girlfriend) wants to get married. I'm not ready
for that. So we've been fighting a lot, and I feel stressed.

You should . . .

You ought to . . .

◇**The Sound of It:
Listening for
Stressed Words—
Can or *Can't*?**

In the interviews about stress and health habits, you heard several
examples of *can* and *can't*. Listen to the examples again:

Person 1: I lie awake at night . . . can't go to sleep, thinking or worrying. Then I'm tired the next day, and I can't think clearly.

Person 2: I can eat and eat and eat . . . anything.

Person 3: I start smoking more—one cigarette after another. Just can't
stop.

Person 4: I can't eat.

Here are some more examples. Listen to the difference in stress:

I can RIDE a BIKE.

I CAN'T RIDE a BIKE.

He can RIDE a HORSE.

He CAN'T RIDE a HORSE.

**Children who live with
smokers are more than
twice as likely to develop
lung cancer later in life
than children of non-
smoking parents.**

Do you hear the difference? *Can't* is louder and clearer. Listen to
these sentences. Do you hear *can* or *can't*? Check the answer. You
will hear each sentence two times.

	CAN	CAN'T
1.	_____	_____
2.	_____	_____
3.	_____	_____
4.	_____	_____
5.	_____	_____
6.	_____	_____
7.	_____	_____
8.	_____	_____
9.	_____	_____
10.	_____	_____

PART 4: Dealing with Stress

Getting Ready to Listen   **Vocabulary Building**

You are going to hear selections from an interview with a health expert. Before you listen, guess the meanings of the underlined words in the sentences below:

1. My <u>physician</u>, Dr. Jones, tells me that too much stress can hurt my health.

2. He advises me to eat foods with good things in them—vitamins, minerals, and other <u>nutrients</u>.

3. He says it's not possible to <u>utilize</u> all your energy, but you can use more of your hidden energy if you follow some simple steps.

4. Long ago, Americans used to watch a funny TV show, "<u>Candid Camera</u>," with Allen Funt.

5. My grandmother helped my mother a lot for many years. My mother always asked me to thank my grandmother politely for things, to express our <u>gratitude</u>. She was very thankful that my grandmother gave her so much help.

Listen   **Listening 4: Interview with a Health Expert**

Listening for Main Ideas You are going to hear two short selections from an interview with Dr. Joseph Houlton, a health expert.* Earlier in the interview, Dr. Houlton explained that stress is sometimes good for us. We need some stress in our lives in order to do certain kinds of activities (like talking to a group of people or playing music in a formal situation). He explained that we all relax in different ways. For example, a fisherman might work in his garden to relax. A gardener might go fishing to relax. He then talked about stress and negative emotions, which can cause us to get sick. There are some difficult words in the interview, and you won't understand every word. Listen for main ideas only.

*From the series *The Human Condition,* KUT-FM; interviewed by Bert K. Smith of the Hogg Foundation for Mental Health, University of Texas, Austin, Texas 78712.

Section 1: Listen to Section 1 and answer this question: Dr. Norman Cousins had a serious illness; the odds (chances) were against his recovery, and he thought he might die. What did he do to get well?

Section 2: Listen to Section 2 of the interview and answer this question: Dr. Houlton has a motto, or saying, on his business card. It tells the attitude he tries to have toward life. What is the saying? How does it help him in life?

◆**After You Listen**

Creating A Good Motto Write a motto, or saying, for yourself. It should tell how you can be happy in life. It can be something simple, like "Eat chocolate," or something like "Do something nice for someone every day."

PART 5: It's a Matter of Attitude
· · · · · · · · · · ·

◆**Getting Ready to Listen**

In 1776, the average person in North America could expect to live 35 years.

Thinking Ahead Work in groups. You are going to hear part of a television show about older people.* Barbara de Angelis talks to some older Americans about their views of life. In groups, discuss these questions:

1. Do you know any very old people?

2. Are they happy? Are they active?

3. Do they give advice to younger people? If so, what do they say?

◆**Listen**

Listening 5: It's a Matter of Attitude

Listening for Specific Information Listen to the selection from the television show and answer the questions. You may have to listen several times. You may not understand everything. Just listen for the answers to the questions. First, read the information and the questions on page 84:

*© 1991 100% Productions, Inc. Kushner-Locke Company. Used by permission.

Person 1: Lottie Hicks, 105 Years Old Lottie Hicks celebrated her 102nd birthday by riding in a Goodyear blimp out to Catalina Island, near Los Angeles. She celebrated her 104th birthday by riding in a helicopter around Burbank and Hollywood. What does she want to do for her 106th birthday?

Person 2: Mary Ann Webber, 72 Years Old Mary Ann Webber says that when she was young she was afraid of making a fool of herself, but now she doesn't mind if people call her a "character" (a unique person). What does Mrs. Webber mean when she says that aging is "a matter of attitude"?

Person 3: Leo Salazar, 75 Years Old Leo Salazar lifts weights—he can lift 75 pounds, his age, in weights. What else does he do?

◆ **After You Listen**

Discussion Work in groups. Discuss these questions.

1. Are Lottie Hicks, Mary Ann Webber, and Leo Salazar like older people that you know?

2. Do you want to live to be 100 years old? Why or why not?

PART 6: Planning for a Long and Healthy Life

The CNN video segment for this chapter, about healthy aging, includes interviews with people from several different countries. The video is about things you can do at any age—even when you are young—to be healthy in the future.

◆ **Vocabulary Match**

Which definition on the right matches the word or expression on the left? Write its letter on the line.

_____ 1. longevity   a. food

_____ 2. pension   b. person who remains alive

_____ 3. tidal wave   c. giant ocean wave, huge amount

_____ 4. nutrient   d. great length of life

_____ 5. survivor   e. money you get on a regular basis
                               when you stop working

TUNING IN: "Healthy Aging"

Making Predictions Watch the video the first time without sound. What topics do you think that the video will cover? The teacher will write your answers on the board.

LANGUAGE LEARNING STRATEGY

B e aware that not all accents in English are the same. English is a global language, and it is different in different places. One accent is not necessarily "better" than another. In the interviews on the video, you will hear accents in English that you may not be familiar with. Don't worry if you do not understand every word. Just notice and enjoy the different varieties of English.

Apply the Strategy

Look at the video again. How many of the topics on the board are in the video? Notice the variety of accents in English. Can you hear the differences? Can you guess what country any of the speakers is from?

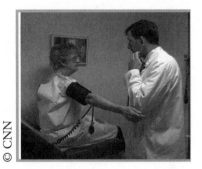

© CNN

Understanding Details True or false? Mark *T* if the sentence is true or *F* if it is false.

_____ 1. The antioxidant vitamins C and E do not benefit young people, but older people can benefit from them.

_____ 2. Success in giving children the chance to grow up is building a large number of adults who may need care.

_____ 3. The same nutrients that help prevent cancer also help prevent osteoporosis (bone disease).

_____ 4. Researchers say that each year in the near future there will be ten million deaths related to osteoporosis.

_____ 5. In a German study, scientists looked at how patients felt about their health and how their doctors felt; after two decades (twenty years), the people who were healthiest were the ones who had the best attitude about their health.

Health Recommendations Work in groups. Make a list of health recommendations from the video. Compare your lists with those of other groups.

PUTTING IT ALL TOGETHER

Food Journal For several days, make a list of foods that you eat. Write what you have for breakfast, lunch, dinner, and snacks. Then look at the "Food Guide Pyramid" on page 87. This shows how much of each type of food you should eat each day. Are you eating right? If not, what foods should you eat more of? Less of? (Remember that most fast foods—hamburgers, fried chicken, french fries, soft drinks—contain a lot of fat and sugar and are at the top of the pyramid.)

Day 1	
Breakfast:	
Lunch:	
Dinner:	
Snacks:	
Day 2	
Breakfast:	
Lunch:	
Dinner:	
Snacks:	
Day 3	
Breakfast:	
Lunch:	
Dinner:	
Snacks:	

Food Guide Pyramid
A Guide to Daily Food Choices

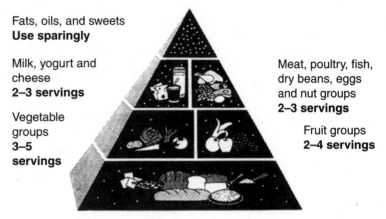

Fats, oils, and sweets
Use sparingly

Milk, yogurt and
cheese
2–3 servings

Meat, poultry, fish,
dry beans, eggs
and nut groups
2–3 servings

Vegetable
groups
**3–5
servings**

Fruit groups
2–4 servings

Bread, cereal, rice and pasta groups **6–11 servings**

United States Department of Agriculture

Gathering Information In North American culture, there are certain old sayings about foods. Fish is "brain food"; people say it's good for the brain. They say carrots are good for the eyes. Another saying is "An apple a day keeps the doctor away." In your native culture, are there certain foods that people say are good for you? Ask four or five people this question and complete the chart.

Culture/Country	Food	Belief or Saying
Person 1:		
Person 2:		
Person 3:		
Person 4:		
Person 5:		

- Before the invention of the refrigerator, Americans ate ¼ as much fat as they do now.

- Before the invention of the light bulb, Americans slept 9½ hours a night (about two hours a night more than they do now).

- Smoking, drinking alcohol, and breathing other people's cigarette smoke are the three main causes of preventable deaths in the United States. That is, they are the three causes that people could avoid by changing their health habits.

Just for Fun Ann Landers has a column in many newspapers across the United States every day. Below is one of her columns. It includes a "stress diet." Read it and answer this question: Would you like to go on a diet like this? Why or why not?

Ann Landers: A Diet to Die For

Dear Ann:

During these tension-filled days, we are hearing a lot about stress. People need a good laugh.

I am sending on a stress diet that a friend dropped in my mailbox last week. It really lifted my spirits. Please share it with your readers.

Kitty L.
principal, S.S.E. School, Decatur, Ill.

© Ann Landers, Chicago Tribune

THE STRESSER'S DIET

Breakfast
   ½ grapefruit
   1 piece whole-wheat toast
   8 oz. skim milk

Lunch
   4 oz. lean broiled chicken
   1 cup steamed lima beans
   1 Oreo cookie
   Herb tea

Midafternoon snack
   Rest of the package of
      Oreo cookies
   Quart of rocky-road ice cream
   Jar of hot-fudge sauce

Dinner
   2 loaves garlic bread
   Large mushroom-and-
      pepperoni pizza
   Large pitcher of beer
   3 Milky Ways
   Entire frozen cheesecake, eaten
      directly out of the freezer.

From: *The Joy of Stress,* by Pam Pettler (Quill, NY 1984, page 47).

Test-Taking Tip

Pronunciation is important in speaking tests. Before a speaking test, practice pronunciation areas that are difficult for you. Make a list of words that have these difficult pronunciation areas. Practice these words with a classmate. Say the words and ask your partner to correct your pronunciation. Then listen to your partner and help with his or her pronunciation.

CHECK YOUR PROGRESS

On a scale of 1 to 5, rate how well you have mastered the goals set at the beginning of the chapter:

1 2 3 4 5   get information and order food in restaurants.

1 2 3 4 5   brainstorm.

1 2 3 4 5   work in groups to improve your English.

1 2 3 4 5   give advice about health, including foods, exercise, and relaxation.

1 2 3 4 5   hear the difference between *can* and *can't*.

If you've given yourself a 3 or lower on any of these goals:

- visit the *Tapestry* web site for additional practice.
- ask your instructor for extra help.
- review the sections of the chapter that you found difficult.
- work with a partner or study group to further your progress.

W hat have your experiences with other cultures been like? Have you traveled abroad? Are you living abroad now? Has cross-cultural contact changed your life in any way?

5

WHEN CULTURES MEET

When we say that "the world is getting smaller," we mean that it is easier to travel, to communicate with people in other countries, and to learn about other cultures than at any time in the past. In this chapter, you'll learn about some effects of this global trend, including culture shock: What is culture shock, and how do people deal with it? You'll also discuss ways in which people and cultures are influenced by other cultures.

Setting Goals

In this chapter you will learn:

- to take notes when you listen to a lecture.
- to use expressions for making suggestions.
- to understand reductions.
- to distinguish between main ideas and details.
- to avoid forming stereotypes.
- about some customs in the United States and Canada.

◆**Getting Started**

How has your country been influenced by other cultures? (Think of food, styles, music, language, ideas, and customs.) List here the evidence of such influence and the country from which it came. For example, a student from the United States might write:

INFLUENCE   FROM

foods and restaurants   Mexico, China, Italy, Thailand

music   India, Ireland, Africa, Latin America

INFLUENCE   FROM

_____   _____

_____   _____

_____   _____

_____   _____

_____   _____

◆**Getting Ready to Read**

Thinking Ahead Listen to this excerpt from a famous traditional African-American song.

1. What mood (feeling) does it express?

2. Do you sometimes feel like this when you're away from your family, friends, or country?

Sometimes I Feel Like a Motherless Child

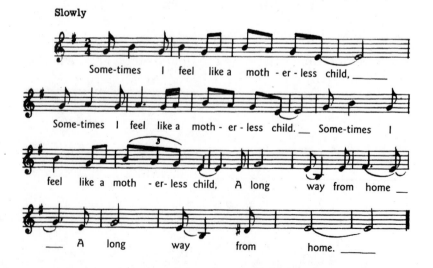

◆ **Vocabulary Match**

These are some words that you'll see in the reading. Use a dictionary to help you match each word on the left with its meaning on the right. Write the letter on the line.

_____ 1. to slip   a. a dirty mark

_____ 2. streaked   b. covered with a kind of light-color paint

_____ 3. to huddle   c. marked with long, thin lines

_____ 4. smudge   d. to crowd closely together

_____ 5. to slink   e. to look without being able to see well

_____ 6. whitewashed   f. to escape or pass unnoticed

_____ 7. to peer   g. to move in a secretive, guilty way

◆ **Read**

Read these entries from the journals of two students living abroad. As you read, try to understand the mood of the two writers.

There is no education like diversity.

—BENJAMIN DISRAELI

Entry 1
· · · · · · · · ·

The city, in the rain, is a gray **smudge** against the hills. Strange. In the summer, everything is bright white, and the tourists run around, laughing and taking pictures. But now, in winter, there are no tourists, and the **whitewashed** buildings are **streaked** with gray. The streets are empty. People **huddle** indoors. They **peer** sadly out of windows, waiting, waiting. What are they waiting for? I don't know. An occasional cat **slips** wetly from under a parked car and **slinks** into a doorway. The cat watches and waits, waits. But nothing happens. I think the rain will never stop.

—from the journal of a U.S. student living in Europe

Entry 2
· · · · · · · · ·

I've decided to cook a big chicken soup. This sounds easy, but it's not. My problem is finding a chicken. Back in Vancouver, all the chickens are in plastic at the supermarket. They're all cleaned and cut up. But here, I can't find any that look like that. Here, the only chickens that I've seen are at the outdoor marketplace, and they're ALIVE. What am I going to do? How do people buy chickens here? I don't understand. Do I have to take a LIVE chicken home with me and kill it in my kitchen? Oh! I can't do that. Maybe the chicken man at the marketplace will kill it for me. But that doesn't seem much better. I don't want to ride home on the bus with a DEAD CHICKEN. I guess I'll have to get out my dictionary and practice: "Please take off the head, take off the feathers, and cut it up for me."

—from the journal of a Canadian student living in Asia

◆ **After You Read**

Discussion With a partner, answer these questions:

1. What is the mood of the first student? Why might the student feel like this? Do you sometimes feel like this?

2. What is the second student's problem? Have you ever had any small problems like this in another country?

PART 1: Culture Shock

◆ **Getting Ready to Listen**

Thinking Ahead In a small group, discuss this question: What do you think culture shock is?

◆ **Vocabulary Match**

These are some words that you'll hear in the lecture. Match each word on the left with its meaning on the right. Write the letter on the line. Use a dictionary if necessary.

_____ 1. misconception   a. not different; almost the same

_____ 2. homesickness   b. change

_____ 3. transition   c. very sad

_____ 4. stage   d. feeling of sadness, of missing a place

_____ 5. expert   e. step; period of time

_____ 6. similar   f. mistaken idea

_____ 7. depressed   g. person who knows a lot about a subject

◆ **Listen**

Listening 1: The Stages of Culture Shock

You're going to hear someone give a short lecture about culture shock. The person will talk about four stages of culture shock and what happens in each one.

LANGUAGE LEARNING STRATEGY

Take notes when you listen to a lecture. Taking notes will help you remember details later. Also, when you take notes, you usually pay closer attention than if you just listen.

Apply the Strategy

As you listen, take notes in the following chart. Listen several times if necessary.

Stages of Culture Shock	What Happens
1	
2	
3	
4	

After You Listen

Discussion With a partner, answer these questions:

1. What misconception do many people have of culture shock?

2. What *is* culture shock, according to this listening passage?

3. What happens at each stage of culture shock? (Compare your chart with your partner's chart. Are your answers similar?)

4. Read the entries from students' journals (page 93) again. What stage of culture shock are these people in? Why do you think so?

LANGUAGE YOU CAN USE: MAKING SUGGESTIONS

In Chapter 4, you saw some ways to give advice:

should
shouldn't   } + simple form of the verb
ought to

These forms are also used to make suggestions. Other expressions for making suggestions include:

It might be nice (good) if you . . .

Why don't you . . .

If I were you, I would . . .

(continued on next page)

It's more polite to use expressions for making suggestions than to use an imperative. Notice this contrast:

Get out and take a dance class. (less polite)

You should get out and take a dance class. (more polite)

USING NEW LANGUAGE

With a small group (3–4 people), give advice to people who are in Stage 2 of culture shock. These people are confused and depressed. What can they do to move on to Stage 3? What can they do to become happier? What can their family and friends do to help them? Use expressions for making suggestions in your answers. (Choose a group secretary to write your answers.)

Imagine that you have a friend from another country who is going to live in your home country for a few years. This person has never been there before and doesn't know anything about your culture. Write one paragraph with suggestions for your friend. What will probably be difficult for your friend in your home country? What will be irritating or confusing or shocking? What should your friend do?

The Sound of It: Understanding Reductions

A. In normal or fast speech, you'll hear "reductions"—that is, a shortened version of a word or group of words. Although reductions are common in speech, they are not correct in writing. Listen to these examples. Can you hear the difference between the long forms and the short forms?

LONG FORM	REDUCTION	SHORT FORM
She made a lot of friends.	lot of → lotta	She made a lotta friends.
He had lots of problems.	lots of → lotsa	He had lotsa problems.
He wasn't able to relax.	to → ta	He wasn't able ta relax.
Could you help me with this?	could you → cudja	Cudja help me with this?
I'll see you later.	you → ya	I'll see ya later.
Do you know her?	her → er	Do you know er?
Do you know him?	him → im	Do you know im?
I was hurt and angry.	and → n	I was hurt n angry.

B. Listen to these sentences. Do you hear a reduction? Check *Long Form* or *Short Form* as you listen. You will hear each sentence two times.

	LONG FORM	SHORT FORM
a. She made a lot of friends.	X	
b. She made a lot of friends.		X
1. They spent a l ot of time with us.		
2. Could you explain this?		
3. Everything was new and exciting.		
4. He had lots of new experiences.		
5. After some time, I was able to enjoy the new culture.		
6. Let's invite her.		
7. Let's invite him.		
8. I'll call you tomorrow.		

C. Listen to these conversations. You'll hear reduced forms. Write the long forms. You will hear each sentence two times.

1. A: Do you know _____?

   B: Yeah. She's in my history class.

   A: _____ introduce me to _____?

2. A: I'm sick _____ tired of feeling like a foreigner.

   B: I know what you mean. There are a _____ problems in the beginning, but things will get better.

3. A: Where's Bill? Didn't you invite _____?

   B: Yeah, but he wasn't able _____ come.

PART 2: Adjusting to a New Culture
· · · · · · · · · · ·

Vocabulary Check

The following words and phrases are from the next listening passage. Check the ones you already know. Add new words to your Vocabulary Log.

_____ sort of   _____ to associate

_____ weird   _____ for good

_____ in reverse   _____ weaving

_____ severe   _____ reservation

Vocabulary Building

> No culture can live, if it attempts to be exclusive.
>
> —MOHANDAS KARAMCHAND GANDHI

Guessing Meaning from Context Guess the meanings of the underlined words in the sentences below:

1. This will sound <u>sort of</u> <u>weird</u>, and I guess maybe it *is* kind of strange, but it's true.

2. He put the car <u>in reverse</u> and slowly backed up.

3. I went into such a very <u>severe</u> culture shock that my parents were worried about me.

4. She <u>associated</u> only with people from her own country. She didn't have any friends from anyplace else.

5. I guess I'm going to live here <u>for good</u>. I'm not happy about it, but my husband and children were all born here, so I guess we'll be here permanently.

6. I took a class in Indian <u>weaving</u>—you know, making baskets, rugs, cloth, things like that.

7. We went to the Navajo Indian <u>reservation</u>, where we studied with Navajo weavers who lived there.

Getting Ready to Listen

Thinking Ahead Think of the good and bad things about the country you are currently living in. Write them on a piece of paper, in two columns—"Good" and "Bad." Then share your answers with a small group.

Listen

Listening 2: Talking About Culture Shock

You are going to hear three people talk about their experience with culture shock. Two of the three now live in the United States, and one lives in Canada.

LANGUAGE LEARNING STRATEGY

Apply the Strategy

Learn to distinguish between the main idea and supporting details when listening to a speaker. Details are often interesting, but the "big picture"—the main idea—is more important. You can usually express the main idea in one general sentence.

Read the questions below. Then listen to the people talk about their experiences with culture shock. Listen for the answers to the questions. Remember that the details are less important than the main ideas.

Person 1

Main Idea:

In general, did the speaker have a good or bad experience in Canada?

_____

Details:

Where is he from? _____

How did he feel when he arrived in Canada? _____

_____

What happened when he went back to his country? _____

_____

Person 2

Main Idea:

In general, did she have a good or bad experience in the United States?

_____

(continued on next page)

Details:

Where is she from? _____

Who did she associate with? _____

Why? _____

What happened when she went back to her country? _____

_____

_____

Person 3

Main Idea:

In general, did she have a good or bad experience in the United States?

_____

Details:

Where is she from? _____

What was her initial (first) experience in the United States? _____

_____

What were two experiences that influenced her decision? _____

_____

What did she decide to do? _____

_____

◆ **After You Listen**

Discussion

1. Do you have any friends who have experienced culture shock similar to these people?

2. If so, what were their experiences?

LANGUAGE YOU CAN USE:
PRESENT AND PAST PARTICIPLES AS ADJECTIVES

You can use many present and past participles as adjectives. Present participles end in *-ing*. Most past participles end in *-ed*.

Present participles show the *cause*:	Past participles show the *effect*:
English is a *confusing* language.	I'm really *confused*.
The homework was *boring*.	The students were *bored*.

Here are some other common participles that you can use as adjectives:

depressing	depressed	irritating	irritated
exciting	excited	shocking	shocked
interesting	interested	tiring	tired

USING NEW LANGUAGE

> He that travels much knows much.
>
> —THOMAS FULLER

A. Complete the paragraph with words from the participle list above. In some sentences, there is more than one possible answer.

When I first arrived in this country, I was really happy. I was
_____ (1) to be here. Everything was new and _____
(2). But then I started to have some problems. I had trouble with the
language. A lot of the customs were strange and _____
(3). Some new customs bothered me a little bit; they were just
_____ (4). But others seemed really terrible. I was
_____ (5) by some of them. I worked hard to learn the
language. I spent five hours in English class every day and two hours
on homework. This was very _____ (6), so I didn't have
much energy for other things. Mostly, I was homesick. I missed my
friends and family. I stayed in my apartment all weekend and was
_____ (7).

Slowly, things got better. I began to make friends and to go
places. My English got better. I began to understand the customs.
Now I'm _____ (8) in life again, and I'm much happier.

B. In a small group, discuss your answers to the following questions.
(Use participles and other adjectives.)

1. If you are living abroad, how did you feel when you first came to this country? What seemed strange to you? What things did you notice?

2. How do you feel now? Which stage of culture shock are you in?

3. Is it possible to be in two stages at the same time? Is it possible to stay in one stage forever?

PART 3: Understanding Cultures

 Getting Ready to Listen

Discussion People's first impressions of another culture are sometimes strange ones. From this experience, they often make generalizations about the new culture. They usually learn later that these generalizations are incorrect. In a small group, discuss these questions about first impressions:

1. If you are now living abroad, what were your first impressions of the country you are living in now? From this experience, did you make any generalizations about the culture?

2. As you learned more about the culture of the country you are living in now, did you discover that your generalizations were incorrect?

3. If you have traveled to another country, what were your first impressions of that country? From this experience, did you make any generalizations about the culture?

4. As you learned more about the culture of that country, did you discover that your generalizations were incorrect in some ways?

Listen

Listening 3: Two Cross-Cultural Experiences

You are going to hear two people tell about experiences that they had when they first arrived in a country new to them. They will explain how they formed a generalization from their experience.

ACADEMIC POWER STRATEGY

Avoid making stereotypes. Keeping your mind open will help you learn more about other cultures. A stereotype is a generalization about a group of people. The idea may be wrong, but many people believe it. It's common to form stereotypes of a new culture, but it's important to remain open to the possibility that your first impression might not be accurate. In the academic world, you will probably meet people from many cultures, and your experiences will be more positive if you have an open mind.

Apply the Strategy

Listen to these two stories. What generalizations did people make that were based on one early experience with a new culture? How were these inaccurate? Take notes in the chart.

Generalization (Stereotype)	How This Was Inaccurate
Person 1	
Person 2	

After You Listen

What generalizations did the two people make that were based on one experience each? How were they wrong? Compare your chart with other students' charts. Then take this short quiz to find out how much you already know about customs in the United States.

Minds are like parachutes. They only function when they are open.

—LESTER R. BITTEL

Quick Quiz: Some Customs In the United States

1. Someone tells you, "That's a nice sweater." You say:

   a. Thank you.

   b. Oh, not really. It's very old.

   c. Would you like it?

2. Your teacher sometimes sits on her desk. You think:

   a. She's not polite.

   b. She's not very serious about teaching.

   c. It's not strange.

3. Someone has invited you to a party at 8:00. It's probably best to arrive:

(continued on next page)

a. a few minutes before 8:00

b. at 8:00 exactly

c. a few minutes after 8:00

4. You have a business appointment for 10:30. It's probably best to arrive:

a. at 10:25 to 10:30.

b. at 10:35 to 10:45.

c. at 11:00.

5. You go out to lunch with an American friend. Who pays?

a. Your friend pays because lunch was his suggestion.

b. You both pay.

c. You pay because you're a little older than your friend.

6. Your American friend comes to your house for dinner. She has already eaten one serving of food. You say, "Would you like some more?" She says, "No, thank you. It was really delicious, but I'm so full!" What do you do?

a. Ask her two or three more times.

b. Say, "Are you sure? Well, if you change your mind, please help yourself."

c. Put some more food on her plate.

7. Last week, you had a short conversation with your American friend. He said, "Let's get together sometime for a movie or dinner or something. I'll give you a call." But he hasn't called. What do you think?

a. Nothing is strange.

b. He isn't polite.

c. He hasn't called because he has a problem.

8. Your American neighbors are rich, but their two children (who are in high school) work part time. One of them does babysitting on weekends. The other helps neighbors with the gardening on Saturdays. Your neighbors probably:

a. are bad parents.

b. care more about money than they care about their children.

c. love their children and are teaching them to be independent.

9. You tell your teacher, "I'm going to take the TOEFL exam to-morrow." Your teacher says, "Well . . ." and crosses two fingers (the index finger and the middle finger). You think that your teacher:

a. is *very* impolite.

b. is telling you "good luck."

c. is angry because you're going to be absent.

10. You are taking a college history class. The person at the desk next to you looks like she is over fifty years old. Probably:

a. This situation is very strange.

b. She is waiting for her son or daughter, who is in the class.

c. She has decided to go back to school; the situation isn't strange.

Don't judge a book by its cover.

Discussion Share your answers with a small group. Which ones do you agree on? Which ones do you disagree on? Are you confused by any of them? Ask your teacher for his or her opinion.

Write a short letter to your teacher. Choose *one* of these topics:

Write About It.

- an experience that you had when you were in a new country (and how this experience led you to a generalization)

- a stereotype that you once had and how this was inaccurate

- a custom from your native culture and the explanation for it

- a U.S. or Canadian custom that confuses you

PART 4: A Changing Society

The CNN video segment for this chapter explores changes in British society. British people have always been renowned (famous) for two cultural characteristics: their "stiff upper lip"—in other words, not showing emotions—and their belief in a class system—clear divisions among the lower, middle, and upper classes.

◆**Vocabulary Match**

Which following definition on the right matches the word or expression on the left? Write its letter on the line. Use a dictionary if necessary.

© CNN

_____ 1. weep	a. to relax, be natural, show emotions
_____ 2. mutating	b. equal
_____ 3. reserved	c. doing something in a "bigger" way than other people do it
_____ 4. to loosen up	
_____ 5. outdoing	d. not showing emotions
_____ 6. egalitarian	e. cry
_____ 7. quivering	f. changing
_____ 8. climate	g. famous
_____ 9. renowned	h. to tell someone what to do or how to feel
_____ 10. extraordinary	i. shaking
_____ 11. grieving	j. not ordinary, amazing
_____ 12. to dictate	k. atmosphere
	l. suffering sadness

TUNING IN: "Britain's Changing Society"

Making Predictions The video you will watch discusses a change in British culture. Watch the video the first time without sound. What kind of a change in British culture do you think the program discusses?

Talk shows are very popular in the United States. Oprah Winfrey is one example of an American talk-show host. On her program, people often talk about very personal subjects and frequently express emotions freely.

Getting the Big Picture Watch the video again, this time with sound. Then answer these questions. Work with a partner.

1. In what way has British society recently changed?

2. What are two possible explanations for this change, according to people in the video segment?

Discussion In a small group, answer these questions:

1. In the video, one person gives his opinion: "It would be sad if the world moved to some sort of McDonald's-ization of emotions. I think that national cultures are still there, but they're mutating." What does he mean by a "McDonald's-ization of emotions"? What are some examples of cultures that are "mutating"?

2. At the end of the segment, the reporter concludes by saying that the British now "*wear their hearts on their sleeves.*" What do you think this idiom means? Guess from the context of the whole story.

PUTTING IT ALL TOGETHER

Choose *one* of the following three projects:

Project 1: Interviews

If there are people at your school who have traveled abroad or are now living outside their own country, do this exercise. Interview three people who have had experiences with another culture. Ask them these three questions, and record their answers in the following chart.

1. Did you have any strange or funny first impressions or experiences in the new country?

2. What general ideas did you have about the culture, based on this experience?

3. Did you later discover that your general idea was wrong?

Person	First Impression	Generalization	Wrong?
1 new country:			
2 new country:			
3 new country:			

Project 2: Examining Cultural Influences

In many ways, the world is getting smaller. Each society is influenced by other cultures. One example is the appearance of some restaurant chains (such as Kentucky Fried Chicken, McDonald's, and Pizza Hut) in many countries where most people had never eaten such food before.

Ask two or three people this question: In what ways have other cultures influenced your culture in recent years? (Note: If people have difficulty finding an answer, suggest that they consider food, stores, fashion, music, language, or ideas.) Write their answers here.

Influences from Other Cultures	
Person 1 from (country):	
Person 2 from (country):	
Person 3 from (country):	

Project 3: Investigating Culture

Write a list of U.S. or Canadian customs that are confusing to you. You might choose some from the quiz on pages 103–105 or any other customs. Then interview an American or a Canadian. Explain that you are confused by certain customs and ask if this person can explain them. Write the customs and explanations on the chart below.

Customs	Explanations
Example: People usually say "thank you" after receiving a compliment.	They're thinking: "Thank you for saying that." It doesn't mean that they agree with the compliment.

Test-Taking Tip

Do everything you can to be physically ready for a test: get enough sleep the night before and have a nutritious breakfast on the day of the test. Also, get plenty of exercise. Exercise makes you more alert, helps you think more clearly, and increases your energy level.

CHECK YOUR PROGRESS

On a scale of 1 to 5, rate how well you have mastered the goals set at the beginning of the chapter.

1 2 3 4 5   take notes when you listen to a lecture.

1 2 3 4 5   use expressions for making suggestions.

1 2 3 4 5   understand reductions.

1 2 3 4 5   distinguish between main ideas and details.

1 2 3 4 5   avoid forming stereotypes.

1 2 3 4 5   learn about some customs in the United States and Canada.

If you've given yourself a 3 or lower on any of these goals:

- visit the *Tapestry* web site for additional practice.

- ask your instructor for extra help.

- review the sections of the chapter that you found difficult.

- work with a partner or study group to further your progress.

Do men and women communicate differently? What kinds of misunderstandings might people have in a new language that they don't have in their own language?

WHAT DO YOU MEAN? THOUGHT AND COMMUNICATION

A t times, it might seem that English is an impossible language. Even when you know all the words, there are misunderstandings. People sometimes talk fast. They sometimes say one thing but mean another. Men and women sometimes misunderstand each other—even when they speak the same language. In this chapter, you'll learn about some problems in communication—between men and women, between two people on the phone, and between people in business. You'll learn how to solve some of these problems. Also, you'll have an opportunity to view a CNN video segment about communication in the workplace.

Setting Goals

In this chapter you will learn:

- ◈ about differences between men's and women's communication styles.

- ◈ to become aware of your stereotypes and be open-minded about changing them.

- ◈ to understand reductions in speech.

- ◈ to pay attention to speakers' use of intonation to express emotion.

- ◈ to make an appointment.

- ◈ how to answer a negative question.

◇ Getting Started

Before you begin the activities in this chapter, consider what you already know about the topics—and what you need to know. Read these questions and think about the answers:

What Do I Know About the Topic?

1. Do men and women think in different ways?
2. What's different about men's and women's styles of conversation?
3. What are some gender stereotypes people have about how men and women are different?

What Do I Know About the Language?

1. How do people express emotion with their intonation?
2. How can I make an appointment in English?
3. How should I answer a negative question?

◇ Getting Ready to Read

Look at the cartoon. What does the artist believe about communication between men and women? Which answer(s) do you agree with? Check (✓) your answer(s). Then discuss the cartoon with a small group.

_____ Women talk more than men.

_____ Women are more direct; men are more indirect.

_____ Women are clearer; men are less clear.

_____ Women are honest; men aren't.

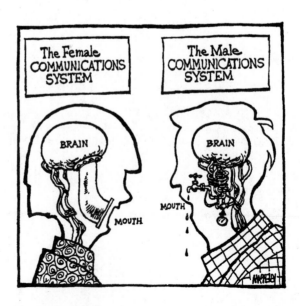

Reprinted by permission of Jeff MacNelly, San Jose Mercury News.

_____ Women say everything they're thinking; men say only important things.

_____ Women are less secretive than men.

_____ Other: _____

Mind Games Where do communication differences begin? Here is a test. Scientists say that on this kind of test, men usually do better on Question 1. Women usually do better on Question 2. Take this test just for fun.

Question 1: Which picture (a, b, c, or d) is the same as the picture on the left?

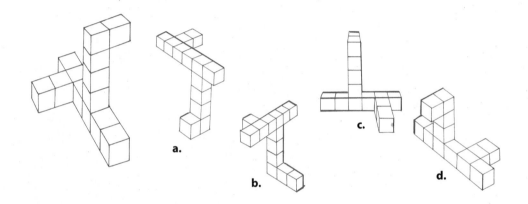

Question 2: For one minute, look at the items in this box (Box A). Then turn the page and look at the items in Box B. Cross out (X) anything that wasn't in Box A. How many items can you find?

Thinking Ahead Think about how little boys and girls (in your native culture) play and speak. Discuss your answers to these questions with the whole class:

1. Do boys and girls usually play together—or boys with boys and girls with girls?

2. Are their games similar or different?

3. Who plays in large groups with a leader—boys or girls?

4. Who plays in small groups or with one other child—boys or girls?

5. Who probably has one "best friend"—boys or girls?

6. Who gives *commands* (for example, "Give me that!" or "Get out of here!")—boys or girls?

7. Who gives *suggestions*, not commands—boys or girls?

8. Who probably tells other children "I'm better than you are"—boys or girls?

◆**Vocabulary Match**

Which definition on the right matches the word on the left? Put its letter on the line.

_____ 1. anthropologist   a. fight with words

_____ 2. research   b. person who studies human culture

_____ 3. tend to   c. chance to do something

_____ 4. argue   d. studies (noun)

_____ 5. turn   e. be likely (probable) to

◆**Read**

Read this excerpt from a book by a linguist, Deborah Tannen. She is writing about children in U.S. culture.

It Begins at the Beginning

1 Even if they grew up in the same neighbor-hood, on the same block, or in the same house, girls and boys grow up in different worlds of words. **Anthropologists** Daniel Maltz and Ruth Borker summarize **research** showing that boys and girls have very different ways of talking to their friends. Although they often play to-gether, boys and girls spend most of their time playing in same-sex groups. Their favorite games are different, and their ways of using language in their games are separated by a world of difference.

2 Boys **tend** to play outside, in large groups. Their groups have a leader who tells others what to do and how to do it. Boys' games have winners and losers and systems of rules. Finally, boys frequently **argue** about who is best at what.

3 Girls, on the other hand, play in small groups or in pairs; the center of a girl's social life is a best friend. In their most frequent games everyone gets a **turn.** Many of their ac-tivities (such as playing house) do not have winners or losers. Girls are expected not to show that they think they are better than the others. Girls don't give orders; they express their preferences as suggestions. Whereas boys say "Gimme that!" and "Get outta here!" girls say, "Let's do this," and "How about doing that?" Much of the time, they simply sit to-gether and talk.

—Adapted from Deborah Tannen, *You Just Don't Understand* (New York, Ballatine Books, 1990), pages 43–44. Permission granted by ICM, Copyright © 1990 by Deborah Tannen.

◆**After You Read**

Answer these questions with a partner:

1. Look at your predictions in Thinking Ahead. Were your answers the same as Tannen's?

2. Were you surprised by anything in the reading?

3. Deborah Tannen was writing about children in the United States. Are children in your native country similar or different?

PART 1: Men's Language and Women's Language

Getting Ready to Listen

Taking a Poll You're going to listen to people talk about how men and women think and speak. Do they think and speak differently? Talk with as many people as possible—students in your class, other people at the school, and people in your neighborhood. (Talk with the same number of men and women.) Ask them one question: "Who talks more—men or women?" What do men believe? What do women believe? Count their answers and complete the chart below. (You can use lines: ЖΙ= 5 people, for example.)

Question: Who talks more—men or women?

MEN'S ANSWERS		WOMEN'S ANSWERS	
Men talk more	Women talk more	Men talk more	Women talk more

> Speech is a mirror of the soul.
>
> —PUBLILIUS SYRUS

Vocabulary Building: Guessing Meaning from Context

You are going to hear part of a talk by Deborah Tannen (an expert on language) and Helen Fisher (an expert on human culture).* Before you listen, guess the meanings of the words underlined in the sentences below:

1. She told us a funny <u>anecdote.</u> She knows a lot of these short, interesting stories.

2. There was one <u>couple</u> sitting on the couch. The husband was about forty years old, and his wife was a little younger.

3. My family is very <u>vocal.</u> Everyone in my family talks a lot.

4. He <u>complains</u> a lot. He's always saying, "This is a terrible situation," or "I'm so tired," or "I hate my job," or "She really bothers me."

5. I'd like to talk to you in <u>private.</u> I don't want other people to hear this.

6. <u>Intimacy</u> isn't always easy. Closeness to another person takes time, patience, and love.

7. If you want to <u>please</u> children, give them some ice cream. They'll be happy.

*From an interview with Deborah Tannen and Helen Fisher on *Modern Times with Larry Josephson.* Used by permission.

Listen

Listening 1: Men's Language and Women's Language

Getting Main Ideas Listen for the answers to these questions.

Section 1

According to Deborah Tannen, who talks more—men or women?

Section 2

According to Helen Fisher, how can men make women happy? How can women make men happy?

 **After You Listen**

Follow Up Read the selection below and then answer the questions in the chart on the following page. Check *Men* or *Women*.

Love Is Never Enough
. . . .

Like Deborah Tannen (page 115), Dr. Aaron T. Beck has made use of studies by anthropologists Daniel Maltz and Ruth Borker. In his book *Love Is Never Enough,* Beck summarizes some of the differences that they have found in the communication styles of men and women:

- In a conversation between a man and a woman, the woman asks most of the questions because she wants to keep the conversation going.

- Women see conversation as a way to get closer to another person.

- Men see conversation as a way to exchange information.

- Women think, "If I don't ask, he'll think I don't care."

- Men think, "If she wants to tell me something, she'll tell me. I don't need to ask."

- Women use the pronouns *you* and *we* more than men do.

- Men state more facts and opinions than women do.

- If there are problems in a marriage, women feel the need to discuss these problems with their husbands. They think, "Everything will be OK if we can just keep talking."

- In a marriage, many men don't like to discuss problems. They prefer to find a quick solution. They think, "We're in serious trouble if we have to keep talking about it."

COMPREHENSION CHECK		
Male–Female Conversation		
In general . . .	Men	Women
Who asks most of the questions?		
Who uses the words *you* and *we* a lot?		
Who thinks "Questions keep a conversation going"?		
Who asks questions mostly to get information?		
Who makes more statements of fact or opinion?		
Who thinks it's important to talk over problems?		
Who thinks it's important *not* to talk over problems?		

ACADEMIC POWER STRATEGY

Become aware of your stereotypes and be open-minded about changing them. This is extremely important in the academic world. As you saw in Chapter 5, a stereotype is an oversimplified idea about a group of people. In other words, it is too general to be correct. A stereotype might have some basis in reality, but it is mostly wrong. A stereotype often begins with the word *all*. Many people have certain stereotypes about gender: "*All* women . . ." or "*All* men. . . ." Before we can break our own gender stereotypes and begin to see people clearly, we need to identify what stereotypes we actually have.

Apply the Strategy

For a few minutes, write about your own gender stereotypes. Have you been surprised by anything so far in this chapter? If so, what? Have your gender stereotypes changed? If so, how?

_____

_____

_____

_____

_____

Discussion In a small group (three or four students), discuss these questions:

1. In your native culture, do people complain "Women talk too much, and men don't talk enough"?

2. Deborah Tannen said that women talk a lot in private and men talk a lot in public. Is this true in your culture?

3. Helen Fisher said, "If a man wants to please a woman, sit down and _talk_ to her. And if a woman wants to get along with a man, she should _do_ something with him." Do you agree with this?

4. What do you like to talk about with your friends and family?

5. What do you like to do with your friends and family?

The Sound of It: Understanding Reductions

In normal or fast speech, you will hear reductions of some words. Listen to these examples. Can you hear the difference between the long forms and the short forms? (Note: The short forms are not correct in writing.)

Long Form	Reduction	Short Form
Get out of here.	out of → outta	Get outta here.
Give me that book.	give me → gimme	Gimme that book.
Let me ask you something.	let me → lemme	Lemme ask you something.
I don't know.	don't know → dunno	I dunno.
You like it, don't you?	don't you → doncha	You like it, doncha?
You liked it, didn't you?	didn't you → didncha?	You liked it, didncha?

A. Listen to these sentences. Do you hear a reduction? Check *Long Form* or *Short Form* as you listen. You will hear each sentence two times.

	LONG FORM	SHORT FORM
Examples:		
a. *Let me* help you.	X	
b. *Let me* help you.		X
1. I *don't know* him.		
2. *Give me* a minute, will you?		
3. *Don't you* believe it?		
4. I took it *out of* the closet.		
5. We *don't know* her.		
6. *Let me* talk with him.		
7. *Give me* your opinion.		
8. You believed it, *didn't you?*		

B. Listen to these conversations. You'll hear reduced (short) forms. Write the long forms. You will hear each conversation two times.

1. A: _____ talk with him about how you feel?

   B: Well, I tried to, but he doesn't like to discuss problems.
   I _____ why.

2. A: _____ the ball!

   B: No! This is our game. You get _____ here!

3. A: _____ think there's a problem?

   B: Yeah, well maybe. _____ just think about it for a while.

PART 2: Expressing Emotion

Getting Ready to Listen

Here are some sentences that men say in the listening passage. Are these emotional situations or not? What do you think?

Examples: Beautiful sunrise, dear.

That's a very sexy swimsuit.

This is the happiest day of my life.

Tickets for the Olympics?

Making Predictions Say the sentences out loud. What do you think the intonation should be? How will the men show their enthusiasm (excitement)?

Listen

Listening 2: Understanding Intonation

Listen to men say these four sentences. Which men are enthusiastic? Which aren't? Circle the answer.

1. Oh, yeah. Beautiful sunrise, dear.

      enthusiastic   not enthusiastic

2. Yeah. That's a very sexy swimsuit.

      enthusiastic   not enthusiastic

3. This is the happiest day of my life, too, honey.

      enthusiastic   not enthusiastic

4. Tickets for the Olympics? This is fantastic.

      enthusiastic   not enthusiastic

After You Listen

Discussion In a small group, discuss this question: In your native language, do people express enthusiasm, friendliness, or sincerity with their intonation? If so, how? If not, how do they express these emotions?

LANGUAGE LEARNING STRATEGY

Pay attention to people's intonation, not just their words. In English, people show emotion with intonation. When they are enthusiastic (excited) or very happy, their voices go up on stressed words. There are more "mountains" and "valleys" in their speech:

    It's really wonderful.   

When people are *not* very enthusiastic or happy, their voices usually don't go up. In the example below, the person *says* "It's really wonderful," but probably doesn't truly think so:

    It's really wonderful.   ———————

(continued on next page)

When a person likes another person and wants to be friendly, the voice usually goes up:

Oh, hi. How are you?

When a person does not feel very friendly toward another person, the voice does not usually go up:

Oh, hi. How are you?

Apply the Strategy

A. Listen to these sentences. Are the speakers enthusiastic or friendly, or not? Check your answers. You will hear each sentence two times.

	Not Very Enthusiastic or Friendly	Enthusiastic or Friendly
1. Good morning.		
2. Good morning.		
3. Yeah, I like it.		
4. Yeah, I like it.		
5. It was a good movie.		
6. It was a good movie.		
7. Is this for me?		
8. Is this for me?		
9. It's good to see you.		
10. It's good to see you.		

B. When a person shows quiet sincerity (honest, true feelings), the voice might not go up much, but there is probably a small pause between words or word groups.

Example: He . . . is a great . . . friend.

When the person is not very sincere, there is usually no pause.

Example: He'sagreatfriend.

Listen to these sentences. Are the speakers sincere or not? Check your answers. You will hear each sentence two times.

	SINCERE	NOT SINCERE
1. This is a wonderful meal.	_____	_____
2. This is a wonderful meal.	_____	_____
3. I had a good time.	_____	_____
4. I had a good time.	_____	_____
5. We're very glad to see you.	_____	_____
6. We're very glad to see you.	_____	_____
7. She is a really special person.	_____	_____
8. She is a really special person.	_____	_____

PART 3: Dealing with Communication Problems

◆ **Getting Ready to Listen**

Thinking Ahead You are going to hear three telephone conversations about some of the notices below. These are all from a college bulletin board. Read the notices. If you don't understand something, ask other students. (If nobody understands, ask your teacher.) What's one question that you might have about each notice?

 Listen

Listening 3: Talking About Notices

Getting Main Ideas Listen to the three conversations. Write the number of the conversation (1, 2, or 3) in the box next to the notice that goes with it.

Listening for Specific Information Listen to Conversation 1 again and answer these questions:

- How long has the woman been teaching?
- Can she give lessons at the man's house?

Taking a Message Listen to Conversation 2 again. Complete this form with the man's message.

Time: _____
While You Were Out
_____ called.
Telephone Number:_____
☐ returned your call
☐ wants to see you
☐ please call back
☐ will call again
☐ other
Message: _____
_____
_____

Listening for Stressed Words Listen to Conversation 3 again. Complete the conversation with the stressed words.

Woman: Good _____. Startime _____

Company.

Man: Hello. I'm _____ about your help

_____ ad at the _____. Uh, what

kind of _____ is it?

Woman: Well, you'd be _____ fliers.

Man: _____? Could you _____ more

about that?

Woman: We're _____ a new _____

theater. We need you to stand on the _____

and give _____ to people walking by—you

know, to advertise the _____.

Man: Oh, OK. Could I make an _____ for an

_____?

Woman: Yes, of _____. How's _____

morning at _____?

Man: I'm afraid I have a _____ at that time. Could

we make it in the _____?

Woman: _____. How about _____?

Man: Great.

After You Listen

Writing a Notice Write one or two notices for your class bulletin board or for a class "newspaper." These can be serious or funny. Do you want to sell or buy something? Do you need to find a roommate? Do you want to take or give lessons? Put it in your notice!

LANGUAGE YOU CAN USE: MAKING AN APPOINTMENT

When you make an appointment, both speakers need to agree on the time. What can you say if the other person suggests a time that is not possible for you? You can say several different things. Here's an example from the previous section.

A: Could I make an appointment for an interview?

B: Yes, of course. How's Tuesday morning at 10:00?

A: I'm afraid I have a class at that time. Could we make it in the afternoon?

B: Sure. How about 3:00?

A: Great.

Don't be shy about asking for a different time or day!

USING NEW LANGUAGE

Creating a Conversation Work with a partner. Look at the conversation below. One student is A, and one student is B. Take roles and have a conversation. Choose words from the lists. Then change roles and have another conversation. Choose different words from the lists.

A: Could I make an appointment
{ for an interview?
with a counselor?
with the doctor? }

B: Yes, of course.
{ How about
How's
We have an opening on }
{ Tuesday at 10:00?
Friday at 3:00?
the 14th at 9:00. }

A: I'm afraid
Oh, I'm sorry, but
{ I have a class at that time.
I can't make it that day. }

Could we make it
{ another time?
a little later?
a different day? }

B: Oh, sure.
{ How about Thursday?
How's that same day at 4:00?
We can fit you in on Friday afternoon. }

A: Great. See you then.

Role Play Work with a partner. Student A wants to make an appointment with the dentist. Student B is the dentist's receptionist (secretary). Student A uses the calendar at the top of page 127. Student B uses the appointment book at the bottom of page 127. Have a conversation. Use some of the expressions from the previous exercise.

Student's Calendar

Sunday	9	*picnic 11:30*
Monday	10	*class 9—12* *work 1—5*
Tuesday	11	*class 1—4*
Wednesday	12	*class 9—12* *work 1—5*
Thursday	13	*meet J. 10:00* *class 1—4*
Friday	14	*class 9—12*
Saturday	15	*movie w/ S!*

Monday   10

9:00 – 10:00   *Ann Evans–teeth cleaning*
10:00 – 11:00 _____
11:00 – 12:00   *F. Dale–check-up*
closed for lunch
2:00 – 3:00   *Marian Forbes–extractions*
3:00 – 4:00 _____
4:00 – 5:00   *E. Chavez–check-up*

Tuesday   11

9:00 – 10:00   *Bill Wong*
10:00 – 11:00 _____
11:00 – 12:00 _____
closed for lunch
2:00 – 3:00 _____
3:00 – 4:00 _____
4:00 – 5:00   *N. Sarkisian–cleaning*

Wednesday   12

9:00 – 10:00 _____
10:00 – 11:00 _____
11:00 – 12:00 _____
closed for lunch
2:00 – 3:00   *conference with Dr. Allen*
3:00 – 4:00 _____
4:00 – 5:00 _____

Thursday   13

9:00 – 10:00   *G. Porter–check-up*
10:00 – 11:00 _____
11:00 – 12:00 *M. Forbes–fit for denture*
closed for lunch
2:00 – 3:00 _____
3:00 – 4:00 _____
4:00 – 5:00   *Ed Cohen–fill cavity*

Friday   14

9:00 – 10:00   *L. Miles–cleaning*
10:00 – 11:00 *meet w/ Dr. Fahmian*
11:00 – 12:00 _____
closed for lunch
2:00 – 3:00 _____
3:00 – 4:00 _____
4:00 – 5:00 _____

Notes

_____
_____
_____
_____
_____
_____

Now change roles. Student A is the dentist's receptionist, and Student B wants to make an appointment. Have another conversation. After you finish, write one of your conversations. Your teacher may want you to present it to the class or put it on tape.

LANGUAGE LEARNING STRATEGY

Learn how to respond to a negative question—or, more specifically, a negative statement with intonation that goes up at the end. People often use statement word order to ask a negative question if they think the answer will be "no." Their intonation goes up. Here's an example from Conversation 1:

Example: Question: You don't have one?

In many languages, people answer "yes" because they're thinking, "Yes, that's right. I don't have one." But in English the answer is "no."

Example: Question: You don't have one?
Answer: No (I don't).

Apply the Strategy

A. With a partner, take turns asking and answering these questions. In each case, answer "no" and give the correct answer. Then listen and check your answers.

Example: a: The main language of Quebec isn't English?

b: <u>No, it's French.</u> (French)

1. a: It's not strange to experience culture shock?

   b: _____ (normal)

2. a: Osaka isn't the capital of Japan?

   b: _____ (Tokyo)

3. a: Men don't usually talk much at home?

   b: _____ (in public)

4. a: Women don't usually talk much in public?

   b: _____ (at home)

5. a: English isn't easy?

   b: _____ (hard)

6. a. You're not from Canada?

   b: _____

7. a: Today isn't Sunday?

   b: _____

8. a: You haven't been to Antarctica?

   b: _____

9. a: You can't call a teacher by her first name in your native country?

   b: _____

10. a: College textbooks aren't free?

    b: _____

B. You show surprise in a negative question if your intonation goes down low and then up high at the end.

Example: Question: You don't have one?
              Answer: No, I don't.

With a partner, take turns asking and answering these questions. Person A will show surprise in the question. Person B will answer "no" and add a short negative answer. Then listen and check your answers.

Example: a: The main language of Quebec isn't English?

              b: _No, it isn't._____

1. a: We don't have class tomorrow?

   b: _____

2. a: You didn't see it?

   b: _____

3. a: He doesn't like it?

   b: _____

4. a: They won't even try it?

   b: _____

(continued on next page)

5. a: She hasn't studied English before?

    b: _____

6. a: You're not from around here?

    b: _____

7. a: You don't know him?

    b: _____

8. a: They can't help us?

    b: _____

9. a: There won't be a problem with that?

    b: _____

10. a: She doesn't eat meat at all?

    b: _____

C. Sometimes a person thinks that the answer to a question will be "no," but that person isn't right. How do you answer?

Example: Question: You don't have one?
             Answer: Yes, I *do*.

It's very important to stress the affirmative verb in the answer (*do* in the example). Ask and answer Questions 1–10 from the previous exercise. This time, Person B will answer "yes" and correct Person A.

PART 4: Workplace Communication

As more and more women enter business, there is a growing perception that gender differences in communication exist in the workplace, just as in other areas of life. The CNN video that you are about to see deals with how people are responding to problems communicating at work. Before you view the video, complete the following activities.

Thinking Ahead In a small group, discuss the answers to these questions:

1. In your opinion, who are more creative—men or women? Who are more analytical (careful to analyze, or study each part of a problem)—men or women?

> . . . when men and women agree, it is only in their conclusions; their reasons are always different.
>
> —GEORGE SANTAYANA

2. Here are some possible ways to give criticism—in other words, to tell another person that he or she has done something badly. Which are more polite? Which are less polite? Do men and women have different "styles" of giving criticism? Can you think of other ways to give criticism?

   • Could you please rework this report a little? If you include some examples, I think your main ideas will be clearer.

   • This report is badly written. You'll have to rewrite it.

   • You have some interesting ideas here, but the report is too general. Some specific details would improve it a lot.

   • If I were you, I might include several examples for each main point in the report.

3. When someone says "I'm sorry," what does the person mean? Can *I'm sorry* have more than one meaning?

◆ Vocabulary Match

If necessary, use a dictionary to help you match the following words or expressions with their definitions. Write the letters on the lines.

_____ 1. upper management

_____ 2. firm (noun)

_____ 3. issue

_____ 4. seminar

_____ 5. blunt

_____ 6. to buffer

_____ 7. to jibe

_____ 8. assertive

_____ 9. aggressive

a. not trying to be polite or nice

b. class to study a specific subject

c. to make something less shocking or unkind

d. corporation

e. very confident about one's own opinions

f. higher-ups; bosses

g. pushy; ready to attack

h. a point to consider

i. to match, agree with

© CNN

TUNING IN: "Workplace Communication"

Getting the "Big Picture" Watch the video once. Try to answer this question: What are the women in these seminars learning?

Understanding Important Details Watch the video again—perhaps several times. Listen for the answers to the following questions:

> **When work is a pleasure, life is a joy! When work is a duty, life is slavery.**
>
> **—MAXIM GORKY**

1. When Carmen de Brock gives a seminar at a company, what is the number one thing she is asked by the men at the company?

2. If women are better communicators than men, why are so many communication training seminars directed at women instead of men?

3. According to Deborah Tannen, how do bosses sometimes interpret female speech patterns (such as saying "I'm sorry")?

4. When a woman says "I'm sorry," what does she often mean?

Discussion In small groups, discuss your answers to these questions:

1. Have you ever experienced or noticed differences between men and women in workplace communication?

2. People in the video give several examples of different ways in which men and women express themselves at work. What are some others?

3. In the video, you saw women learning how to better communicate in the workplace. Should men also attend seminars in order to improve their workplace communication skills?

PUTTING IT ALL TOGETHER

A Typical Conversation What's a typical (usual, common) conversation that you have had with your husband, wife, boyfriend, girlfriend? Or what's a conversation that your parents often had? Tell a small group about this conversation.

Example: My mother: Oh, I had such a hard day at work! Everyone in the office is complaining about the new boss. I didn't even have time for lunch, and I'm so hungry! . . . So how was your day, dear?

My father: OK.

My mother: Well, what happened at work?

My father: Nothing.

At the Movies Rent a movie that deals with the business world. Examples of such movies are *9 to 5* and *Wall Street*. Watch the movie and make notes on what you notice about the way people communicate. Do the men and women communicate differently? How do people express emotion, make appointments, or talk on the phone?

Write About It.

When you finish, write 1–2 paragraphs about the results of your project. What did you learn from your project? Were you surprised by anything?

Test-Taking Tip

Read statements carefully on true/false tests. Look for words called *absolutes*. These kinds of words often make a statement false. Examples include words such as *always, never, only,* and *all*. Also, be careful of statements with two clauses. If the statement contains *and,* both clauses must be true for the statement to be true. If the statement contains *or,* only one clause has to be true for the statement to be true.

CHECK YOUR PROGRESS

On a scale of 1 to 5, rate how well you have mastered the goals set at the beginning of the chapter:

1 2 3 4 5   understand some differences between men's and women's communication styles.

1 2 3 4 5   become aware of your stereotypes and be open-minded about changing them.

1 2 3 4 5   understand reductions in speech.

1 2 3 4 5   pay attention to speakers' use of intonation to express emotion.

1 2 3 4 5   make an appointment.

1 2 3 4 5   answer a negative question.

If you've given yourself a 3 or lower on any of these goals:

- visit the *Tapestry* web site for additional practice.

- ask your instructor for extra help.

- review the sections of the chapter that you found difficult.

- work with a partner or study group to further your progress.

*S*ome friendships and romantic relationships are very brief. Some last a lifetime. How do people ever get together— or *stay* together? What are the obstacles to meeting people? What are the pleasant surprises in getting to know them?

MAKING FRIENDS AND FINDING LOVE

In this chapter, you'll listen to people talking about meeting and getting together with other people. You'll listen to a personal "radio essay" about affectionate nicknames, and you'll give your own ideas on relationships. You'll also have the opportunity to view a CNN segment on romance in Japan.

Setting Goals

In this chapter you will learn:

◈ to make invitations and suggestions in English.

◈ to pay attention to a speaker's choice of words when that person is making an invitation.

◈ the difference between general and specific invitations.

◈ how to accept or decline invitations.

◈ how to share ideas and work together with your classmates.

◈ how to make inferences by paying attention to the entire context.

◈ how to ask personal questions in a polite way.

◈ the importance of intonation in understanding meaning.

◈ to organize and give a short report.

◆**Getting Started**

Here are some quotations about friendship and love. What do you think each one means? Do agree with them or not? Discuss them in a small group.

> A true friend is the most precious of all possessions and the one we take the least thought about acquiring.
> —La Rochefoucauld, *Maxims*

> Who ever loved that loved not at first sight?
> —Christopher Marlowe, *Hero and Leander*

> There is no more lovely, friendly, and charming relationship, communion, or company than a good marriage.
> —Martin Luther, *Table Talk*

◆**Getting Ready to Read**

Thinking Ahead The man and woman in this picture are exchanging gifts for Valentine's Day—a day on which many people in some countries send cards or give small presents to people they love. Each person is hoping for certain gifts. Read the thoughts in their minds and answer the questions that follow. Work with a partner.

> **The verb "to love" in Persian is "to have a friend." "I love you" translated literally is "I love you as a friend," and "I don't like you" simply means "I don't have you as a friend."**
>
> **—SHUSHA GUPPY**

1. What's the only item on the list that the man and woman agree on?

2. What do they probably think about each other's lists?

3. Do people celebrate Valentine's Day in your native culture? If so, how?

> **The course of true love never did run smooth.**
>
> —WILLIAM SHAKESPEARE

4. What would *you* like to receive on Valentine's Day? Write your wish list here:

_____

_____

_____

 Read

In *Male and Female Realities,* Joe Tanenbaum reports the findings of his surveys on the opinions that men and women in the United States have of each other. Here is some of what he learned.

MEN WANT WOMEN TO:	WOMEN WANT MEN TO:
talk less	talk more
be less emotional	be more emotional
be less "romantic"	be more "romantic"
be less involved with others' problems	care more about people
be more serious	have more fun
put job/career first	put family first
change less	be more flexible
be on time	be more flexible with time

Excerpted from Joe Tanenbaum, *Male and Female Realities* (Sugar Land, Texas: Candle Publishing Company, 1989), p. 18.

After You Read

Discussion This list was written about men and women in the United States. In your opinion, which items on the list are true in your native culture?

LANGUAGE YOU CAN USE: EXPRESSING DESIRED ACTIONS

To express an action that a person desires, you can use this simple structure:

someone + want(s) + infinitive

Examples: She wants to take a walk up the beach.

He wants to go to a soccer game.

But how can you express an action that a person wants *another* person to do?

Use this structure:

someone + want(s) + someone + infinitive

Examples: Men want women to talk less.

            Women want men to talk more.

            A teacher wants all students to participate.

USING NEW LANGUAGE

With a partner of your own gender, answer this question: Are there items that you would like to add to the list—specific items about your own spouse or siblings or friends of the opposite sex? If so, what?

PART 1: Meeting People

Getting Ready to Listen

Getting Someone's Attention Imagine this situation: You're walking down the street. You see a *very* attractive person. You would like to get this person's attention—to meet him or her. In your native culture, is it ever acceptable to do this? If so, what are some things that people typically say or do to get the attention of an attractive stranger? Discuss this with a partner.

Vocabulary Match

Look at the picture on the following page. Match the words in the box to items in the picture. Write the letters by the items.

a. briefcase	c. dime	e. Cadillac convertible
b. pocket	d. parking meter	f. sidewalk

Making Predictions Answer these questions about the picture:

1. What is happening in the picture?

2. Whom does the man notice?

3. What is the man thinking?

4. What will he do?

Listen

Listening 1: A New York Story

Getting Main Ideas You are going to hear a famous American story-teller, Garrison Keillor,* tell about an experience on a New York City street. Don't worry if you don't understand every word. As you listen, think about the answers to these questions:

- What did the man do? Why?
- What did the woman do? Why?

Note: *to lean against* = to stand against

After You Listen

Discussion Work in a group of four to five students. Discuss this question: What are different ways to meet people—either new friends or a possible romantic partner? Make a list of all the group's ideas. The ideas can be serious or silly. Choose one person to be the group's "secretary." This person will write everyone's ideas.

In your journal, write your own ideas about different ways to meet someone. These can be serious, funny, or both.

PART 2: Getting Together

◇ **Getting Ready to Listen**

Making Invitations People in any relationship (friendship, business, or love) need to know how to make invitations and how to respond to (answer) them. Work with a partner. How do people make invitations in English? Write several ways on a piece of paper.

◇ **Listen**

Listening 2: Understanding Invitations

Serious or Not Serious? Take this short quiz to see how much you already understand about invitations in English. You are going to hear four conversations. In each one, someone invites another person to do something. Don't worry if you don't understand every word. Just listen for the answer to this question: Which are serious invitations? (In other words, from which conversations do you really expect the people to get together later?) If you're not sure, just put a question mark.

	Serious Invitation	Not a Serious Invitation
Conversation 1		
Conversation 2		
Conversation 3		
Conversation 4		

LANGUAGE LEARNING STRATEGY

Pay attention to a speaker's choice of words when the person is making an invitation. If you do this, you'll know what to expect. There are two kinds of invitations and suggestions in English: specific and general.

SPECIFIC	GENERAL
Can you come to dinner next Friday at 8:00?	Why don't we get together sometime soon?
Would you like to go to a movie tomorrow night?	Let's have dinner or something in a couple of weeks.

Specific invitations are serious. The speaker really wants to get together and needs an answer. General invitations are friendly expressions but are not very serious. The two people might or might not get together. You need to listen for words or expressions that are specific and words or expressions that are general.

SPECIFIC			GENERAL		
next Saturday	this evening	on May 24th	sometime	sometime soon	someday
tomorrow evening	at 7:30		in a couple of weeks	one of these days	

Apply the Strategy

Listen to these sentences. Are they serious invitations? Check *Serious* or *Not Very Serious*. You will hear each sentence two times.

	SERIOUS	NOT VERY SERIOUS
1.	_____	_____
2.	_____	_____
3.	_____	_____
4.	_____	_____
5.	_____	_____
6.	_____	_____
7.	_____	_____
8.	_____	_____

Now check your answers to the short quiz on page 140. Listen again to the four conversations. Were your answers correct?

LANGUAGE YOU CAN USE: RESPONDING TO INVITATIONS

 **After You Listen**

How do you respond to an invitation? If the invitation is *general,* you accept it (say "yes") in a general way.

Examples: That sounds good.   Great. I'll give you a call.

Sure. Good idea.   OK. I'll call you.

If the invitation is *specific,* you need to answer in a specific way. If you want to accept, ask for or give a specific time or place in your answer.

Examples: That sounds good. *What time* do you want to meet?

Sure. Good idea. *Where* should we meet?

Great. I'll give you a call *tonight*.

OK. I'll call you *tomorrow morning*.

If you want to decline (say "no"), you need to tell the person "no" and say a few more words to be polite.

Examples: No, I'm sorry. I'm busy that night.

Oh, I can't do it that day. I have an appointment.

No, I can't make it then. Maybe another night?

No, that's a bad day for me. But let's get together soon.

USING NEW LANGUAGE

Work with a partner. Practice invitations. One person will make an invitation. The other person will accept or decline. Then change roles. Use some of these phrases.

MAKING AN INVITATION

Why don't we . . .	$\left\{\begin{array}{l}\text{have a cup of coffee}\\ \text{see a movie}\\ \text{go to a game}\end{array}\right.$	$\left.\begin{array}{l}\text{next weekend?}\\ \text{sometime soon?}\\ \text{on Friday night?}\end{array}\right.$
Can you . . .		
Would you like to . . .		

Let's $\left\{\begin{array}{l}\text{get together}\\ \text{have lunch}\end{array}\right\}$ $\left\{\begin{array}{l}\text{some day.}\\ \text{one of these days.}\end{array}\right.$

ACCEPTING AN INVITATION (SPECIFIC OR GENERAL)

That sounds good.

Sure. Good idea.

Great. I'll give you a call.

OK. I'll call you.

ACCEPTING A SPECIFIC INVITATION

What time . . . ?

Where . . . ?

. . . this evening.

. . . tomorrow morning.

. . . on Thursday.

DECLINING A SPECIFIC INVITATION

No, . . . $\left\{\begin{array}{l}\text{I'm sorry.}\\ \text{I can't make it then.}\\ \text{that's a bad time for me.}\\ \text{I'm busy that day.}\end{array}\right.$ $\left\{\begin{array}{l}\text{Maybe another day?}\\ \text{But let's get together soon.}\end{array}\right.$

ACADEMIC POWER STRATEGY

Share ideas and work together with your classmates. Your English class is a perfect place to learn about different cultures and to compare ways of saying things in your own language and in English.

Apply the Strategy

With a partner, discuss this question: What are the similarities and differences between making (and accepting or declining) invitations in your first language and in English?

PART 3: My Honey

Getting Ready to Listen   **Discussion**

1. In your first language, what are some common nicknames that friends have for each other? (Nicknames are names that we use with family or friends instead of their real names.) How do people acquire (get) nicknames?

2. In your first language, are there some special nicknames that married people or people in love use for each other? If so, what are some of them?

3. Are there special nicknames that only *younger* people use for the one they love? Are any nicknames old-fashioned?

Vocabulary Check

The following words and phrases are from the listening passage. Check the ones you already know. Add new words that you learn to your Vocabulary Log. (You'll find these words in the exercise that follows.)

_____ monikers   _____ idiosyncrasies

_____ affection   _____ initially

_____ rocky times   _____ startled

_____ the bottom line   _____ reverted

_____ pet names   _____ vow

_____ bound (past tense of *bind*)

◇ Vocabulary Building

> No one acts more fool-
> ishly than a wise man
> in love.
>
> —**WELSH PROVERB**

Guessing Meaning from Context Guess the meanings of the under-lined words in the sentences that follow. These will help you under-stand the listening passage.

1. In English, some <u>monikers</u> of <u>affection</u>—such as Sweetheart, Honey, and Babe—are pretty common. But many couples create special <u>pet names</u> for each other.

2. They had some <u>rocky times</u> in their marriage, but even in the middle of a terrible experience, <u>the bottom line</u> was their love for each other. This always <u>bound</u> them together.

3. <u>Initially</u>, when I met George, his little <u>idiosyncrasies</u> irritated me. After a while, though, these strange little habits didn't bother me anymore.

4. She was <u>startled</u> the first time he called her "Honey." She was surprised because she hadn't realized how comfortable their rela-tionship had become.

5. For many months, he called her "Susie." Then he started calling her "Babe." But when he discovered that she hated that nick-name, he <u>reverted</u> to "Susie" and made a <u>vow</u> never to call her "Babe" again.

◇ Listen

Listening 3: My Honey

Getting Main Ideas In this passage, Robert Rand* talks about af-fectionate nicknames that his parents used for each other and ones that he and his wife Eriko use for each other. (Note: Rand uses many new words in addition to the ones that you've just seen. However, you don't need to know them in order to understand the main ideas of this passage.) Listen for the answers to these questions:

1. What's similar about the way that Robert and Eriko use nick-names and the way that Robert's parents used them?

2. Which nickname does Robert refuse to use for his wife? Why?

Listening for Names Listen to the passage again. Which real names do you hear? Which affectionate nicknames do you hear? Write them in the following table.

*Robert Rand is a public radio producer and editor.

REAL NAMES	AFFECTIONATE NICKNAMES
Robert	
Florence	Schnookums
	Poopsie-Woopsie

◆ **After You Listen**

LANGUAGE LEARNING STRATEGY

Apply the Strategy

Make inferences in English, as in your first language, by paying attention to the entire context. In this way, you can often understand people even when they don't explicitly say what they mean.

Robert Rand tells us about the first time Eriko casually called him "Honey." He says: "I could not dismiss the fact that Eriko, in one word, had turned my legs into noodles and my heart into chocolate pudding." What do you think he means? Did he like it when she called him "Honey"?

LANGUAGE YOU CAN USE: ASKING PERSONAL QUESTIONS

Sometimes you want to ask someone a personal question, but it might be awkward to do this. Before you ask a personal question, you need to make sure the person doesn't mind answering. In order to do this, you can say something like:

- May I ask you a personal question?
- Do you mind if I ask you something personal?
- I have a question for you. You don't have to answer, but. . . .

USING NEW LANGUAGE

Most people in the United States marry between the ages of 25 and 29.

Talk with five people who are married. Politely ask them if they use any special affectionate nicknames with their spouse. Write their answers below.

	Nickname
Person 1	
Person 2	
Person 3	
Person 4	
Person 5	

PART 4: A Radio Drama

◆ **Getting Ready to Listen**

Brainstorming Vocabulary You are going to hear a commercial for a pasta company.* The commercial is in the form of a radio drama. You won't hear much English because every word in the drama is a kind of pasta! Before you listen, think of as many kinds of pasta as you can. Write them on the lines below. Don't worry about spelling.

Love is a kind of warfare.

—OVID

KINDS OF PASTA

_____ capellini _____ _____ _____

_____ vermicelli _____ _____ _____

_____ rigatoni _____ _____ _____

Sharing Answers Share your answers with the class. One person will put the words on the board. Add words to your list.

*RONZONI Pasta radio commercial is used courtesy of Hershey Food Corporation.

Listen

Listening 4: More Than Pasta

Getting Main Ideas Very often, you can understand more from people's intonation than from their words. You might surprise yourself, in fact, by how much you can understand even if you don't know *one word!* Listen to the commercial once or twice. It's a wonderful example of the importance of intonation. As you listen, think about the answers to these questions:

1. Who are the people?

2. How do they feel about each other?

3. What happens in this drama?

After You Listen

Making Inferences Work in groups or with the whole class. Play a bit of the tape, stop, and guess what the people are saying. Write it down. Play a bit more of the tape, stop, and write. Continue this way and write a conversation in English. There are no "correct" or "incorrect" answers. Do this activity just for fun.

The Sound of It: Listening for Stressed Words

A. Listen to these sentences and repeat them. Notice the stressed words.

1. How ARE you?

2. Let's get TOGETHER sometime.

3. I'll give you a CALL.

4. Let's have LUNCH sometime soon.

5. What do you want to get MARRIED for?

6. I was HOPING she would NOTICE.

7. I'll be GLAD when final EXAMS are over.

B. Listen to the important (stressed) words in these sentences. Underline them. (Some sentences have two stressed words.)

1. Who is that?

2. May I ask you a question?

3. I'm busy that night.

4. I'll call you tomorrow morning.

5. I have a question for you.

6. That sounds good.

C. Work with a partner. Figure out which word(s) should be stressed *in the answers* below. Underline those words. When you finish all five, listen to the tape to see if you were right. Then practice saying the questions and answers.

1. Question: Where does she want to GO?

   Answer: She wants to go to a movie.

2. Question: Where does SHE want to go?

   Answer: She wants to go to a movie.

3. Question: What did they DO?

   Answer: They got married.

4. Question: WHEN did they get married?

   Answer: They got married last year.

5. Question: What TIME should we MEET?

   Answer: Let's meet at about 8:00.

PART 5: Romance in Japan

◆Vocabulary Match

Which definition on the right matches the word or expression on the left? Write its letter on the line. (Use a dictionary if necessary.)

_____ 1. obligated   a. person with whom you work

_____ 2. colleague   b. image or idea of a perfect situation

_____ 3. off the mark   c. to give or receive a score

_____ 4. to rate/rank   d. required

_____ 5. fantasy   e. not reaching a goal

To the ancient Greeks, Eros was the god of romantic love. To the ancient Romans, the same god was called Cupid. People believed that if Cupid shot someone with his arrow, that person would fall in love. These days, you'll see pictures of Cupid on Valentine's cards.

TUNING IN:
"Romance Survey in Japan"

The CNN video segment for this chapter refers to two surveys by Harlequin Publishing Company—a company that is famous for producing romance novels. In one of these surveys, men in nineteen countries rated the "romance level" of women from their country. In the other survey, women in the same nineteen countries rated the "romance level" of men.

Making Predictions How do you think Japanese men and women rated each other in the surveys by Harlequin Publishing Company? In other words, are the Japanese romantic?

Getting the "Big Picture" Watch the video once and listen for the answer to this question: In general, what do Japanese men and women think about each other's ability to be romantic?

Understanding Details Mark *T* if the sentence is true or *F* if it is false.

_____ 1. Japanese women are expected to buy sweets for the men they work with, not just for their sweethearts.

_____ 2. Japanese women seldom say "I love you."

_____ 3. According to the surveys, both Japanese men and women are the most romantic in the world.

_____ 4. There are three words in the Japanese language for the word *romantic*.

_____ 5. The Japanese seem to separate romance and reality.

PUTTING IT ALL TOGETHER

Give a short oral report (1–2 minutes) on one of the topics below—A, B, or C—to a small group or to the class.

Topic A: Meeting the Person of Your Dreams

In your native country, how do people meet someone to marry? (Where? In what situations?) How did people find spouses in the past—fifty or a hundred years ago? Were the customs different from today? For example, how did your parents meet? How did your grandparents meet?

Topic B: Romance

What does *romantic* mean? Are people from some cultures more romantic than others? What are some characteristics of a romantic person? How would you rate your native culture on "romance level"?

Topic C: A Typical Wedding

Describe a typical wedding in your native culture. What are some of the most important wedding customs? Are weddings these days different from weddings a hundred years ago?

To prepare for your report, follow these steps:

1. Brainstorm. Write quick notes on all of your ideas.

2. Work on vocabulary. If you need some new words, ask a classmate, your teacher, or a friend—or use a dictionary.

3. Put your ideas in order. Discard (throw out) any ideas that don't belong.

4. Put notes on an index card.

5. Give your report. When you speak, don't read from the index card. Just refer to it when you need to remember your ideas.

Test-Taking Tip

For multiple choice and matching tests, look for clues to the right answer within the test itself. Clues can sometimes be found in the grammar of the test questions and answers. For example, if a question is past tense, but one of the answers is present tense, you know you can rule out that answer. Similarly, if a question is singular, but one of the answers is plural, you know that that cannot be the correct answer. Rule out any grammatically incorrect answers. Also, sometimes you can find important information in one question that can actually help you answer a different question on the test.

CHECK YOUR PROGRESS

On a scale of 1 to 5, rate how well you have mastered the goals set at the beginning of the chapter:

1 2 3 4 5   make invitations and suggestions in English.

1 2 3 4 5   pay attention to a speaker's choice of words when that person is making an invitation.

1 2 3 4 5   understand the difference between general and specific invitations.

1 2 3 4 5   accept or decline invitations.

1 2 3 4 5   share ideas and work together with your classmates.

1 2 3 4 5   make inferences by paying attention to the entire context.

1 2 3 4 5   ask personal questions in a polite way.

1 2 3 4 5   understand the importance of intonation in understanding meaning.

1 2 3 4 5   organize and give a short report.

If you've given yourself a 3 or lower on any of these goals:

- visit the *Tapestry* web site for additional practice.
- ask your instructor for extra help.
- review the sections of the chapter that you found difficult.
- work with a partner or study group to further your progress.

Women in the United States spend about seven hours a week shopping, and men in the United States spend about five hours a week shopping; about half of the total time is buying food and clothing. People in the United States spend 40 to 50 percent of their income on housing and food.

- About how much time do you spend shopping each week?
- Do you spend more or less than half your income on housing and food? Do you enjoy shopping?
- Why or why not?

TELL ME WHAT I WANT: ADVERTISING . . . AND SHOPPING

In this chapter, you'll hear some radio advertisements, find out some practical things about shopping in a place where people speak English, and have the opportunity to see a CNN video segment about advertising.

Setting Goals

In this chapter you will learn:

- ◈ to use the yellow pages of the telephone book.
- ◈ to think ahead and predict what people will say.
- ◈ to understand messages on message machines.
- ◈ to find opportunities to practice English outside the classroom.
- ◈ to make a purchase.
- ◈ to return something to a store.
- ◈ to express agreement and disagreement.
- ◈ to understand incomplete sentences and short answers to questions.
- ◈ about how advertising works to create an "image."

◆ **Getting Started**

Look at the photos and pictures in this chapter. What topics will the chapter probably cover? Work with a partner. Choose one picture and describe it.

◆ **Getting Ready to Read**

Vocabulary Check The following words and phrases are from the reading. Check the ones you already know. You can add new words that you learn to your Vocabulary Log.

_____ advertisement, ad

_____ to cheer up

_____ fashion

_____ like a kid in a candy store

_____ window shopping

◆ **Vocabulary Match**

Which word or phrase above has the same meaning as the following?

_____ 1. like a child in a place with lots of good or appealing things

_____ 2. shopping without spending any money

_____ 3. to make happy

_____ 4. commercial

_____ 5. style

◆ **Read**

1 People everywhere today see and hear **advertisements** constantly: in signs, in newspapers or magazines, on television, on the radio, even on the Internet! No matter where you are, you are probably going to see or hear advertisements, or commercials. Some people say that advertising has a bad influence, or effect. Says writer Noreene Janus:

Advertisers use mainly a few themes again and again: happiness, youth, success, status, luxury, **fashion,** and beauty. They hide class differences and problems in the workplace. Many **ads** suggest that you can solve all human problems by buying things. . . . They suggest that modern things are good and traditional things are bad. . . . As one ad professional said, "Once the TV set goes to work, the family is **like a kid in a candy store.** They watch 450 commercials a week. They see all the beautiful things. And they want everything that they see." (Adapted from Noreene Janus, *Cultural Survival Quarterly,* summer 1983.)

2   However, not everyone thinks that advertising is a bad thing. Some people say that advertising sometimes gives us useful information about different products—for example, the advantages of buying one product instead of another. Also, shopping sometimes makes us feel good. When people see a famous person on TV talking about a certain kind of shoes or jacket, they like how they feel when they buy the same shoes or jacket. According to writer Judith Williamson:

The meaning in most people's lives comes much more from what they use than from what they produce in their jobs. Clothes, furniture, all the things that we buy involve **deci-**

sions and the use of our own choice. . . . Shopping is a social event . . . . It makes you feel normal. Most people find it **cheers them up**—even **window shopping.** (Adapted from Judith Williamson, *Consuming Passions: The Dynamics of Popular Culture* [London and New York: Marion Boyards, 1986].)

◆ **After You Read**

Discussion

1. What are some of the themes that advertisers use?

2. What do many advertisements suggest?

3. Does shopping "cheer you up"?

4. Do you go window shopping when you don't have money to buy things?

5. What kinds of things do you like to shop for? What kinds of things do you *not* like to shop for?

PART 1: Understanding Advertising; Using the Yellow Pages

◆ **Getting Ready to Listen**

Phone books in the United States have a lot of useful information in them. You can find out about community services, postal services, public transportation, recreation, government offices, where to shop, what to do in an emergency, and, of course, how to use telephone services.

The **"Yellow Pages"** Have you ever looked at the yellow pages of your telephone book? They give you a lot of useful information. Here are some examples of things that you can look up in the yellow pages:

- barber shops
- beauty salons
- bicycles
- computers
- pharmacies
- restaurants
- shoes
- sporting goods

The yellow pages have an index that shows where to look for the item you need. Then you look on the page the index gives you. Here is a section of an index. If you want to rent a car, what page would you look on? Circle it.

Car Radios—See	
Automobile Radios & Stereophonic Systems	123
Car Rental—See Automobile Renting	124
Car Telephone—See Cellular Telephones	260

Understanding Yellow-Page Ads Below are three ads from the yellow pages of three different telephone books (for different cities). For each ad, find the following information:

- What is the advertisement for?
- Is there an address for the business?
- What is the telephone number of the business?

a.

b.

c.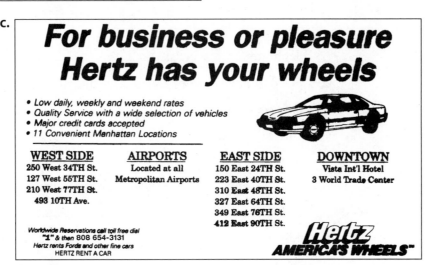

 Listen

Listening 1: Understanding a Radio Advertisement

Listen to the radio advertisement. There may be words in it that you don't understand. The first time you listen, just try to identify the business. Look at the ads from the yellow pages above. Which yellow page ad is for the same business as the ad you hear? Write a, b, or c: _____.

Understanding the Ad Listen again. What does Doris need to do? Why?

◆**After You Listen**

Using Your Local Telephone Book Get a copy of your local telephone book. (If you don't have one at home, ask your teacher for one or go to a public telephone.) Find a business for each of the items below. Write the name, address, and telephone number of the business.

1. a copy shop

   Name of business: _____

   Address: _____

   Telephone: _____

2. soccer or tennis balls

   Name of business: _____

   Address: _____

   Telephone: _____

3. a pharmacy that is open at night

   Name of business: _____

   Address: _____

   Telephone: _____

4. a place to have clothes cleaned (cleaners)

   Name of business: _____

   Address: _____

   Telephone: _____

5. a pizza restaurant that delivers (brings pizza to you)

   Name of business: _____

   Address: _____

   Telephone: _____

6. a place to get a haircut

   Name of business: _____

   Address: _____

   Telephone: _____

7. a bank

   Name of business: _____

   Address: _____

   Telephone: _____

PART 2: Understanding Messages
············· on Business Answering Machines

◆ Getting Ready to Listen

Think ahead and predict what people will say. This will help your listening comprehension. For instance, if you walk into a fast-food restaurant, what questions will you probably hear? (Examples: "Do you want fries with that?" "What would you like to drink?") Thinking ahead and considering the situation will help you understand more.

Apply the Strategy

Work in pairs. Look at the following ad for a bicycle shop from the yellow pages of the telephone book. What things do you think you might hear on a telephone message for this store? Make a list. Then compare your answers with your partner's.

1. _____

2. _____

3. _____

NEW & USED BIKES
328•8900
Quality Repairs & Parts
for all makes

Specializing in:
- Used Bikes
- Inexpensive New Bikes
- Mountain Bikes
- Hybrids
- Sport Touring

- 3-Speeds
- Kid's Bikes
- Accessories
- Buy-Back Program
- Layaways

- Free Estimates
- One Day Service
- Complete Parts Dept.
- Large Repair Facility
- Affordable Rates

GENERAL
RALEIGH   YOKOTA
              HARO   REDLINE
                         MT SHASTA

recyclery

1955 El Camino Real, Palo Alto
Located across from Stanford University

Listen   **Listening 2: Understanding a Message on a Business Machine**

Listen to the message on the answering machine in the bicycle store. Answer the questions.

1. What days is the shop open?

   _____

2. During what hours is it open?

   _____

3. What is the location? El Camino and _____
   (cross street).

After You Listen

Getting Information Look in the yellow pages of the telephone book for the number of a business or service that interests you and that has a message in English. (If you are not in an English-speaking country, call a business that tourists use; your teacher will help you find one.) Call the business late in the evening or early in the morning. What does the message on the answering machine say? Take notes and share the information with the class.

_____

_____

_____

ACADEMIC POWER STRATEGY

Find opportunities to practice English outside the classroom. This will improve your language skills. Turn on the TV, listen to the radio, go to the movies, listen to music in English, and make small talk with English speakers. Talk with clerks in stores and shops about the items that they are selling. Don't be shy. You can find out information and practice English at the same time.

An excellent way to practice English that many students do not take advantage of is listening to recorded telephone announcements. Many businesses and other organizations have long recorded messages twenty-four hours a day. You can use these to practice listening to English without having to respond.

Apply the Strategy

Call a company or organization that has a long recorded message in English, such as the INS (Immigration and Naturalization Service), a large bank, an airline, or—if you are not in an English-speaking country—a consulate or tourist office. Take notes on the message. Share the information with the class. (If you can understand the entire INS message, you should get an A+ for the week!)

Telephone Quiz On the left are some expressions that you might hear on the telephone. Match them with expressions on the right that have the same meanings.

_____ 1. The number you have dialed has been temporarily disconnected and is no longer in service.

_____ 2. You can dial that direct.

_____ 3. There is no one here by that name.

_____ 4. I have a collect call from Sue. Will you accept the charges?

_____ 5. This is a recording.

_____ 6. What number did you dial?

a. The person that you want is not at this number.

b. This is a taped message.

c. This number is not "good" anymore.

d. Will you pay for a call from Sue to you?

e. What number were you trying to call?

f. You don't need an operator; you can make the call yourself.

Note: If people call you by mistake, you don't have to give them your number. You can ask them what number they called and tell them "Sorry, you have the wrong number."

Many large organizations have numbers that you can call for free, without paying. You can find out if a company has a toll-free number by calling 1-800-555-1212.

This is the information operator for toll-free numbers. You can get a directory of these numbers by contacting your local telephone company.

PART 3: Buying Things

◆ **Getting Ready to Listen**

◆ **Vocabulary Building**

Guessing Meaning from Context You will hear a conversation in a store. Before you listen, guess the meanings of the underlined words in the sentences below.

1. I <u>recommend</u> that you buy a new computer—your old one is not working very well, so it would be a good idea to get another one.

2. There's a <u>sale</u> at the shopping center—let's go buy a new desk while the price is low.

3. They have other office <u>equipment</u> on sale too—like laser printers and fax machines.

4. I don't know how to use a computer. I hope my new computer comes with an <u>instruction manual</u> that is easy to read.

5. Do you pay <u>cash</u> for things you buy? Or do you charge them on your credit cards?

6. I always write <u>checks</u> to pay for things so that I have a record of what I spend.

Making Predictions Work with a partner. You will hear a conversation in a store. A woman wants to buy a computer, and a salesclerk shows her different models. Then the woman buys a computer. What questions do you think the woman will ask? What questions will the salesclerk ask? Make lists.

People have three stages as consumers, or shoppers: Young people want "possession experience"; they want to buy a house and fill it with objects. Middle-age people spend money on things like travel, education, and sports. Older adults want "being experiences"; they get the most happiness from simple pleasures and human contact.

QUESTIONS THAT THE WOMAN WILL ASK	QUESTIONS THAT THE SALESCLERK WILL ASK
1. _____	1. _____
2. _____	2. _____
3. _____	3. _____
4. _____	4. _____
5. _____	5. _____

 Listen

Listening 3: Buying a Computer

Checking Your Predictions Listen to the conversation at the computer store. As you listen, look at your lists of questions above. Which questions does the woman ask? Which questions does the salesclerk ask? Check them on your lists.

Revising Listen to the conversation again. Look at your lists of questions. Does the woman ask any questions that aren't on your list? Does the salesclerk ask any questions that aren't on your list? Add any new questions to your lists.

> The oldest paper money is from China: 2697 B.C.

Getting the Main Idea You will hear an advertisement for Apple and Macintosh Computers. The ad is about two different kinds of buyers. You don't have to understand everything in the ad. Just listen to answer this question: What is the difference between the two kinds of buyers? Are you like Buyer 1 or Buyer 2?

After You Listen

Creating a Conversation Work with a partner. Have a conversation. One student is shopping in a store, and the other student is a clerk. The shopper asks several questions. The clerk answers the questions and tries to persuade the shopper to buy the product (you choose a product). Finally, the shopper buys the item. Your teacher may want you to present your conversation to the class or put it on tape. Note: You may want to use one of the products from the old-time ads below. If you do, imagine that you are living many years ago, 1900 for instance. After you finish, write your conversation.

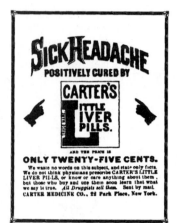

Write About It.

Imagine that you win a lot of money. You can buy anything that you want. What would you buy? Write a short description. Why would you buy it? Share your answer with a classmate.

_____

_____

_____

_____

PART 4: Returning Things to a Store

 Getting Ready to Listen

Vocabulary Building

You will hear an advertisement for AT&T Communications. First, for each expression on the left, tell which expression on the right has the same meaning. Write the letter on the line.

> You can't have everything. Where would you put it?
>
> —ANN LANDERS

_____ 1. reliable   a. warranty

_____ 2. to switch   b. dependable

_____ 3. guarantee   c. money that you get back

_____ 4. refund   d. safe, no danger

_____ 5. no-risk   e. to change

 **Listen**

Listening 4: Understanding an Advertisement

Getting the Main Idea Listen to the advertisement for AT&T Communications and answer these questions:

- Who is Emerson?

- What idea does he give the boss (the head of the company)?

After You Listen

LANGUAGE YOU CAN USE: RETURNING THINGS TO A STORE

New Kind of Hat
Worn 10 Minutes a Day
Grows Hair in 30 Days
~or No Cost

How many people do you think tried to return this?

You can use the following phrases to return something to a store:

- I'd like to return this.

- I'd like to make an exchange.

- I have the receipt (sales slip) right here.

- I'd like a refund.

- This _____ is broken (too large, the wrong size).

USING NEW LANGUAGE

Work with a partner. Look at the conversation below. One student is A, and one student is B. Take roles and have a conversation. Choose words from the lists. Then change roles and have another conversation. Choose different words from the lists.

A: Hi, I'd like to return this ⎰ radio.
                                 ⎱ television set.
                                    _____ (your idea).

B: What seems to be the ⎰ problem?
                               ⎱ trouble?

A: It's ⎰ broken.
           ⎨ not working.
           ⎩ out of order.

B: Do you have the ⎰ guarantee?
                          ⎱ warranty?

A: Of course, and I have the ⎰ receipt ⎱ right here.
                                    ⎱ sales slip ⎰

B: Well, I can ⎰ give you credit.
                   ⎱ exchange it for you.

A: Thank you, but I'd prefer to get ⎰ my money back.
                                         ⎱ a refund.

Note: If what you return is clothing, you can give other reasons for returning it, especially if it was a gift that someone bought for you:

A: Hi, I need to return this ⎰ dress.
                              ⎨ shirt.
                              ⎩ pair of pants.

B: Why is that?

A: It's ⎰ the wrong color.
           ⎨ too big (small).
           ⎩ not the right size.

Taking a Poll Have you ever returned anything to a store? What? What reason did you give for returning it? Did you get your money back? Did you get credit? Did you buy another item? Ask several people these questions. Write their answers in the chart below. Try to get at least three examples of items that people returned.

	ITEM	REASON FOR RETURNING IT	WHAT HAPPENED? (DID YOU GET A REFUND? CREDIT?)
Person 1			
Person 2			
Person 3			
Person 4			

PART 5: Expressing Agreement and Disagreement

 Getting Ready to Listen

Discussing Past Experiences You are going to listen to an advertisement for Fox Television programming. The advertisement is about a woman who is in a big hurry to get home in time to see her TV shows (on the Fox weekend lineup on Channel WXIN 59). A policeman stops her for speeding (driving too fast). First, with a partner, answer these questions:

1. Has a police officer ever stopped you (or a friend that you were riding with)? Why?

2. What did you do when the police officer stopped you? Did you pull over right away? Did you argue with the police officer? Did you get a ticket?

Listen

Listening 5: Expressing Agreement and Disagreement

Getting the Main Idea Listen to the following advertisement. There are some difficult words that you won't understand. Just listen and answer these questions:

- Does the woman argue with the police officer?

- Does he give her a ticket?

Note: *I bet you will.* = I think you will.

　　　to chat = to talk

After You Listen

Disagreeing Using *So, Too,* and *Not* Work with a partner. Have a conversation where people disagree, using *so, too,* and *not.* First, make short conversations following these examples:

Examples: I always watch public television.

You do not!

I do so (I do too)!

I never watch public television.

You do so (You do too)!

I do not.

1. I always listen to the radio news.

2. I love Crunchies cereal.

3. I never eat Crunchies cereal.

4. I always wear Guy's shoes.

5. I never wear Guy's shoes.

6. I always buy Powdermilk Biscuits.

7. I never buy Powdermilk Biscuits.

Have a conversation like one of the ones that you practiced, but use your own ideas. Your teacher may want you to present it to the class or put it on tape.

Agreeing Using *Too, Either,* or *Neither* Work with a partner. Have a conversation where people agree. Use *too, either,* or *neither.* First, make short conversations following these examples:

Examples: I always watch public television.

I do too.

I never watch public television.

I don't either. (Neither do I.)

1. I always listen to the radio news.

2. I love Crunchies cereal.

3. I never eat Crunchies cereal.

4. I always wear Guy's shoes.

5. I never wear Guy's shoes.

6. I always buy Powdermilk Biscuits.

7. I never buy Powdermilk Biscuits.

Have a conversation like one of the ones that you practiced, but use your own ideas. Your teacher may want you to present it to the class or put it on tape.

After you finish, write your conversations.

Short Answers to Yes/No Questions

1. With the verb *be:*   Yes, I am. / No, I'm not.

    Yes, he is. / No, he's not (he isn't).

    Yes, they are. / No, they're not (they aren't).

2. With the verb *do:*   Yes, I do. / No, I don't.

    Yes, she does. / No, she doesn't.

    Yes, we do. / No, we don't.

3. With *there is/are:*   Yes, there is. / No, there isn't.

    Yes, there are. / No, there aren't.

Understanding Missing Words Below are six questions and short answers. What words are missing in the answers? Write them in the blanks.

Example: Do you buy your food at ABC Market?

Yes, I do (**buy my food at ABC Market**).

1. A: Is Koji home?

   B: Yes, he is (_____).

2. A: Do you want to go to the movies now?

   B: Yes, I do (_____).

3. A: Is there a movie on TV now?

   B: No, there isn't (_____).

4. A: Are you going shopping today?

   B: Yes, I am (_____).

5. A: Do they shop downtown?

   B: No they don't (_____).

6. A: Do you need to go to the supermarket today?

   B: Yes, I do (_____).

The Sound of It: Understanding Incomplete Sentences

LANGUAGE LEARNING STRATEGY

Understanding incomplete sentences will help your comprehension. Sometimes people leave out (don't say) certain words, but you can still understand the meaning. People leave out words more often in informal speech than in formal speech or writing. The words that they leave out would not be stressed.

Apply the Strategy

A. Listen to these examples of incomplete sentences from this chapter:

Example	Complete Sentence
You ready, Doris?	Are you ready, Doris?
We're open Saturday; closed on Sunday.	We're open Saturday; we're closed on Sunday.
You practice this?	Do you practice this?
Bet I will.	I bet I will.
If you already know what an Apple can do . . . I do.	If you already know what an Apple can do . . . I do already know what an Apple can do.
. . . and you're ready to buy one now . . . I am.	. . . and you're ready to buy one now . . . I am ready to buy one now.

Notice the last two examples: *I do. I am.* It is very common to answer a question with a short answer.

B. You will hear eight questions. For each question, circle the correct answer.

Example: Do they have a computer?

a. Yes, they are.   (b.) Yes, they do.

1. a. Yes, I am.   b. Yes, I do.

2. a. Yes, she is.   b. Yes, she does

3. a. No, he isn't.   b. No, he doesn't.

4. a. No, I'm not.   b. No, I don't.

5. a. Yes, there is.   b. Yes, there does.

6. a. No, we aren't.   b. No, we don't.

7. a. No, there aren't.   b. No, there don't.

8. a. No, we're not.   b. No, we don't.

PART 6: Advertising and Image

In today's world of television, image (or appearance) is very important. Advertising tries to create an image for a product; for instance, because of the many ads for Coca-Cola that emphasize youth, someone once said that Coca-Cola is 140 years young. Other products try to create images of beauty, fashion, or wealth. Even politicians use advertising images in their ad campaigns, and sometimes they win or lose elections because of these ads.

Many ads feature models (people who wear or use a product) who weigh much less than most of us. This is especially true of female models. The CNN video you are about to see deals with this topic. Before you view the video, try to do the following activities.

More Than Average or Less Than Average? Which of the following words on the next page refer to someone who weighs more than average? Less than average? Check (✓) *More* or *Less*.

MORE	LESS	
_____	_____	1. underweight
_____	_____	2. overweight
_____	_____	3. skinny
_____	_____	4. heavy
_____	_____	5. skin and bones
_____	_____	6. thin
_____	_____	7. full-figured
_____	_____	8. slim-figured
_____	_____	9. with a little more body fat
_____	_____	10. with a slim waistline (waist = one's middle)

Vocabulary Match

Match the words or expressions that mean the same thing.

_____ 1. body curves   a. bad

_____ 2. damaging   b. body contours

_____ 3. eating disorder   c. biological elements that determine things like hair color or height

_____ 4. genes

_____ 5. resolution   d. promise

    e. eating problem

TUNING IN: "Jeans for Everyone"

Making Predictions Watch the video the first time without sound. What topics do you think that the video will cover? The teacher will write your answers on the board.

Getting the "Big Picture" Look at the video again. How many of the topics on the board are in the video? Try to answer this question: What are jeans companies doing now that they did not do in the past?

Determining Point of View Watch the video a third time. Dr. Kahan is the man who counsels women with eating disorders. Sometimes these problems start because the women want to look very thin. What does Dr. Kahan think about the kind of advertising you saw in the video? Does he approve or disapprove of it? Why?

Discussion Certain well-known people have had eating disorders. (For instance, a very famous case was Princess Diana.) Do you know anyone with an eating disorder? Does "image" (for instance, the desire to look thin) have anything to do with the problem? How do you think these problems begin? How might dolls or toys (like the Barbie doll) add to the problem? Do you think advertising is part of the problem?

PUTTING IT ALL TOGETHER

What's in an Ad? Bring an ad from a magazine or newspaper to class (or choose one that your teacher brings in). In pairs, try to answer these questions:

- Who is the ad for? That is, who is going to buy the product or use the service—older people, women, men, etc.?
- What image is the ad trying to create (youth, beauty, fashion, happiness, wealth)?
- Is the ad effective (good) or not effective (bad)? Why?

Complete the following chart:

This ad is for: _____ women.   _____ older people.

_____ men.   _____ other (Who? _____)

_____ children.

The image the ad tries to create is: _____

(The images could be of youth, beauty, fashion, wealth, etc.)

The ad is good because:

_____ 1. it has pretty or interesting images.

_____ 2. it is colorful.   _____ 4. it has a good slogan.

_____ 3. it is humorous.   _____ 5. it provides useful information.

The ad is not very good because: _____ 6. other (What? _____)

_____ 1. it is not attractive.

_____ 2. it is not colorful.   _____ 4. it doesn't have a slogan.

_____ 3. it is boring.   _____ 5. it doesn't give any information.

_____ 6. other (What? _____)

Describe the ad to the class. Include the information in the chart.

An Ad to Remember Think of an ad that you have seen or heard on TV or the radio. Describe it to a classmate. Was it funny? Serious? Terrible? Did it have special music or sounds? What kind of image was it trying to create for the product? Did it have a special kind of slogan, like "It's finger-lickin' good" (KFC™), "Just do it!" (Nike™), or "Good to the last drop" (Maxwell House™ coffee)? Why do you think you remember this ad when you forget some other ads? Tell a classmate one reason why you noticed and remembered the ad.

Buy These Jeans! There are a lot of ads for jeans because jeans are so much the same: If two products are very similar, the one with the best advertising may sell better. Work in groups. You are going to create an ad for a jeans company. First, either make up a name or choose a kind of jeans (one that someone has on or another kind). Create a slogan for your product, like some of the ones you saw on the video or others that you have seen. What kind of image will you use with the slogan? Design a written ad that includes a slogan and a picture of what the ad will contain. You can describe the picture or draw it. One person from each group reports on the ad to the class. Which group created the best ad? Why?

Test-Taking Tip

Deal with test-anxiety. Some anxiety is actually good for motivation and can even help your performance on tests. But if you have too much anxiety, it can have a negative effect on your test performance. Before the test begins, take a few slow, deep breaths and concentrate on relaxing your whole body. During the test, think about test items, not about how well you're doing. If you feel you cannot get control over your test anxiety, get some help from a teacher or counselor.

CHECK YOUR PROGRESS

On a scale of 1 to 5, rate how well you have mastered the goals set at the beginning of the chapter:

1 2 3 4 5   use the yellow pages of the telephone book.

1 2 3 4 5   think ahead and predict what people will say.

1 2 3 4 5   understand messages on message machines.

1 2 3 4 5   find opportunities to practice English outside the classroom.

1 2 3 4 5   make a purchase.

1 2 3 4 5   return something to a store.

1 2 3 4 5   express agreement and disagreement.

1 2 3 4 5   understand incomplete sentences and short answers to questions.

1 2 3 4 5   understand how advertising works to create an "image."

If you've given yourself a 3 or lower on any of these goals:

- visit the *Tapestry* web site for additional practice.

- ask your instructor for extra help.

- review the sections of the chapter that you found difficult.

- work with a partner or study group to further your progress.

How do you get news? Do you watch TV? Listen to the radio? Read a newspaper or news magazine?

9

WHAT'S IN THE NEWS?

In this chapter, you'll hear some weather reports and news stories. You'll also have the opportunity to view a CNN segment on violence in the media.

Setting Goals

In this chapter you will learn how to:

- ◈ understand weather reports.
- ◈ describe weather.
- ◈ understand numbers.
- ◈ understand news headlines and stories.
- ◈ summarize what you hear or read.
- ◈ improve your language by watching the news in English.
- ◈ express agreement and disagreement.

Getting Started

Think about what you know about the topic of this chapter: the news. How did people communicate news before the invention of television? How did television change the way people got the news? What new inventions are changing the way we get news today?

Getting Ready to Read

Vocabulary Check

The following words and phrases are from the reading. Check the ones you already know. You can add new words you learn to your Vocabulary Log.

_____ satellites   _____ fax machine

_____ cultural environment   _____ inform

_____ electronic mail   _____ technology

_____ entertain   _____ videotape

Vocabulary Building

Complete the sentences with words from the list.

1. The ___fax___ machine and _electronic mail_ are two recent inventions that help us communicate.

2. If you see an important event happening and you have a camera, you can make a _____ recording.

3. The physical world is part of our environment, but other things create our _____ _____, like the way we live and work, our system of beliefs, and the art and music we have.

4. Technology like communication _____ makes it possible to send messages instantly around the world.

5. Some people say that many TV news programs _____ more than they _____.

Read

1 For most of human history, the only communication between people was face to face. The invention of writing changed that, but for a long time most people could not read or write. Those who _could_ read and write (people at the top of the religious or political system) often had great power. The invention of the printing press in the middle of the 1400s gave people the printed word, which caused a huge change in human culture. People could now get information, look at that information themselves, and (more importantly) ask questions about it and form their own opinions.

2   Later inventions made a very big difference in the way people communicated with each other. The telegraph and then the telephone made communication very rapid. More recently came the **fax machine;** in 1990 students made history by faxing information about the problems in Tienanmen Square all over China. In 1991 Mikhail Gorbachev made history by using **electronic mail** to communicate with the world when the Soviet military tried to take over his government. (They would not allow him to use the telephone, but he was able to use a computer instead.) Today many international organizations use fax machines and electronic mail for instant communication. In addition, the Internet provides information about news everywhere in the world: hundreds of newspapers and news magazines are on the Internet for anyone anywhere to see. Home **videotapes** appear on television news shows, and the video revolution makes it impossible for governments to decide what people should—or should not—see on their TVs. Also important is the **communication satellite,** which sends messages through space in seconds.

3   Some people say the world is getting smaller. Are we all part of a "global village" because of our ability to communicate quickly?

4   Some people worry about the use of communication **technology** in the news industry. George Gerbner, former dean of the Annenberg School for Communication and founder of the Cultural Environment Movement, says that news is a big business that is international in size. According to Gerbner, the purpose of most news shows is to make money, and making money often

The Global Village

means **entertaining** people more than **informing** them about the truth. TV news, especially, is a very powerful influence and often focuses on sex or violence. In the case of the famous trial of athlete and actor O. J. Simpson in 1994–95, for instance, he writes that it was wrong to allow TV cameras into the courtroom. What he calls "The O. J. Show" lasted for a year and had 150 million people watching in the United States alone on an important day of the trial. This, says Gerbner, was entertainment, not news, and had a negative influence on the **cultural environment**.

After You Read

Checking Your Understanding

1. Throughout most of human history, how did people communicate news?

2. What major invention in the 1400s changed the way people got their news and had a very important influence on human culture?

3. What did students use in 1990 to inform people in China about the Tienanmen Square demonstrations?

4. How did Mikhail Gorbachev communicate with the world during the 1991 Soviet crisis?

5. How have communication satellites changed the news?

6. Why do some people, like George Gerbner, worry about how we get our news?

ACADEMIC POWER STRATEGY

Use today's technology to find out about the news and practice your English at the same time. You can listen to the news on the radio or on television, or you can use the Internet. Hundreds of newspapers and news magazines have sites on the Internet. Examples are the *New York Times* and the *Chicago Tribune*. Just type the name of a newspaper or magazine in a search engine (such as AltaVista, Infoseek, Yahoo, or Excite), and you should be able to find the most recent edition in very little time. You can also search specific topics that you are interested in to find recent information about them. Also, many radio and television networks (CNN, ABC, and so on) have sites on the Internet. If your computer has sound capability, you may be able to hear the news. If it has video, you can see news segments at some of these sites.

Apply the Strategy

Use a search engine to explore the Internet site of a newspaper or news magazine in English. What is the main story of the day? Besides today's news, what other topics does the edition include? Then look at a radio or TV network site, such as CNN or NBC, and answer the same questions. Share the information with your classmates.

PART 1: Understanding Weather Reports

◇ **Getting Ready to Listen**   Look at the pictures and read the weather expressions below:

It's sunny/warm/dry/fair.

It's cloudy/partly cloudy/overcast.

It's rainy. There are thunderstorms/ scattered showers.

**There's snow/ice.
It's freezing/icy.**

It's cool/chilly/foggy.

It's windy/breezy.

ATLANTA ✈	BOSTON ✈	CHICAGO ✈	CLEVELAND ✈	COLUMBUS, OHIO	DALLAS FT. WRTH ✈	DENVER ✈
Many clouds showers around, high 75, low 61, **Tomorrow:** partly sunny, a bit warmer, high 78, low 58.	Staying cool more clouds than sun, cool east wind, high 56, low 51. **Tomorrow:** showers then clearing, high 69, low 47.	Plenty of sun nice, quite cool along lakeshore, high 66, low 48. **Tomorrow:** sun then clouds, high 65, low 54.	Cloudy start shower, risk, thunder, clearing later on, high 71, low 45. **Tomorrow:** partly sunny and cool, high 62, low 48.	Rain early maybe thunder, clearing late day, high 75, low 46. **Tomorrow:** mostly sunny and pleasant, high 71, low 51.	Hot sun few clouds build up but day looks dry, high 91, low 66. **Tomorrow:** some sun, chance t'storm. high 87, low 67.	Intervals of sun some afternoon thunderstorms, high 76, low 51. **Tomorrow:** good supply of sunshine, high 76, low 48.

DETROIT ✈	HOUSTON	INDIANAPOLIS	KANSAS CITY	LOS ANGELES ✈	MIAMI	MPLS.-ST. P. ✈
Clouds early maybe a shower, then skies clear out, high 73, low 43 **Tomorrow:** sunny to partly cloudy, high 66, low 45.	Very balmy under mostly sunny skies, drier air, high 89, low 68. **Tomorrow:** sun, scattered t'storms, high 88, low 71.	Sun develops after some clouds early, high 76, low 48. **Tomorrow:** sunshine, couds late, high 75, low 55.	Sun, clouds looks good comfortable readings, high 75, low 59. **Tomorrow:** scatered showers, high 77, low 61.	Not bad some morning clouds then sunny afternoon, high 78, low 62. **Tomorrow:** milder, high 81, low 65.	Warm, humid seasonable, a mix of clouds and sun, high 84, low 70. **Tomorrow:** partial sun, risk storm, high 85, low 72.	Partly sunny light winds, just a bit on the cool side high 64, low 48. **Tomorrow:** intervals of clouds and sun, high 67, low 50.

NASHVILLE	NEW ORLEANS	NEW YORK ✈	ORLANDO ✈	PHILADELPHIA	PHOENIX	PITTSBURGH
Lots of clouds showers end, brighter afternoon, high 77, low 54. **Tomorrow:** nice, dry and partly sunny, high 79, low 60.	Sunny intervals humid, isolated thunderstorm possible, high 84, low 68. **Tomorrow:** lots of sun, warmer, drier, high 86, low 65.	Changeable blend of clouds, sun, a bit milder, high 71, low 56. **Tomorrow:** clouds then sun, breezy, high 73, low 54.	Sun at times thunderstorm or two around, high 87, low 66. **Tomorrow:** some sun, chance t'storm high 86, low 68.	Mainly sunny a few clouds, risk of showers tonight high 75, low 57. **Tomorrow:** clouds early then sun, high 76, low 52.	Hot sunshine humidity continues high for the season, high 99, low 73. **Tomorrow:** more sun, high 98, low 71.	Overcast mild, chance of a t'shower, high 77, low 49. **Tomorrow:** cooler but largely sunny, high 69, low 46.

ST. LOUIS ✈	SALT LAKE CITY	SAN DIEGO	SAN FRAN. ✈	SEATTLE	TAMPA-ST.P.	WASH., D.C. ✈
Delightful warm sun, drier, breezy this morning high, 79, low 58. **Tomorrow:** clouds return, high 77, low 62.	Sun prevails a few passing clouds, warm, high 79, low 54. **Tomorrow:** warm with lots of sun, high 81, low 55.	Cloudy morning partly sunny midday, afternoon, high 73, low 64. **Tomorrow:** sunshine slowly develops, high 75, low 65.	Splashes of sun patchy morning low clouds and fog, high 69, low 54. **Tomorrow:** a mixture of clouds and sun, high 69, low 56.	Milder trend fine day under lots of bright sun, high 65, low 44. **Tomorrow:** more sun, nice again, high 66, low 49.	Sun, clouds late-day t'storm not out of question, high 84, low 67. **Tomorrow:** some sun, high 83, low 68.	Sunny intervals some clouds shower or two tonight, high 77, low 60. **Tomorrow:** cloudy to partly sunny, high 77, low 54.

Source: *USA Today*, May 13, 1992. p. 12A. Copyright © 1992, *USA Today*. Reprinted with permission.

Understanding a U.S. Weather Chart Work with a partner. Look at the chart about U.S. weather and answer the questions.

1. What's the weather like in New Orleans? Chicago? Washington, D.C.?

2. What's the high temperature for the day in New York?

3. What's the low temperature for the day in Miami?

4. Is it going to rain in Columbus?

5. Is it going to be windy in Boston?

Comparative and Superlative Adjectives Look at the following chart. Notice how regular comparatives and superlatives are formed.

Adjective	Comparative	Superlative
cold	cold**er**	the cold**est**
dry	dri**er**	the dri**est**
sunny	sunni**er** (**more** sunny)	the sunni**est** (the **most** sunny)
humid	**more** humid	the **most** humid

Comparing Weather in Different Places Work with a partner. Look at the weather chart on page 182. Ask and answer questions about the weather in different places. Take turns. Compare cities.

Examples: What's the weather like in . . .?

What's the high (low) in . . .?

Is it sunny (cloudy, foggy, etc.) in . . .?

Is it going to be foggier (rainier, colder) in San Francisco or Nashville?

Which city will have the hottest (coldest, windiest) day: San Francisco, Nashville, or Atlanta?

Identifying Items of Clothing Look at the list of clothing items below. For each item, write the letter of the picture in the blank.

_____ 1. scarf

_____ 2. snow boots

_____ 3. rain boots

_____ 4. heavy gloves

_____ 5. umbrella

_____ 6. raincoat

_____ 7. overcoat

> Animals are good at predicting the weather. Frogs croak when the air pressure falls. Before rain, ants move to higher ground and sheep's wool uncurls.

A.   B.   C.   D.

E.   F.   G.

Listen

Listening 1: Understanding Weather Reports

You will hear four short weather reports from the morning news. For each report, write what you would probably wear or take with you for the day. Use items from the list on page 183.

Weather Report 1: _____

Weather Report 2: _____

Weather Report 3: _____

Weather Report 4: _____

Understanding the Daily High and Low Temperatures Listen again. For each report, tell the high and low temperatures the reporter gave.

	High	Low
Weather Report 1:	50s	
Weather Report 2:		
Weather Report 3:		
Weather Report 4:		

After You Listen

Understanding an International Weather Chart Look at the chart on page 185 and answer the following questions about the weather on this day in April:

1. What was the high temperature in Cairo? Hong Kong? Tokyo?

2. What was the low temperature in Bangkok? Singapore? Madrid?

3. How many inches of precipitation (rain or snow) fell in Moscow? Guadalajara? Beijing?

4. Which city had the hottest weather?

5. Which city had the coldest weather?

6. Which city had the most precipitation?

Lightning strikes somewhere on earth about 6,000 times a minute.

INTERNATIONAL FOREIGN CITIES

FOREIGN CITIES   Following are the highest and lowest temperatures and daily precipitation (reported in inches) for the 24 hours ended 7 P.M. (E.D.T.).

Cities	High	Low	Precipitation	Cities	High	Low	Precipitation
Acapulco	87	73	0	Madrid	63	44	.08
Athens	67	52	.08	Mexico City	76	50	0
Bangkok	100	78	0	Montreal	51	32	0
Beijing	69	44	.03	Moscow	48	31	.1
Belgrade	46	34	.1	Nairobi	75	58	0
Bombay	89	75	0	Nassau	81	69	0
Budapest	70	50	.09	Oslo	51	34	.09
Buenos Aires	68	50	0	Paris	60	42	.1
Cairo	83	60	0	Prague	55	41	.07
Caracas	81	59	0	Quebec	43	31	0
Dakar	77	58	0	Rio de Janeiro	80	69	0
Damascus	75	68	0	Rome	69	45	.06
Dublin	50	39	.5	San Jose (CR)	80	62	0
Glasgow	53	38	.4	San Juan	83	71	0
Guadalajara	78	60	.03	Seoul	62	43	.01
Havana	81	70	0	Singapore	88	74	.02
Helsinki	43	29	.2	Stockholm	44	30	.1
Hong Kong	80	67	.01	Sydney	73	58	0
Istanbul	61	45	0	Taipei	78	63	.02
Jerulsaem	73	52	0	Tokyo	65	48	0
Johannesburg	77	51	0	Toronto	51	34	0
Lagos	89	77	0	Vancouver	56	40	.2
Lisbon	80	65	.06	Vienna	57	42	.07
London	56	40	.3	Zurich	60	42	.08

A hurricane can release as much energy as 400 20-megaton H-bombs every second.

Note: If you are in the United States, for 95 cents a minute you can call 1-900-740-3033 to get weather information in the United States and also internationally. You can even get a wake-up call with the day's weather! If you don't mind spending 95 cents a minute, this is one way to practice your English.

Describing the Weather in Your Home Town What is the weather like in your home town? Are there four seasons (spring, summer, fall, winter) or two (rainy, dry)? What's the best time of year, in your opinion? The worst? Complete the chart on the following page about the "best" and "worst" seasons.

HOME TOWN: _____

Best Season	**Worst Season**

Months: _____

Weather: _____

_____

_____

What happens (what people do): _____

_____

_____

Months: _____

Weather: _____

_____

_____

What happens (what people do): _____

_____

_____

Making Small Talk About the Weather Work with a partner. Look back at Chapter 1, where you learned about making small talk. Very often, people make small talk about the weather. Make small talk about today's weather in this situation: You are at a bus stop. You have been waiting for the bus for a long time.

The Sound of It: Understanding Numbers

There are many situations where you will need to understand numbers, such as in prices, telephone numbers, and addresses. Learning to understand numbers will improve your listening comprehension in many circumstances. For example, you heard numbers in the weather reports for temperatures.

A. Practice listening for ordinal numbers, which describe order: *first, second, third, fourth, fifth,* and so on. Circle the number that you hear. You will hear each number two times.

> It is safer to be in a car during a thunderstorm than in a house. If lightning strikes a car, it goes through the tires to the ground.

1. 14	14th		4. 32	32nd	
2. 20	20th		5. 63	63rd	
3. 21	21st		6. 78	78th	

B. Practice listening to numbers that end in *-teen* and numbers that end in *-th*. Circle the number that you hear. You will hear each number two times.

1. 13	13th		4. 18	18th	
2. 15	15th		5. 19	19th	
3. 16	16th				

C. Practice listening to other numbers. Circle the number that you hear. You will hear each number two times.

1.	13	30	30th	6.	17	70	17th
2.	4	14	4th	7.	8	80	18th
3.	5th	50	1st	8.	2	22	22nd
4.	16	60	16th	9.	17	70	70th
5.	15	50	50th	10.	9	90	90th

PART 2: Understanding Headlines and News Reports

◆ **Getting Ready to Listen**   **Understanding Headlines** Read the headlines (titles) of news stories below:

A. **Families to spend more on entertainment**

B. **Rain forests in serious danger**

C. **Most cancer due to how we live, work**

D. **More people staying single and liking it**

E. **The Smokeout: Millions to quit smoking**

Most headlines are not complete sentences. Here are the complete sentences for the headlines above.

Families *are going* to spend more on entertainment.

The rain forests *are* in serious danger.

Most cancer *is* due to how we live *and* work.

More people *are* staying single and liking it.

The Smokeout: Millions *of people are going* to quit smoking.

The words *a, an,* and *the* usually do not appear in headlines. Verbs like *is* and *are* often do not appear. *To* plus a verb usually means future *(be going to): Millions to Quit = Millions Are Going to Quit.* A comma sometimes appears instead of *and: live, work = live and work.*

Completing Headlines Write the missing words in the headlines below.

Example: Eastern Europe _____is_____ seeing more tourists

1. More people _____ avoiding meat

2. Major storm _____ to arrive tonight

3. _____ Japanese _____ living longer

4. Scientists _____ to study _____ world's warmer weather

5. _____ Chinese diet _____ among _____ healthiest

Note: Sometimes the verb *be* (for instance, *is, are, was, were*) is missing before a past participle (like *gone, made, completed*):

Kidnapped millionaire found in Los Angeles = A kidnapped millionaire *was* found in Los Angeles.

Traffic reports completed = Traffic reports *were* completed.

◆ Vocabulary Building

Guessing Meaning from Context You will hear five news stories. Before you listen, guess the meanings of the underlined words in the sentences below.

1. I tried to <u>quit</u> smoking, but I couldn't stop.

2. Many accidents are <u>preventable</u>; if people were more careful, these accidents would not happen.

3. Last year the number of accidents in that city <u>doubled</u>, going from 40 to 83. It was a 100 percent increase.

4. Which is more important—<u>heredity</u> or <u>environment</u>? Do our genes and physical characteristics—our heredity—determine who we are? Or does the situation or world that we live in—our environment—determine who we are?

5. Each part of your body has thousands of small <u>cells</u>.

6. Emiko is making enough money to <u>support</u> herself, so she doesn't live with her parents anymore.

7. I don't need my old credit card, so I <u>destroyed</u> it—I cut it in half.

8. <u>Tropical forests</u> have thousands of varieties of plants and animals in them, but the land is not good for agriculture.

9. The president is having a <u>press conference</u> tonight to answer questions from reporters about the Middle East.

◆Listen

Listening 2: Identifying News Stories

Listen to the five news stories. Match the report with one of the headlines on page 187. Write the letter of the headline on the line.

News Report 1: __*e*__   News Report 4: _____

News Report 2: _____   News Report 5: _____

News Report 3: _____

Listening for Numbers Listen to the reports again. Practice listening for numbers. Answer these questions:

1. News Report 1: How many people in the United States smoke?

   a. 15 million   b. 30 million   c. 50 million

2. News Report 2: How fast will the Internet industry grow each year until 2007?

   a. 26 percent   b. 56 percent   c. 66 percent

3. News Report 3: Up to what percentage of all cancer might we be able to prevent?

   a. 60 percent   b. 70 percent   c. 80 percent

4. News Report 4: What percentage of men between the ages of 30 and 34 have never married?

   a. 25 percent   b. 30 percent   c. 35 percent

5. News Report 5: In how many years will we destroy the rain forests, at the present rate of destruction?

   a. 55 years   b. 105 years   c. 155 years

> **One of the biggest news agencies, Reuter's, started in 1850. It began when a German bank clerk, Paul Julius Reuter, used pigeons (birds) to carry information about the Paris stock market.**

◆After You Listen

LANGUAGE LEARNING STRATEGY

Summarize what you hear or read. To *summarize* means to sum up, to tell the important part of a message or story. If you can summarize, you will be able to tell someone the main facts or ideas of a message or story without telling all of the details. Summarizing is a good way to be sure you've really understood what you heard or read.

(continued on next page)

Apply the Strategy

Work in groups of five. Each person in the group chooses one of the news stories. (Each person should choose a different story.) Listen to the story again and take notes. Tell the group everything important about the story, making a summary. Other people in the group can ask questions. Write your notes here:

_____

_____

_____

_____

LANGUAGE LEARNING STRATEGY

Improve your language skills by watching the news on television on an English channel. The pictures will help with understanding. At first you won't understand everything, but as your English improves you will understand more. You might want to watch the news first in your native language.

Apply the Strategy

From now until the end of the course, watch two local and two national or international news programs a week in English. Your teacher can give you information about when you can see the news and on what channels. Complete the following table for each news program that you watch. Write a very short summary of the most interesting story on a separate page.

DATE	FIRST NEWS STORY: TOPIC	VOCABULARY
_____	_____	_____
_____	_____	_____
_____	_____	_____
_____	_____	_____
_____	_____	_____

_____   _____   _____
_____   _____   _____
_____   _____   _____
_____   _____   _____
_____   _____   _____

Choose a news story that made you especially happy or especially sad. Describe it to a partner. Your partner will ask you questions about the story. Tell why the story made you happy or sad. Write about the story in your journal. Then write a summary of the story and your reactions to it.

PART 3: Special Reports

 Getting Ready to Listen   **Vocabulary Match**

For each expression on the left, tell which expression on the right has the same meaning. Write the letter on the line.

_____ 1. to cope   a. not nice, unkind

_____ 2. somewhere else   b. to deal with (a problem)

_____ 3. to play catch   c. to break, destroy

_____ 4. best buddies   d. to throw and catch a ball
                                  (with another person)
_____ 5. mean
                               e. another place
_____ 6. to shatter
                               f. very good friends

 Listen   **Listening 3: Understanding an Ad for Eyewitness News**

Getting the Main Idea You are going to hear a commercial for the Channel 3 Eyewitness News. Listen and answer the questions below. You may have to listen several times.

• A child is talking. What problem does she have?

• What will the subject of the news report be?

After You Listen

Reporting on a Current Event Look in a newspaper or TV magazine for a list of local TV programs. Find a news show or documentary about a current event or problem. Watch the show. Then complete this table:

Name of program: _____

Day and time: _____

Subject: _____

What the program showed/What I learned: _____

_____

_____

_____

_____

PART 4: Violence in the Media

The CNN video segment for this chapter is about violence in the media. Violence means aggressive or hurtful behavior, like fighting or use of force. First, think about some of the television shows you like to watch. Do they have a lot of violence? Do they show realistic violence or *fantasy violence* (the kind that you see in cartoons)?

Vocabulary Building

Choose the correct word to complete each sentence.

1. His behavior was very _____ (aggressive/fighting).

2. There was a _____ (fortunate/shocking) incident last week when a youngster shot and killed his older brother.

3. When you go to court because of a crime, you may get a *conviction*; that means they find you guilty of the crime. If you have been "*d*riving *u*nder the *i*nfluence" (of alcohol or drugs), your conviction is called a _____ (DUI/XYZ) conviction.

4. A serious crime is called a *felony*. If you have a felony conviction, that means that you face prison and other serious _____ (fantasy/consequences).

TUNING IN: "Violence in the Media"

© CNN

Making Predictions Watch the video the first time without sound. What topics do you think that the video will cover? The teacher will write your answers on the board.

Understanding Numbers There are many words that you may not understand in the video. Don't worry if you don't understand every word. Look at the following sentences from the video and complete each blank with the number that you hear. You may have to listen several times.

1. An _____- and _____-year-old allegedly (reportedly) kill _____ classmates and a teacher.

2. _____ shocking incidents [occurred] within _____ months.

3. We have a _____ studies which show that there is a link (connection) between media violence and aggressive behavior.

4. Leonard Eron followed more than _____ third-graders into adulthood.

5. If you look at youngsters (children) who at age _____ were not aggressive in school but were watching violent television, by the time they were _____ they were significantly more aggressive than those youngsters who at age _____ were highly aggressive but were not watching violent television.

6. Studies show it [the media] accounts for _____ to _____ percent [of violence].

7. Some studies show [that] a change in media violence could reduce violence among children by as much as _____ percent.

Recommendations Many children watch television. What recommendations does the report make to their parents? Check the correct responses.

_____ 1. Limit TV viewing (don't let children watch too much TV).

_____ 2. Watch TV with your children.

_____ 3. Put a control on the TV to turn it off after one hour.

_____ 4. Explain the consequences of violent actions—that is, what will happen to the people who do something violent.

_____ 5. Write a letter to the TV station and complain about violent programs.

PUTTING IT ALL TOGETHER

In Chapter 8, you practiced some ways to agree and disagree with someone, using phrases like _It does too_ or _It doesn't either_. You're going to practice more ways of agreeing and disagreeing with others. First, read these expressions to agree or to disagree with someone.

LANGUAGE YOU CAN USE: EXPRESSING AGREEMENT AND DISAGREEMENT

TO AGREE	TO DISAGREE
Of course! Certainly! Sure! Naturally!	I disagree (completely). I don't agree (at all).
That's true. True.	That's not true. That's not right.
That's right. Right.	That's ridiculous! What nonsense! (not polite)
That's a good point. Good point.	I'm sorry to disagree, but . . . .
I agree (completely).	I see your point of view, but . . . .
I think so too.	
You said it!	
You're absolutely right.	

USING NEW LANGUAGE

Ask three people if they agree or disagree with the following statement: Watching violence on television makes people violent. Record their answers in the following table.

	AGREE OR DISAGREE?	WHY?
Person 1	_____	_____
Person 2	_____	_____
Person 3	_____	_____

Practicing a Conversation Work with a partner to create a conversation. In the conversation, you should each give your point of view on the following issue:

> Is there too much violence on television? Does watching violence on television make people violent? Should there be a law against so much television violence?

Use some of the expressions to agree or disagree in your conversation.

Test-Taking Tip

During a speaking-based test, make sure to speak! Although this may seem obvious, many instructors are frustrated by students who answer questions during interview-type tests with simple "yes" or "no" answers. Remember that the reason you are being asked questions is so that the instructor can listen to how you answer the question. Try to give full answers and show your instructor your willingness to speak.

CHECK YOUR PROGRESS

On a scale of 1 to 5, rate how well you have mastered the goals set at the beginning of the chapter:

1 2 3 4 5   understand weather reports.

1 2 3 4 5   describe weather.

1 2 3 4 5   understand numbers.

1 2 3 4 5   understand news headlines and stories.

1 2 3 4 5   summarize what you hear or read.

1 2 3 4 5   improve your language by watching the news in English.

1 2 3 4 5   express agreement and disagreement.

If you've given yourself a 3 or lower on any of these goals:

- visit the *Tapestry* web site for additional practice.
- ask your instructor for extra help.
- review the sections of the chapter that you found difficult.
- work with a partner or study group to further your progress.

I am a passenger on the spaceship Earth.

—R. Buckminster Fuller,
*Operating Manual
for Spaceship Earth*

The nation that destroys
its soil destroys itself.

—Franklin D. Roosevelt,
letter to state governors,
February 26, 1937

We have forgotten how to be good guests, how to walk lightly
on the Earth as its other creatures do.

—Stockholm Conference,
Only One Earth, 1972

- In what ways are we humans not "good guests"
  who "walk lightly on the Earth"?
- How are we destroying the environment?
- What can we do to save the environment?

10

PLANETHOOD

N ow that we have photographs of our planet, Earth, from space, it should be clearer than ever before how fragile our world is. We humans create artificial borders between countries and then fight wars over them. Photos from space remind us that, in reality, there *are* no borders. They remind us that the war we should be fighting is the "war" to protect our planet, our environment. In this chapter, you'll listen to and discuss some creative solutions to environmental problems. You'll also have the opportunity to view a CNN segment about one of these solutions—ecotourism.

Setting Goals

In this chapter you will learn how to:

◈ locate many countries on a world map.

◈ use ecology-related vocabulary.

◈ use new words as soon and as often as possible.

◈ notice and understand parts of words to guess meaning.

◈ highlight new words.

◈ choose the correct definition in a dictionary.

◈ work with other students to think of solutions to environmental problems.

Getting Started

Decide if you think the following statements are true or false:

_____ Plastic is not biodegradable.

_____ Tourism is not good for the environment.

_____ The amount of carbon dioxide in the air isn't a problem because trees absorb it all.

_____ The ozone protects the earth from harmful sunlight.

_____ Cities in poor countries can't do anything to improve the environment because of lack of money.

Getting Ready to Read

Think Ahead In small groups, discuss the answers to these questions:

1. How have borders changed in the past twenty years? In other words, which new countries have appeared? Which countries don't exist anymore? Which countries have changed their names?

2. What changes to the world map do you expect in the next century? Which areas might become independent countries? Which countries will join with other countries?

3. Do changing borders affect (influence) the environment—the water, land, and air?

Read

1 By the end of the twentieth century, many changes had taken place in world geography. The African colonies of various European countries had become independent countries: Zimbabwe, Angola, and Burkina Faso, for example. The U.S.S.R. had "disappeared," and in its place there appeared many independent countries: Ukraine, Armenia, Kazakhstan, and Russia, to name a few. Czechoslovakia divided into two countries—the Czech Republic and Slovakia. East Germany and West Germany joined to become one country.

2 Geographers sometimes make predictions about possible changes to the world map in the twenty-first century. Some believe that Scotland will become an independent country, as well as Zululand and Samiland. They think that the Basque region will separate from Spain and Brittany from France. They say that Brazil, Mexico, and Australia may each break into smaller countries. If their predictions turn out to be true, countries may correspond more closely to the ethnic groups within their borders.

3 How will these changing borders and changing governments affect the environment? Geographers can't answer this question. Plants and animals do not recognize borders. The wind blows across borders, and the oceans connect all continents. If our planet is going to be livable in the twenty-first century, we'll need to shift our focus from the idea of "*my* country" and "*your* country" to "*our* world." We'll need to turn our attention from the placement of borders to the health of the environment.

◆After You Read

Labeling a World Map Find your native country on the world map below. Draw in the borders and add the name of your country. (If your country is small, you might need to write the name outside the map and draw a line to it.) Then do *one* of the following:

- Exchange information with each student in your class from a different country. Ask each one "Where is your country?" Then add that student's country to your map. (Draw in the borders and write the name of the country.)

- Break into five groups. Each group should then find the countries for *one* of the groups below and put them on the map. If you need help, ask each other or look at an atlas. Then exchange information with students from the other groups.

GROUP 1	GROUP 2	GROUP 3	GROUP 4	GROUP 5
Afghanistan	Angola	Argentina	Brazil	Egypt
Canada	Chile	China	Denmark	Greece
Ethiopia	France	Germany	India	Iran
Japan	Kenya	Korea	Morocco	Mexico
Nigeria	Poland	Russia	Spain	Myanmar
Saudi Arabia	Turkey	United Kingdom (Great Britain)	U.S.A.	Venezuela

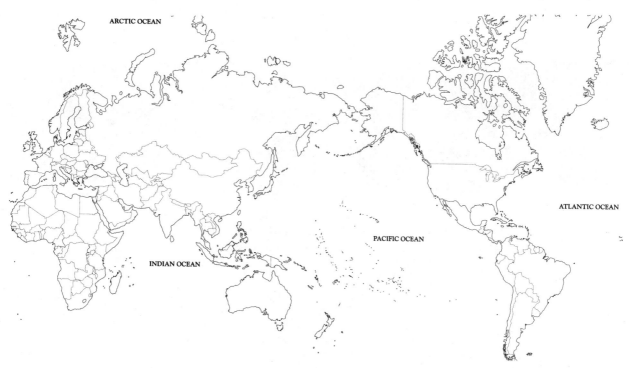

PART 1: Environmental Problems

◆ **Getting Ready to Listen**

Highlighting New Words You are going to hear six people answer this question: "What do you do to help the environment?" Before you listen, look at these photos of environmental problems and read about them. Take a highlighter pen and mark the new words below the photos. Marking them will help you to find them later.

☐ We burn oil, wood, and coal. This puts carbon dioxide (CO_2) into the air. Usually trees and oceans absorb CO_2, but now there's more than they can absorb. This causes the temperature of the earth to go up.

☐ Plastics are *not* biodegradable. They will remain in landfills for hundreds or thousands of years.

☐ Many products (such as batteries, motor oil, detergent, and household cleaning chemicals) pollute the water and land. These toxic chemicals kill plants and make people sick.

☐ Smog (air pollution) from factories and cars causes health problems such as lung cancer. "Acid rain" (a kind of air pollution) kills fish and plants in lakes and rivers.

☐ People are cutting down rain forests in Central and South America, Southeast Asia, and Africa. They want trees for wood or land for cattle. Usually rainforests absorb CO_2, produce oxygen, and give us plants for medicine. But now we're cutting down 80 acres of forest every minute, a high price to pay for beef.

☐ CFCs (from refrigerators, air conditioners, and white styrofoam cups) go into the atmosphere (air around the earth). Usually the ozone protects the earth from harmful sunlight. But CFCs are causing the ozone to get thinner. This causes skin cancer in animals and people.

◇ Vocabulary Building

Look for these words in the text below the photos. Guess their meanings. Match the meanings to the words. (Write the letters on the lines.) Add new words to your Vocabulary Log.

> **Every time a ton of steel is recycled, it means 2500 pounds of iron ore, 1000 pounds of coal and 40 pounds of limestone will not have to be mined from the earth.**
>
> **—ABSOLUTE TRIVIA WEB SITE**

_____ 1. biodegradable

_____ 2. smog

_____ 3. landfill

_____ 4. cattle

_____ 5. atmosphere

_____ 6. carbon dioxide

_____ 7. to pollute

_____ 8. ozone

_____ 9. styrofoam

_____ 10. CFCs

_____ 11. acid rain

_____ 12. temperature

_____ 13. toxic chemicals

_____ 14. to absorb

a. area that is filled in with garbage

b. air around the planet

c. to make air, water, or land dirty and dangerous

d. a kind of plastic; we use it for plastic cups for hot drinks

e. a kind of air pollution that falls to earth when there is precipitation

f. something in air conditioners and refrigerators

g. able to become part of the earth again, after some time

h. CO_2

i. heat or cold

j. something in the atmosphere that protects the earth from sunlight

k. poisonous compounds

l. animals that people raise for beef

m. to take in or "drink" in

n. air pollution

◇ Listen

Listening 1: Helping the Environment

Getting the Main Idea On page 200, there are small boxes below the photos. Listen to six people talk about how they help the environment. Ask yourself, "Why do these people do these things?" How—in small ways—are they helping? Put the number of each speaker in the box under the picture that shows the problem that this person is helping to solve. (In some cases, there are two possible answers.)

◇ After You Listen

Matching Causes and Effects On the following page are some environmental problems and their causes. Decide which causes and effects belong together. In other words, which cause leads to which effect (or result)? Draw lines. (You can look at page 200.)

CAUSES	EFFECTS
Factories, homes, and cars burn oil, wood, and coal.	People are cutting down rain forests to open land for cattle.
People are using poisonous products to clean things or to kill grass.	The ozone is getting thinner.
"Acid rain" falls into lakes and rivers.	There is a lot of CO_2 in the atmosphere.
People are eating more beef.	Fish are dying.
People are using a lot of styrofoam products and air conditioners with CFCs.	There are toxic chemicals in our land and water.

LANGUAGE LEARNING STRATEGY

Apply the Strategy

U se new words as soon—and as often—as possible. If you *use* a word in speaking or writing soon after you see or hear it for the first time, you'll remember it better.

Use the words from page 200 as you do this exercise.

A. What are some environmental problems in your home country or city? List them here.

Environmental problems in _____.
                                             (my home country)

_____   _____

_____   _____

_____   _____

_____   _____

B. Share your list with a small group. Discuss which problems you have in common and which are different.

LANGUAGE YOU CAN USE: ASKING FOR CLARIFICATION

You need to ask for clarification when you don't understand something in a conversation. If you simply didn't hear a word or phrase, you can ask the speaker:

• Pardon?   • Excuse me?   • Could you repeat that?

If you didn't understand the meaning, you can ask the speaker:

• What does that mean?   • Could you explain that?

USING NEW LANGUAGE

Getting Information Talk with classmates, your teacher, people at your school, and people in your community. Ask them, "What do you do to help the environment?" Complete the chart with their answers. Ask for clarification whenever necessary.

PERSON'S NAME	WHAT DOES THIS PERSON DO?	WHY? (HOW DOES THIS HELP THE ENVIRONMENT?)

Discussion In a small group, discuss your charts. What are people doing to help the environment? Is there anything that surprises you? Do people seem to be concerned about the environment?

PART 2: The Plastic of the Future?

Getting Ready to Listen

Thinking Ahead You are going to hear a report about plastic.* Before you listen, think about the contents of your home. How many things in your home are made of plastic or have plastic parts? List them here:

*© Copyright National Public Radio® 1992. Excerpts and audio actualities from National Public Radio's news magazine are used with permission from National Public Radio. All rights reserved.

LANGUAGE LEARNING STRATEGY

Notice and understand parts of words as a way to determine meaning. If you understand *parts* of words—prefixes (at the beginning of words), roots (the main parts), and suffixes (at the end), you can guess the meanings of words more easily. To do this, divide words into parts and analyze each part.

Examples: prefixes: re-   (= back; again)

dis-   (= away; apart)

roots: bio   (= life)

cycl   (= circle)

suffix   -able   (= with ability; possible to)

If you analyze the parts of the word *renewable,* for example, you can guess that it means "can become new again." From its parts, you can guess that the word *biodegradable* means "can become part of the earth."

Apply the Strategy

Complete the sentences. Choose from these words:

breathable   drinkable

changeable   livable

disposable   recyclable

1. We need to clean up the water so that it will be _____.

2. The air pollution is so bad that sometimes the air isn't _____.

3. There are a lot of toxic chemicals in that area, so everyone had to move out of the neighborhood. The area isn't _____.

4. The weather is very _____ these days. One minute it's warm, and then suddenly it's cold.

5. Don't throw away that bottle. It's _____.

6. New parents like to use _____ diapers for their babies. Unfortunately, people in the United States throw away 18 billion of these diapers every year, and they aren't biodegradable.

Vocabulary Check

The following words and phrases are from the next listening passage. Check the ones you already know. Add new words to your Vocabulary Log.

_____ genes   _____ tubers   _____ acre

_____ biogenetic engineering   _____ harvest   _____ soil

_____ derived   _____ granules   _____ finite

Vocabulary Building

Guessing Meaning from Context Guess the meanings of the underlined words in the sentences below:

1. Biologists are studying <u>genes</u> to discover which ones are responsible for which physical and emotional characteristics.

2. By using <u>biogenetic engineering</u>, they hope to create new types of plants.

3. Plastic is <u>derived</u> from petroleum.

4. Potatoes, carrots, and other <u>tubers</u> are an important part of our diet.

5. They worked hard, <u>harvesting</u> wheat and putting it into bags.

6. There were small <u>granules</u> of sugar all over the kitchen table.

7. He owns 100 <u>acres</u> of land. He can't plant crops on much of the land, though, because the quality of the <u>soil</u> is so poor.

8. Anything that comes from something that was once alive—vegetables, fruit, even paper—can be <u>degraded</u> in soil. Plastic, of course, is not degradable because it comes from petroleum.

9. There is only a <u>finite</u> amount of petroleum. When we use it all, we can't produce any more.

> To cherish what remains of the Earth and to foster its renewal is our only legitimate hope of survival.
>
> **—WENDELL BERRY**

Listen

Listening 2: One Solution to the Problem of Plastic

Getting the Main Idea Plastic is not biodegradable. If you throw away a plastic bag today, it will be here on Earth for your great-great-great-great-great-grandchildren. You are going to hear two people talk about a possible solution to the problem of plastic. You won't understand every word. Just listen for the main ideas and complete these sentences:

- Right now, people produce plastic from _____.

- In the future, maybe we can produce plastic from _____.

> **Remember, this planet is also disposable.**
>
> **—PAUL PALMER**

Listening for Reasons When you're listening for reasons, listen for words such as *first*, *second*, and *third*. Listen to the report again. Why do people want to harvest (get) plastic from potatoes? Give two reasons:

1. _____

2. _____

◆ **After You Listen**

Getting Specific Information You are going to read an article about the breakthrough—the discovery—of plastic plants. In the article are some vocabulary words that you heard in the radio interview, but there are also some new words. Don't worry about them. Instead, focus on what you *do* understand. Below are some questions about the article. Look for the answers as you read. When you find the answers, mark them with a highlighter pen and compare your answers with those of another student.

1. What information in this article is the same as something you learned in the radio interview? What information is new?

2. In what part of a plant does plastic develop? In the future, in what part of a plant will there be plastic?

3. What is a British company making from a biodegradable plastic?

4. What is the problem with the plastic from the British company?

Researchers Sow Seeds, Harvest Plastic

1 Guilt-free throw-away plastic bottles, bags and diaper liners could be the fruit of research at two U.S. universities. Scientists have bio-genetically engineered a plant—the green kind, not the factory kind—that makes plastic.

2 And the plastic is biodegradable: It decays without harming the environment.

3 "Just like wood," says Charles Downs at Michigan State University, one research site; the other is James Madison University in Virginia. The breakthrough is reported today in *Science* magazine.

4 Future plastic plants could be a new cash crop for farmers. Now, the plastic develops in the plant's stems and leaves, but researchers hope to produce plants whose "fruit" would be lumps of plastic rather than tomatoes or potatoes.

5 Plastic already is being made, in factories, from plant products such as cornstarch—but it also contains petroleum.

6 A British firm makes bottles from a bio-degradable plastic grown by bacteria cultures. But the plastic costs about $12 a pound vs. 50 cents for plastic made from petroleum. Plastic grown from plants is expected to cost about $1.20 a pound.

—James Kim, From *USA Today* (April 24, 1992) page 1A. © Copyright 1992, USA TODAY. Reprinted with permission.

ACADEMIC POWER STRATEGY

Be careful to choose the correct definition when you use a dictionary. Many words have more than one meaning. You need to find the definition for the word in its context.

Example: "Scientists have bio-genetically engineered a *plant*—the green kind, not the factory kind—that makes plastic."

This dictionary entry has two definitions of *plant*:

---

plant *n.* **1** a life form that is usually held to the ground by roots and makes food from soil, water, and air. Ex. *Trees are large plants.* **2** the machines, buildings, etc. of a factory, business, or institution. Ex. *Automobiles are made in that plant.*

You need to look at a sentence and then choose the correct definition of a word:

She bought a *plant* for the garden.   A lot of people work at that *plant*.

(Plant = Definition 1)   *(Plant* = Definition 2)

Apply the Strategy   Choose the correct definition for each underlined word below. Write the number of the definition in the space.

---

earth *n.* **1** the planet on which humans live. Ex. *The earth travels around the sun.* **2** ground; soil; dirt. Ex. *He planted the tree in the earth.*

---

1. Soon we might dig potatoes out of the earth and find plastic in them.

   (Definition _____)

2. The ozone protects the earth from harmful sunlight.

   (Definition _____)

---

sow *v.* **1** plant seed on or in the earth. Ex. *The farmer will sow his wheat next week.* **2** plant in the mind. Ex. *The enemy agents tried to sow discontent among the people.*

---

3. They sowed confusion everywhere. (Definition _____)

4. Scientists are sowing seeds to try to grow plastic.

   (Definition _____)

(continued on next page)

culture *n*. **1** the ideas, arts, and way of life of a people or nation at a certain time. Ex. *We have learned from the culture of ancient Greece.* **2** a specially prepared material in which bacteria and cells will grow, used in scientific experiments.

5. How do people do this in your <u>culture</u>? (Definition _____)

6. A British company is making plastic in bacteria <u>cultures</u>.

(Definition _____)

Think about all the plastic items that you bring home, throw away, or recycle in one week. Be sure to include plastic containers (such as milk bottles), packages, and bags. Write a paragraph about your current use of plastic and how you can use less or recycle more.

_____

_____

_____

_____

_____

The Sound of It: Pronouncing the *t* in the Middle of Words

In some words with a *t* in the middle, followed by the sound *-un*, the *t* is not usually pronounced as English language learners might expect. Listen to these words:

mountain   bitten   certain

To make this sound, the tongue goes up to the roof of the mouth but doesn't come down before the *-un* sound. Listen again and pronounce the words after the speaker: mountain, bitten, certain.

Listen to these sentences and write the missing words. You'll hear each sentence two times.

1. We spent our vacation in _____.

2. I haven't _____ to them for several months.

3. He was concerned that the water in the drinking _____ might not be clean, so he drank only bottled water.

4. She found a tiny lost _____ on the sidewalk. She had no idea where the mother cat was.

PART 3: Creative Solutions

. . . .

Getting Ready to Listen

Vocabulary Building

Guessing Meaning from Context You are going to hear a report from National Public Radio about a city in Brazil. Before you listen, guess the meanings of the underlined words in the sentences below:

1. I don't want to live in that <u>ramshackle</u> area. It's such a horrible, poor neighborhood—a real <u>slum</u>.

2. He found a job with the <u>municipality</u>. It's the first time that he's ever worked for the city.

3. We recycle all of our <u>non-organic trash</u>—glass, plastic, and metal garbage.

4. The streets used to be <u>filthy</u>, but they're clean now.

5. They <u>transformed</u> the city. It's completely different now.

6. Do you see this machine? They made it from <u>scrap metal</u>. Can you believe that they found all that metal in the garbage and landfills?

7. They made a continual effort to solve the problem. They never gave up. This <u>perseverance</u> finally allowed them to find a solution.

8. Health problems, filthy streets, and crime are often part of the <u>syndrome</u> of poverty.

9. The children can go out to play only <u>on the condition</u> that they finish their homework first.

Listen

Listening 3: Finding Solutions to Environmental Problems

Listening for Specific Information Curitiba is a city in Brazil. (It is pronounced "Cureecheeeba.") It's a poor city with environmental problems. There are also human problems; many people are very poor, and many children don't go to school. But this city is finding solutions to these problems. The mayor, Jaime Lerner, says, "When you don't have the money . . . you have to be creative." Listen to the report and answer the questions on page 210. You don't have to understand every word. Just listen for the information that you need.

Section 1

1. In the neighborhood of Vista Alegre, what do women get from the municipality?

2. What do the women exchange for this?

3. How has the neighborhood changed as a result?

Section 2

4. In a program called "Garbage That Isn't Garbage," what do people put out for the garbage truck to take?

5. Men and boys work at the recycling center. Before they began this work, what problem did the men have?

6. Before they began this work, where were the boys living? What must they now do every day?

Section 3

7. Mayor Lerner says: "Sometimes there is a kind of syndrome of the tragedy in our cities." Then he explains this sentence. What does he say?

> In Los Angeles, discarded garments are being re-cycled as industrial rags and carpet underlay. Such recycling keeps clothing out of landfills, where it makes up 4 percent of the trash dumped each year.
>
> **—ABSOLUTE TRIVIA WEB SITE**

◆ **After You Listen**

Discussion

1. What do you think about the programs in Curitiba?

2. Does your city have a recycling program? If so, how does it work?

PART 4: Ecotourism in Brazil

◆ **Vocabulary Building**

You are going to see a CNN segment about ecotourism in Brazil. Before you view this, complete each of the following sentences with one of these words: *booming, luxurious, wildlife, primitive, mining, ensure, monitoring.* (Use a dictionary if necessary.)

1. Our hotel was quite _____. We didn't have hot water or clean towels, and there wasn't any electricity.

2. The economy is _____ in that part of the country. Most people have jobs, and there is a lot of income from tourism.

> People in the United States use approximately 2.5 million plastic beverage bottles every hour.

3. The rain forest is rich in _____; there are many species of birds, several primate species, a number of reptiles, and thousands of species of insects.

4. I love nature, but after a long day of trekking through a humid jungle, I want to go back to a _____ hotel room where I can be very comfortable.

5. Scientists are carefully _____ the area because they want to _____ that the tourists are not harmful to the environment.

6. He worked for a _____ company for a few years, digging for gold. But the pay was very low and the work was brutally hard, so he went back to work on his brother's farm.

TUNING IN: "Ecotourism in Brazil"

© CNN

Making Predictions Watch the video the first time without sound. What do you expect it to say about ecotourism in Brazil?

Getting the "Big Picture" Watch the video again, this time with sound. Then answer these questions:

1. What are two good things about ecotourism in the Amazon?

2. What is one possible bad thing about it?

3. What are two groups of people who are destroying the forest for profit?

Discussion

1. What do you think about ecotourism? Would you like to take an ecotour to Brazil? Why or why not?

2. Are there ecotours in your native country? If so, tell your group what you know about them.

3. Is there someplace in the world where you would like to take an ecotour?

PUTTING IT ALL TOGETHER

Work in groups of four to five students. Each group needs to choose *one* of the two following projects. After you have chosen a project, read through the directions. Notice which steps are already given. Decide what other, smaller steps the project can be broken down into. Decide which steps to work on together and which should be done by individual students.

Project 1

1. Imagine that your group is the Environmental Protection Department of Xenrovia (a small, poor country). This country has many environmental problems and doesn't have much money. Make a list of the country's environmental problems. (Air pollution? Toxic chemicals in the water? No more space for landfills? Filthy streets? People cutting down rain forests?) For more ideas, look at your list on page 202.

2. As a group, think of solutions to these problems. Remember, your government doesn't have much money. However, you can write any laws that are necessary.

Project 2

1. Imagine that your group is an advertising company. Many environmental organizations have come to you for help. They want you to organize ad campaigns, but you have time to work for only one of these organizations. Choose *one* of these environmental problems:

   a. The African elephant is disappearing.

   b. Air pollution is so bad that the air in this city isn't breathable.

   c. The rain forests are disappearing.

   d. Plastic is piling up in landfills and is not biodegradable.

   e. People are throwing away too much garbage.

   f. People are throwing garbage in the ocean, and ocean animals are dying.

2. Organize an ad campaign for this problem:

   a. Think of a good slogan, or saying. (For example: "If you're not recycling, you're throwing it all away.")

   b. Design a one-page magazine ad.

c. Plan a five-minute program to teach schoolchildren about the problem.

d. Write a short radio ad to persuade people to change their actions. Record this on a cassette tape.

Test-Taking Tip

Work with a partner to prepare for speaking-based tests. Practice speaking with your partner about subjects you think you may be asked about during the test. First, one of you can play the part of the "interviewer" while the other takes the role of the "interviewee," then you can reverse the roles.

CHECK YOUR PROGRESS

On a scale of 1 to 5, rate how well you have mastered the goals set at the beginning of the chapter:

1 2 3 4 5   locate many countries on a world map.

1 2 3 4 5   use ecology-related vocabulary.

1 2 3 4 5   use new words as soon and as often as possible.

1 2 3 4 5   notice and understand parts of words to guess meaning.

1 2 3 4 5   highlight new words.

1 2 3 4 5   choose the correct definition in a dictionary.

1 2 3 4 5   work with other students to think of solutions to environmental problems.

If you've given yourself a 3 or lower on any of these goals:

- visit the *Tapestry* web site for additional practice.
- ask your instructor for extra help.
- review the sections of the chapter that you found difficult.
- work with a partner or study group to further your progress.

TRANSCRIPTS
CHAPTER 1: THE WHOLE WORLD IS YOUR CLASSROOM

Listening 1, page 8:
Learning a New Language

Section 1

Uh, because it's the beginning of the trimester, I'd like to give you some suggestions as to how you can learn English really fast. And most of my suggestions have nothing to do with this classroom. A lot of you told me that you think the most important thing is to come to class every day. I'm very happy that you're going to come to class every day, umm, but I think you can probably learn more English outside the classroom than inside. I think you can make the whole world into your classroom. You can make every person around you into a teacher. But, in my mind, the best teacher in the world is yourself because each person learns differently, and you know how you learn best. I think you can be a really good teacher to yourself. You can use me, you can use your other teachers, as helpers, but I can't give you some magical English pill. You can't come to class and open your mouth and —ping!—put in the pill and—ah!—you learn English. That doesn't work. But I can help you. I can answer your questions, and I can guide you a little bit, but basically I want you to be in control of your own language learning career here at this school.

Section 2

One way that you can do that, as a few of you mentioned a few minutes ago, is to make small talk. I think that's what you were talking about when you said, "Talk with people in the supermarket or at the bus stop." Great. Talk with strangers. Make small talk. When you're at the bus stop, you know, say, "Oh, boy, this bus is always late, isn't it?" And start a small conversation with the person. In the supermarket, in the produce section, you can start a conversation with a stranger over the tomatoes or something. You can complain: "Boy, look, these tomatoes are almost green. They're terrible." And you'll find that people are very friendly. You can have a very short, safe conversation. When you're waiting in line at the su-permarket—you know a person who's really great to practice on? A mother with a little baby. That may be different in different cultures, but, in this culture, if the woman in front of you has a little baby and you say, "Oh, what a beautiful baby!" the woman is just going to ("gonna") smile. She's going to ("gonna") grin from ear to ear. "Oh, thank you." And you'll start a short conversation. There are many places. . . . Uh, here at school, at break time, don't look for people who speak your language. Look for people who don't speak your language.

Section 3

Let me tell you about a friend of mine. Her name is Sara. I met her many years ago—a hundred years ago—when we were going to college. Not quite a hundred years ago, but almost. We were both going to college, and she was from Paraguay, from South America. Her English was pretty terrible, and my Spanish was pretty terrible, but we managed to communicate. In those days, at least at my college, there were no ESL classes, so she didn't have any help at all with her English. They just threw her into biology classes and history classes and English classes with American students. No ESL. So she had to become her own teacher. She had to teach herself English. And the way she did it was really interesting. She had a little notebook. And she spoke with everybody. She was not shy; that helped. She talked with everybody. She made small talk with strangers everywhere, but also she used her friends, and she used to tell us, "You have to tell me if I make a mistake in my grammar." We didn't. We never corrected her. But she was a very good listener, and if we said something differently from the way she normally said it, she remembered that. Or if we used an idiom, she would take out her little notebook and say, "Wait. Wait. What was that again? How do you spell that? Now what does that mean?" So basically, she taught herself English, but she used us as helpers. You know what she's doing today? . . . Exactly. She's teaching English at a high school here in the city. She taught herself. And she didn't have the benefit of an ESL class.

Section 4

Let me give you one more example. For my senior year in college I went to school in Europe. I went to Greece—to Athens—for a year. I wanted to speak Greek really well, but it was a very difficult language. I remembered my friend Sara, and I thought, "Well, if she can do it, I can do it." So I practiced on everybody, just a little bit. The best place I found to practice was with taxi drivers. I used to sit in the taxi and try to think of something to say. I tried to open the conversation. So I'd say, "Oh, um, it's a nice day, isn't it?" And the taxi driver would say, "Oh, yeah, really nice day." And then if he noticed my accent, he'd say, "Are you from another country?" And I'd say, "Yeah. I'm an American." And he'd say, "Oh, an American. I have a brother in Chicago. Maybe you know him." I learned vocabulary from every single person I spoke with. I didn't wait for my Greek class because, to be honest, I didn't learn very much in my Greek class. But it's good if you're not dependent—if you don't have to depend on your, your language teacher, on your language class. Then you're never disappointed. You are your own teacher. The whole world is your classroom.

Listening 2, page 11:
Making Small Talk

Conversation 1

A: It's a great party, isn't it?

B: Yeah. And the music's wonderful. John really knows how to throw a party.

A: Have you known him long?

B: John? Oh, yeah. We went to middle school together.

Conversation 2

A: Man, that was a hard test, wasn't it?

B: It was terrible! I don't think I did very well—especially on the last part.

A: I didn't either.

Conversation 3

A: Oh, what a cute baby!

B: Thanks. She's pretty happy most of the time.

A: She *seems* really happy. So she's helping you with the shopping, huh?

B: Oh, sure. (to the baby) Wait—no, no, no! Candy isn't good for babies.

Conversation 4

A: The bus is late again, isn't it?

B: It sure seems to be. Honestly, this bus is late so often.

A: I know. I've been late to work three times this month.

Choosing a Response

Conversation 1

A: It's a great party, isn't it?

Conversation 2

A: Man, that was a hard test, wasn't it?

Conversation 3

A: Oh, what a cute baby!

Conversation 4

A: The bus is late again, isn't it?

The Sound of It, page 13:
Understanding Intonation
in Tag Questions

We often begin a conversation with a sentence that includes a tag question. We add a "tag" to a sentence and it becomes a question. Our voice goes up on the tag if we aren't sure about the answer; it becomes a real question. Our voice goes down on the tag if we already know the answer and are making small talk.

Examples: We haven't met before, have we?

We haven't met before, have we?

A. Listen to the conversation. Where does it take place? Check the answer.

A: The food in this place is awful, isn't it?

B: Yeah. You don't see any fresh fruit anywhere, do you?

A: No. There isn't any nonfat yogurt either, is there?

B: Of course not. But there's lots of fat, calories, and sugar, though, isn't there?

A: Oh sure. Why is the food in school cafeterias always so bad?

B: I don't know ("dunno"). You haven't seen a good health food place near here, have you?

B. Listen and repeat.

1. Unsure of the answer: The food is awful, isn't it?

   Sure of the answer: The food is awful, isn't it?

2. Unsure of the answer: You don't see any fresh fruit, do you?

   Sure of the answer: You don't see any fresh fruit, do you?

3. Unsure of the answer: There isn't any yogurt, is there?

   Sure of the answer: There isn't any yogurt, is there?

4. Unsure of the answer: There's lots of sugar, isn't there?

   Sure of the answer: There's lots of sugar, isn't there?

5. Unsure of the answer: You haven't seen a good health food place, have you?

   Sure of the answer: You haven't seen a good health food place, have you?

Language Learning Strategy, page 14:
Paying Attention to Intonation

Listen to these sentences. Are the speakers unsure or sure of the answers? Put check marks on the lines. You will hear each sentence two times.

1. This is a wonderful party, isn't it?
2. You haven't seen my dictionary, have you?
3. This bus is always late, isn't it?
4. This line doesn't seem to be moving, does it?
5. The oranges are on sale this week, aren't they?
6. It's going to be a hard class, isn't it?
7. You don't know where I can find a mailbox, do you?
8. The test was pretty easy, wasn't it?

Listening 3, page 16:
Identifying Conversations

Conversation A

A: Well, I have to run now. See you later.

B: Yeah. Have a good weekend.

Conversation B

A: Oh, excuse me! I'm so sorry.

B: That's OK. It was nothing.

Conversation C

A: I'd like you to meet my parents, Mr. and Mrs. Jones.

B: Nice to meet you.

C: Likewise.

Conversation D

A: Is this for me? How thoughtful of you!

B: Don't mention it.

CHAPTER 2: CHANGE AND CHOICE

Listening 1, page 27:
Understanding Directions

1. The grocery store is across the street from the
2. The bank is next to the
3. The bookstore is around the corner from the
4. The library is down the street from the
5. There's a bus stop in front of the
6. There's a Chinese restaurant beside the

Do you want to have dinner there tomorrow, Susan?

Listening 2, page 33:
Understanding Tone of Voice

Conversation 1

Susan: Excuse me, does this bus go to 7th and Lake streets?

Driver: No, this bus doesn't go there. Take bus number 30 and transfer at Geary to the 38.

Susan: Take the 30 and transfer where?

Driver: At Geary. Get the 38 at Geary.

Susan: And where do I get bus number 30?

Driver: Cross the street. See the bus stop there at the corner?

Susan: Thanks.

Driver: Have a good day.

Conversation 2

Susan: Excuse me, does this bus go to Geary Street?

Driver: Yeah.

Susan: How much is it?

Driver: 85 cents . . . you can't use dollar bills.

Susan: What?

Driver: You have to have exact change. See the sign?

Susan: Oh, OK, here you are.

Driver: Move to the back, lady.

Listening 3, page 36:
Reporting Problems

(phone rings)

Mrs. West: Hello?

Susan: Mrs. West?

Mrs. West: Yes.

Susan: This is Susan Evans . . . in Apartment 101.

Mrs. West: Oh, hi Susan! How are you?

Susan: Well, right now I'm pretty warm. I put the air conditioning on "high," but it doesn't seem to be working.

Mrs. West: Oh, dear. Are you sure you set it correctly?

Susan: Yes. I've tried everything, but it just doesn't work.

Mrs. West: Well then, I'll have to call the repair people.

Susan: And there's another problem: the neighbors next door in Apartment 102 are so noisy. They have music on day and night, really loud. I'm having trouble sleeping.

Mrs. West: Hmmm . . . that's more difficult.

Susan: I almost called you last night at midnight, but I didn't want to wake you up.

Mrs. West: I'll speak to them and ask them to be more considerate. If they have a really loud party late at night, you can tell them that you'll call

the police if they don't quiet down. I'm sorry, Susan.

Susan: It's not your fault, Mrs. West. But I would appreciate it if you would call the air conditioning repair people and speak to the neighbors. I'll have to move if I can't sleep well at night.

The Sound of It, page 36:
Understanding Reductions

A. In normal or fast speech, you will hear "reductions" of some words. For instance, *want to* may sound like "wanna." Learning to understand reductions will help you become a better listener. Listen to these examples of reductions from the conversations in this chapter. Can you hear the difference between the long forms and the short forms? (Note: The short forms are not correct in writing.)

Long form: Do you have any pets?
Short form: Do ya have any pets?

Long form: What's your name?
Short form: Whatcher name?

Long form: Does this bus go to Geary Street?
Short form: Does this bus goda Geary Street?

Long form: Do you want to see the kitchen?
Short form: Do you wanna see the kitchen?

Long form: You have to have exact change.
Short form: You hafta have exact change.

B. Listen to these sentences. Do you hear a reduction? Check *Long Form* or *Short Form* as you listen. You will hear each sentence two times.

Examples:

a. You need bus number 3.

b. Ya need bus number 3.

1. Are you Susan Evans?
2. Ya can't use dollar bills.
3. What's your phone number?
4. Whatcher address?
5. I need to goda the store.
6. Do you go to Parkwood Avenue?
7. Does he wanna pay that much?
8. I don't want to walk.
9. Do you have to go?
10. I hafta buy some furniture.

Listening 4, page 38:
Starting Again

Narrator: Pilar, in your country do people move often?

Pilar: Well, sometimes people go off to a university and then don't come back, or sometimes people move because of work. But, in general, in my country people do not move often. We are part of a large family that stays together. For instance, my mother lives near all of her sisters and brothers. Their children live nearby and help them when they are sick or need something. I came to America because of my husband's work, but when I go back to my country, I will go back to my town, my family, my past.

Narrator: How are things different in America?

Pilar: Here, if someone comes from a family that has problems, they leave that family behind and go off and make a new life. There are many opportunities here that we do not have, and people here follow those opportunities. In America, a poor person from a family that other people look down on can become a rich and respected person. A woman who has a bad husband can leave him and move to a new place and start a new life. In my country, that sometimes happens, but it is more difficult for the average person.

Just For Fun, page 41:
"Oh, California"

I sailed from Salem City with my washbowl on my knee.
I'm going to California, the gold dust for to see.
It rained all night the day I left, the weather it was dry;
The sun so hot I froze to death, oh brothers don't you cry.
Oh, California, that's the land for me.
I'm going to San Francisco with my washbowl on my knee.
I soon shall be in Frisco, and there I'll look around.
And when I find the gold lumps there, I'll pick them off the ground.
I'll scrape the mountains clean, my boys, I'll drain the rivers dry;
A pocketful of rocks bring home, oh brothers don't you cry.
Oh, California, that's the land for me.
I'm going to San Francisco with my washbowl on my knee.

CHAPTER 3: THIS IS WHO I AM

Listening 1, page 48:
Interests and Hobbies

Narrator: What do you do in your free time?

Person 1: I like to go shopping. I like to go shopping at *thrift* shops, where I can buy a *lot* of stuff, but it's really cheap, so I don't feel guilty or go broke.

Person 2: What free time? I don't have any free time. All I do is work.

Person 3: Well, uh, because I sit at a computer all day at my office, uh, I like to do physical things—you know, um, jogging, playing tennis, gardening.

Person 4: Free time? Gosh. I enjoy anything outside. I like hiking and camping in the mountains, sailing at a lake near my home, and I just started taking skydiving lessons. It's really neat, jumping out of a plane.

Person 5: Um, I like the theater a lot—you know, plays, ballet, concerts, opera. And I *love* movies, especially classic foreign films.

Person 6: Oh, I don't know, lots of different stuff. I like books, dancing, animals. Um, I like to try interesting restaurants. Mostly, I really like sleeping. Yeah. Sleep is good.

The Sound of It, page 50:
Understanding Intonation in Questions with *Or*

There are two kinds of questions with the word *or*: *yes/no* questions and *either/or* questions.

1. In *yes/no* questions, the answer is "Yes" or "No." The speaker's voice goes up two times.

Example: Question: would you like coffee or tea?
Answer: Yes, please.

2. In *either/or* questions, the answer is one of the two items from the question. The speaker's voice goes up on the first item and down on the second item.

Example: Question: Would you like coffee or tea?
Answer: Tea, please.

A. Listen to these questions and repeat them. Notice the intonation.

1. Yes/No question: Do you like TV or movies?
Either/Or question: Do you like TV or movies?

2. Yes/No question: Does she enjoy ice skating or roller-blading?
Either/Or question: Does she enjoy ice skating or roller-blading?

3. Yes/No question: Does he swim at the gym or at home?
Either/Or question: Does he swim at the gym or at home?

4. Yes/No question: Is he an actor or a musician?
Either/Or question: Is he an actor or a musician?

5. Yes/No question: Did she work during the summer or after school?
Either/Or question: Did she work during the summer or after school?

B. Listen to the intonation in each question. Is it a *yes/no* question or an *either/or* question? For each *yes/no* question, write *yes* on the line. For each *either/or* question, write one of the two items from the question. You will hear each question two times.

1. Is he in Level 1 or Level 2?

2. Do you like French food or Chinese food?

3. Do you read novels or poetry?

4. Does she live alone or with her family?

5. Would you like cake or ice cream?

6. Do you want to go hiking or swimming?

7. Did they stay at home or go away on vacation?

8. Is he from Thailand or Indonesia?

9. Does she study business or art?

10. Do you want to rent a video or go to a movie?

Listening 2, page 53:
Telling a Story

When I was in high school, I had some small jobs doing babysitting on weekends and some evenings, but my first real job was one summer when I was in college. I got a job as a store detective for a big department store. My job was just to walk around the store all day and look like a shopper and catch people who were trying to steal things from the store. I, I could wear anything. Umm, I could wear jeans or shorts to work because I was supposed to look like a shopper and, you know, catch shoplifters.

Uh, anyway, my boss was this really horrible man. Um, actually, I think he liked me. He used to call me "Tiger," which seemed really stupid to me. But he was, he was this big man, great big man, who used to be in the army. And he didn't really trust or believe anybody who was young or anybody who was not white. This man was a, was a real racist. If, if a group of young people would walk in the store or if, or if anybody would walk in the store who wasn't white, he would come over to me and say, "Keep an eye on them. They're gonna take something." And I'd say, "I don't know why you say that. They look fine to me." And he'd say, "They're gonna take something. Trust me." He was, he was just terrible.

Anyway, the job was pretty boring. Um, I used to like shopping until I got that job, and then when I had to walk around the store and look like I was shopping for six or seven hours a day, I didn't like shopping anymore. And also, I spent all the money I made from the job.

But my main problem was that I was very young, and I wanted to look good all the time, and I was very vain, so I, I never wore my glasses, and I couldn't see anything without my glasses, so of course I never saw anybody take anything. Um, finally, after months, I saw one young girl, I don't know, she was maybe eleven or twelve years old. I saw her putting something into her purse. I don't remember. I think it was a piece of jewelry. Anyway, she had to be pretty stupid for me to catch her because I couldn't see anything. So I, I took her into the office, and I was supposed to call the police to have them take her away, but then she burst into tears. And there she was, crying and crying, and telling me that her father was going to be really angry, and I felt so bad that I made her promise never to take anything again, and then I let her go. I was a really bad store detective. Soon after that, I, I quit the job, and I think probably my boss was glad.

Language Learning Strategy, page 55: Listening for Stressed Words

A. 1. It was a TERRIBLE day.
   2. WE'LL take those.
   3. I was SUPPOSED to catch shoplifters.
   4. They're going to TAKE something.
   5. I couldn't SEE anything.

Listen to the important (stressed) words in these sentences. Underline them. You will hear each sentence two times.

B. 1. That was my BOSS.
   2. That was MY boss.
   3. I don't REMEMBER.
   4. I DON'T remember.
   5. George used to WORK there.
   6. George USED to work there.
   7. What do you DO?
   8. What do YOU do?
   9. She said she didn't TAKE it.
   10. She said SHE didn't take it.
   11. SHE said she didn't take it.

C. 1. What's your favorite SPORT?
      I really like SKIING.
   2. What's HER favorite sport?
      I think SHE likes skiing, too.
   3. Where do they COME from?
      They come from BRAZIL.
   4. Where does HE come from?
      HE comes from Hong Kong.
   5. What are you going to TAKE?

I'm going to take ECONOMICS.
   6. What are THEY going to take?
      THEY have no idea.

D. 1. WHERE did your brother find a job?
      He found a job in CHICAGO.
   2. WHOSE brother found a job?
      MY brother found a job.
   3. WHAT did your brother do?
      Answer: He FOUND a JOB in CHICAGO.

Listening 3, page 58: Taking About Goals

Person 1

I just became a father last week, for the first time, and this has changed everything for me. My goal is to give my daughter a good life. First, I'm going to buy a house. I want her to have a garden to play in. Second, I'm going to change my work times so I can spend more time with her. Third, I'm going to start saving money now for her college education. College is expensive, you know.

Person 2

Well, I'll tell you what my goal is for the future. I'm going to become the first woman president of the country. And I'll tell you exactly how I plan to do that. First, I'm going to go to college, and in college I'm going to study history because I think that's really important if you're going to be in politics. Second, sometime when I'm in college, I think it's important to go and live in another country for a year or two and learn another language—at least one other language. And third, when I come back, I'm going to go to law school and become a lawyer for a few years. Then I'm going to go into politics. I'll start small; maybe I'll be the mayor. And then after a while I'll become a senator and then I'll be in the Senate for a number of years, and I'll be prepared to become the president.

Person 3

Well, I retired a couple of years ago. I have a comfortable life—my grandchildren, my house, garden, animals. Anyway, I don't really need anything—not for myself. But I'm very worried about the future of the earth—the environment. I guess you could say my goal is to make this place—the earth—a better place. And how am I going to do this? Well, first, I give money to different groups—you know, Greenpeace, Save the Earth, World Wildlife Fund, and so on. Second, I write a lot of letters to the government. I want them to change some laws and protect the forests and animals. Third, because I live near the ocean, I'm studying ocean animals, and I try to help them. For example, sometimes there's a terrible oil spill from a ship, and birds get caught in the oil. Without help from people, the birds die. So I'm learning how to clean the birds and then let them go free.

Person 4

Um, I think at this point in my life, uh, the goal I'm most worried about is retirement. And I would like to retire in a quiet area, um, in the mountains, a small town where there's no smog, no traffic, very little crime. And uh, I won't retire for another fifteen or twenty years, so it gives me a lot of time to save some more money. Uh, the house that I'm living in is paid for, so when I sell it, um, I should have enough money with that, the money I've saved, and the money from my retirement pension, to buy a house in a small town in the mountains and hopefully have enough money to live on for the next fifteen or twenty years.

The Sound of It, page 61: Understanding Reductions

A. In normal or fast speech, you will hear "reductions" of some words. Listen to these examples. Can you hear the difference between the long forms and the short forms? (Note: The short forms are not correct in writing.)

Long form: What do you do?
Short form: Whadaya do?

Long form: What are you doing?
Short form: Watcha doing?

Long form: What kind of childhood was it?
Short form: What kinda childhood was it?

Long form: What did you do?
Short form: What didja do?

Long form: What did he do?
Short form: What didee do?

Long form: They used to live here.
Short form: They yoosta live here.

Long form: I'm going to buy a house.
Short form: I'm gonna buy a house.

B. Listen to these sentences. Do you hear a reduction? Check *Long Form* or *Short Form* as you listen. You will hear each sentence two times.

Examples:

a. Whatcha looking at?

b. What are you looking at?

1. Did you enjoy school?
2. I'm gonna study history.
3. What kinda sports do you like?
4. He used to live with his grandmother.
5. Where didee go to school?
6. Whadaya think about it?
7. I'm kind of tired.
8. How are you going to do it?
9. Why did you do that?
10. Whadaya want to do?

C. Listen to these conversations. You'll hear reduced (short) forms. Write the long forms. You will hear each conversation two times.

1. A: Did you see that movie on TV last night?
   B: Yeah. I thought it was going to be funny, but it was really sad.
2. A: What kind of sports do you like?
   B: Oh, tennis, swimming, basketball. I used to play tennis in high school.
3. A: What are you planning to do on the weekend?
   B: Bob and I are going to look for a new car. Did he tell you about the accident with the old car?
   A: Yeah. That's too bad.

[Pronounced: Didja, gonna, kinda, yoosta, Whatcha, gonna, Didee]

D. With your partner, figure out which word(s) you need to stress in each question and answer below. Underline it (or them). Then listen to the tape to check your answers. Repeat each question and answer after the speaker.

1. Question: Where did your brother find a job?
   Answer: He found a job in Chicago.
2. Question: Whose brother found a job?
   Answer: My brother found a job.
3. Question: What did your brother do?
   Answer: He found a job in Chicago.

CHAPTER 4:
HEALTH: GETTING THE MOST OUT OF LIFE

Listening 1, page 72:
Ordering a Meal

Conversation 1

Waitress: Are you ready to order, or do you need a few more minutes?

Woman: I'm ready—I'll have the fried chicken with biscuits and gravy.

Waitress: It comes with potatoes, rice, or corn on the cob.

Woman: Potatoes, I guess.

Waitress: Mashed, baked, or french fries?

Woman: Mashed.

Waitress: Would you like soup or salad with that?

Woman: No, thanks. . . .

Waitress: How was everything here? May I take your plate?

Woman: Uh-huh.

Waitress: Would you care for some dessert? We have lemon cake, chocolate cream pie, ice cream, or fresh strawberries.

Woman: I'll have the chocolate pie, please.

Waitress: Would you like coffee or tea?

Woman: Coffee. And could you bring the check with that?

Conversation 2

Waitress: May I take your order?

Man: Um . . . what's the special today?

Waitress: We have prime rib or fresh sole.

Man: Sole sounds good. How much is that?

Waitress: $9.95.

Man: OK, I'll have the sole.

Waitress: Would you like soup or salad?

Man: What's the soup of the day?

Waitress: Vegetable beef.

Man: I'll take the salad, please.

Waitress: What kind of dressing would you like? French, oil and vinegar, or thousand island?

Man: Oil and vinegar. And can I have some water to drink?

Waitress: Sure. . . . Are you finished here, sir?

Man: Yes, thanks.

Waitress: Would you like anything for dessert? We have apple pie, chocolate cake, ice cream, or a fresh fruit salad.

Man: I'll have the fruit salad.

Waitress: Coffee with that?

Man: No, thanks. Just the check.

Listening 2, page 76:
Talking About Fitness

Narrator: What do you do to get exercise?

Person 1: Um . . . I don't get enough exercise, really, but I do walk to school every day. And I work in the garden on weekends.

Person 2: I take a yoga class. In the summer I swim a lot . . . several times a week.

Person 3: I do jazzercise whenever I can . . . it's an aerobic dance class. That's about it.

Person 4: I'm on a volleyball team. We play all the time. Volleyball's my favorite sport. And I love to dance—does that count as exercise?

Person 5: I go running twice a week. I usually run two miles or so.

Listening 3, page 78:
Stress and Your Health

Interviewer: How does stress affect your health habits?

Person 1: I have trouble sleeping when I feel stress. I lie awake at night . . . can't go to sleep, thinking or worrying. Usually just worrying. Then I'm tired the next day, and I can't think clearly.

Person 2: I eat. I can eat and eat and eat . . . anything. Mostly snack foods—you know, corn chips, candy, stuff like that.

Person 3: I start smoking more—one cigarette after another. Just can't stop. And I drink more beer—not a whole lot, but more than usual.

Person 4: I feel nervous. I can't eat. My stomach is . . . I don't know—I just don't feel hungry.

The Sound of It, page 81:
Listening for Stressed Words—
Can or *Can't*?

In the interviews about stress and health habits, you heard several examples of *can* and *can't*. Listen to the examples again:

Person 1: I lie awake at night . . . can't go to sleep, thinking or worrying. Then I'm tired the next day, and I can't think clearly.

Person 2: I can eat and eat and eat . . . anything.

Person 3: I start smoking more—one cigarette after another. Just can't stop.

Person 4: I can't eat.

Here are some more examples. Listen to the difference in stress.

I can RIDE a BIKE.

I CAN'T RIDE a BIKE.

He can RIDE a HORSE.

He CAN'T RIDE a HORSE.

Do you hear the difference? *Can't* is louder and clearer. Listen to these sentences. Do you hear *can* or *can't*? Check the answer. You will hear each sentence two times.

1. They can ski.
2. I can't swim.
3. He can run a mile.
4. We can play tennis.
5. They can't play soccer.
6. I can hike all day.
7. She can't play the piano.
8. Can you do yoga exercises?
9. She can't dance.
10. Can you hear the difference?

Listening 4, page 82:
Interview with a Health Expert

Interview with Dr. Joseph Houlton, Section 1

BKS: All right, you're saying that our emotions have a great deal to do with the disease process?

JH: Uh-huh.

BKS: Do they have a great deal to do with the healing process?

JH: Absolutely. You probably have heard the story of Dr. Norman Cousins, who laughed himself back to health. He had a serious debilitating condition, was under the care of his physician in a hospital, and he found out what the odds were—there were very high odds of ever recovering. . . . He took some nutrients and vitamin C, but the biggest thing he found was watching Allen Funt, "Candid Camera," and other things like this. He laughed. And while he laughed, his pain eased. And they checked his blood cell count, and it had improved for the better, and so he checked himself out of the hospital and into a hotel with the consent of his doctor, who was willing to work with him. And using his own sense of humor, he produced proper states . . . in his body to come back to health.

Interview with Dr. Joseph Houlton, Section 2

BKS: Dr. Houlton, in our final two minutes, I wonder if you could tell all of us who are interested in knowing what we can do with this sometimes monster called stress. What is really the key to the handling of stress for any of us?

JH: Well, a recognition that we can't avoid stress; we should be in a position to welcome it. And in order to welcome stress, I have a little motto—it's on my business card—it says, "Be thankful." It's an attitude of gratitude to life for life—sets my body in position to take whatever comes along and to utilize it properly. So I guess it all boils down to a particular attitude—an attitude within oneself of gratitude to life for life. A thankful attitude maintains the hormonal system in a proper state of balance so that we are able to take whatever action is necessary in a constructive way.

BKS: Thank you very much, Dr. Houlton.

Listening 5, page 83:
It's a Matter of Attitude

Ms. Hicks: Until I was 100 years old, I hadn't really lived. All these interesting things have happened to me since I was 100 years old.

Barbara: Tell me what's happened since you've been 100.

Ms. Hicks: Well, for one thing, I rode on the—well, I had a blimp ride.

Barbara: The Goodyear blimp.

Ms. Hicks: The Goodyear blimp. And all over the—oh, he took me out so I could see Catalina. Beautiful, beautiful trip. Oh, and I've had helicopter trips, a lot of them, over Burbank, and once he took me so close to the Hollywood sign that I could almost touch it.

Barbara: Now, you've been alive over a century. You have seen a lot of changes—

Ms. Hicks: Everything.

Barbara: —since you were a little girl.

Ms. Hicks: I've seen everything develop.

Barbara: You were born what year?

Ms. Hicks: I was born January 30, 1885, in a small village about 70 miles south of Chicago. I spent a lot of time in Chicago later on.

Barbara: But what have you seen change?

Ms. Hicks: What have I seen change? Oh, my word, everything has changed, you know. Now we have space travel, why we have—look what we've developed into. Marvelous.

Barbara: All right. Now, you for your 100th birthday and your 102nd and your 104th went in a helicopter and a blimp. Your 106th birthday, what do you want to do for your 106th?

Ms. Hicks: Oh, well I want to meet a superstar.

Barbara: I'm not good enough, I guess, that's not it. Who do you want to meet?

Ms. Hicks: I've listened—I've heard all the top stars; now I want to hear a superstar.

Barbara: So who is that?

Ms. Hicks: Michael Jackson.

Barbara: Michael Jackson.

Ms. Hicks: Do you think I ever will?

Barbara: I hope you do. All right. As I said, we have people here who are breaking the stereotypes that getting old means sitting around doing nothing and waiting to die.

All right. Mary Ann, you are 72 and you have gone through quite a change in the last several years, in terms of how you looked at aging and how you look at it now.

Mary Ann Webber: Well, I think my whole attitude about aging has changed. I think the older I got the more comfortable I was with myself and the happier I was. I found that as I got older I no longer ran scared anymore. It's sort of kind of go your best shot, you know, what can you do to me now? It's all been done to me. All that can hap-

pen now is really more of the same. So I'm—I just don't have that fear anymore. I think when you're young you're always afraid that you're going to say the wrong thing, you're not going to be dressed properly, you're going to make a fool of yourself. Now, if I make a fool of myself, they call me a character, and that's wonderful.

Barbara: Now, a lot of people think that part of aging is we don't get to do the things that we could do, we become inactive, we sit around, we watch television, we crochet, but we can't go out and have fun anymore. You disprove that all the time.

Ms. Webber: Oh, I think people are very foolish to have that kind of an attitude. We all can make choices, and it's up to us when we get older to decide what choice we're going to make. And it's a matter of attitude. If you—at my age I say that any morning that I wake up and I'm still alive, it's a wonderful morning.

Barbara: All right. Now, Leo, you do not look your age at all. Not only that, when a lot of other men might be sitting around and watching TV or playing cards all day long, you're pressing your weight, your own weight? And incredibly active. Did you age gracefully? Did you think that when you got older you'd be active? Or did you have to psych yourself up and say, "Wait a minute, I don't want to get old"?

Leo Salazar: I think I had to psych myself up. And just like these ladies, I don't want to get old, either. And I agree with them in all their remarks, too. You know, these young people that talk about—they're afraid to even say the word "old." Well, they should read Browning, you know. "The best is yet to come."

Barbara: Tell me what's great about it.

Mr. Salazar: Well, I have a chance to do the things that I didn't do when I was working and supporting my family. And a lot of people say, "Well, you can't do them." Well, I can. I'm going to school. I'm very active in my community. We go on vacation to Washington, Hawaii and all that. I mean, I'm enjoying life and I'm very active.

CHAPTER 5: WHEN CULTURES MEET

Listening Activity, page 92:
"Sometimes I Feel Like a Motherless Child"

Sometimes I feel like a motherless child,
Sometimes I feel like a motherless child.
Sometimes I feel like a motherless child,
A long way from home, a long way from home.
A long way from home, a long way from home.

Listening 1, page 94,
The Stages of Culture Shock

I want to talk for a few minutes about something called "culture shock." Whenever people go and live in another country, they have new experiences and new feelings. They experience *culture shock*. Many people have a misconception about culture shock: they think that it's just a feeling of sadness and homesickness when a person is in a new country. But this isn't really true. Culture shock is a completely natural transition, and everybody goes through it in a new culture. It's a series of changes in the way you see the new culture, the way you see your own culture, and the way you feel about yourself.

There are different stages, or steps, in culture shock. Some experts believe there are four stages. Some say, no, there are five. Others say six. Anyway, there are different stages. I'm going to tell you about four of them.

When people first arrive in a new country, they're usually excited and happy. Everything is interesting. They notice that a lot of things are similar to their own culture, and this surprises them and makes them happy. They think, "Oh, I'm beginning my new life!" This is Stage One.

But then comes Stage Two. In Stage Two, people notice how *different* the new culture is from their own culture. They become confused. It seems difficult to do even very simple things. They feel angry or depressed. They spend a lot of time alone or with other people from their own country. They think, "My problems are all because I'm living in this country." They think, "My new life is horrible."

Then, in Stage Three, they begin to understand the new culture better. They begin to like some new customs. They make friends with some people in the new country. They're more comfortable and relaxed.

In Stage Four, they feel very comfortable. They have good friends in the new culture. They understand the new customs. Some customs are similar to their culture, and some are different, but that's OK. They can accept that. They are, of course, a member of their own culture. But they also become a member of the new culture. They feel that they *belong* in the new country. They enjoy their new life.

The Sound of It, page 96:
Understanding Reductions

A. In normal or fast speech, you'll hear reductions—that is, a shortened version of a word or group of words. Although reductions are common in speech, they are not correct in writing. Listen to these examples. Can you hear the difference between the long forms and the short forms?

Long form: She made a lot of friends.
Short form: She made a lotta friends.

Long form: He had lots of problems.
Short form: He had lotsa problems.

Long form: He wasn't able to relax.
Short form: He wasn't able ta relax.

Long form: Could you help me with this?
Short form: Cudja help me with this?

Long form: I'll see you later.
Short form: I'll see ya later.

Long form: Do you know her?
Short form: Do you know er?

Long form: Do you know him?
Short form: Do you know im?

Long form: I was hurt and angry.
Short form: I was hurt n angry.

B. Listen to these sentences. Do you hear a reduction? Check *Long Form* or *Short Form* as you listen. You will hear each sentence two times.

Examples:

a. She made a lot of friends.
b. She made a lotta friends.

1. They spent a lot of time with us.
2. Cudja explain this?
3. Everything was new n exciting.
4. He had lots of new experiences.
5. After some time, I was able to enjoy the new culture.
6. Let's invite her.
7. Let's invite im.
8. I'll call ya tomorrow.

C. Listen to these conversations. You'll hear reduced forms. Write the long forms. You will hear each conversation two times.

1. A: Do you know <u>her</u>?
   B: Yeah. She's in my history class.
   A: <u>Could you</u> introduce me to <u>her</u>?
2. A: I'm sick <u>and</u> tired of feeling like a foreigner.
   B: I know what you mean. There are a <u>lot of</u> problems in the beginning, but things will get better.
3. A: Where's Bill? Didn't you invite <u>him</u>?
   B: Yeah, but he wasn't <u>able to</u> come.

[Pronounced: er, cudja/er, n, lotta, im, ableta]

Listening 2, page 99:
Talking About Culture Shock

Person 1

I first came here when I was in high school. I was an exchange student in Vancouver, and, uh, I lived with a Canadian family. I guess the kind of weird thing is that I was so excited about being here and, um, learning new stuff, that I wasn't homesick at all. I mean, I stayed in touch with my family back home, but—and maybe this will sound sort of strange—but when I arrived in Canada, I felt right away like I *belonged* here. Then, at the end of the year, it was time to go back home to Russia, and, um, then I got really depressed when I went home. I guess it was sort of culture shock in reverse.

Person 2

Um, I came here to live because my husband got a very good job here. That was twenty-two years ago. And immediately I went into a very severe—a very serious—culture shock. I was *so* homesick, *so* depressed. I didn't want to learn English, I didn't want to learn about this culture, I didn't want American friends. I just went to stores that were, um, where

there was Spanish, and I watched a lot of Spanish-language TV. My friends were all other people from Mexico. I associated only with people from my country even though, you know, I didn't have anything in common with them, really. I mean, I didn't even *like* some of the people I spent time with. It was just that, uh, we were all from the same culture. Back in Mexico we probably never would have been friends. Anyway, I was unhappy and angry for a long, long time. Finally, after about ten years, I went back to Mexico. I thought it would be for good—permanently—not just for a short trip. But it wasn't as great as I remembered. It wasn't really my home anymore. So after only one month, I turned around and came back here to the States. This is my home now. I'm here for good.

Person 3

When I first came to California, everything was difficult in the beginning. I took English classes, but it just seemed so difficult. You know, for Japanese, English is a very hard language. But I met many nice people in my English class, uh, people from many countries. And I made friends from China and Turkey and Brazil. Sometimes we went shopping together or hiking, and sometimes we had a picnic. Then another nice thing happened. Back in Japan I liked art and making things very much, uh, like sculpture and pottery and such things. So I took a class in weaving—you know, making baskets, rugs, and cloth. In this class I met some Americans, and we became friends. One time we went to the Navajo Indian reservation and studied traditional Indian weaving. This was so exciting. Um, I had friends, and I loved Indian art, so I decided to stay in this country and go to college, with a major in American Indian Studies. I was the only Japanese in the department! And so, you see, my experience with culture shock was mostly a very positive one.

Listening 3, page 102:
Two Cross-Cultural Experiences

Person 1

Several years ago, I went to live in Korea for a couple of years. Everything was new to me at first. Some things were similar to the States, but a lot of things were really different.

I had been in Korea for less than a week when I was invited to a truly wonderful dinner. There were many people seated around a long table. And on the table were many, many dishes with a variety of foods. Some were familiar—rice, fish, beef, vegetables such as spinach and cabbage. But some looked really strange. I had no idea what they were. And then I looked to my left and was *shocked* to see a plate of small fried grasshoppers—yeah, that's right, *insects*—the insects that you usually find in your garden, eating up your flowers. I thought, "My God, it seems that people here eat *insects*. If I'm gonna live here, I'll have to learn to eat them, too." But this was very, very difficult to do. I looked at those grasshoppers for a long time, and I imagined them looking at me. I really, *really* didn't want to eat them. Finally, after a long time, I put one in my mouth. It actually tasted pretty good, but it *felt* terrible. I could imagine all those little elbows and knees crunching as I chewed. I ate one more and felt really proud of myself. That night, I wrote letters home, telling my family how people in Korea eat insects.

Anyway, for the next year and a half, I *never saw* another grasshopper—except sometimes in a garden. I asked someone about this once, and he laughed and said, "Oh, nobody here eats grasshoppers. Maybe 500 years ago, kings and queens ate them sometimes, but not now. Nobody now."

Person 2

I was teaching a low-level ESL class one summer at a college in Los Angeles, California. Each day, students spent about ten minutes writing in a journal. They usually wrote about what they had done the day before. (We were working on the past tense.) Anyway, one of my students was new to the United States. He had arrived only two or three days earlier. I wasn't surprised to read in his journal "Yesterday I went to the beach," but I *was* surprised by what he wrote next: "On the beach I saw many elephants and men with no hair. The men were wearing orange dresses." [pause] Now this seemed a little strange to me. Elephants? Men in orange dresses? My student continued in his paragraph. His conclusion was: "American beaches are different from beaches in my country. American beaches have elephants."

Now, this was an absolute mystery to me at first. Then I remembered. There is a religious group called the Hare Krishnas. The men shave their heads and wear orange robes similar to the Buddhists'. And *one day* every year they have a very colorful religious festival at the beach. Part of this festival involves a parade with elephants. And my student just happened to appear on this one day.

CHAPTER 6: WHAT DO YOU MEAN? THOUGHT AND COMMUNICATION

Listening 1, page 117:
Men's Language and Women's Language

Section 1

L.J.: Uh, my impression is that women like to talk a lot, and men don't like to talk at all . . .

D.T.: . . . Yes, the most frequent complaints by women about relationships with men are—number one—he doesn't talk to me and—number two—he doesn't listen to me. . . . Um, you comment that you think women talk a lot. I'd really like to explain that in terms of the following anecdote. I was giving a talk in a living room in a suburban area, and there were women and men there.

There was one couple sitting on the couch, and the woman didn't talk at all; she didn't open her mouth the whole evening, and the man was very vocal—one of the most vocal people in the group. It was the end of the evening. I made the observation that women complain that their husbands don't talk to them, and he volunteered; he spoke up and he said, "That's absolutely right." He pointed to his wife, and he said, "*She's* the talker in our family." And this, I think, really captures the question: Who talks more—women or men? Uh, everybody laughed in the room as you just did, and he looked hurt, and he said, "But it's true! At the end of the day, I come home, and I have nothing to say, and she talks all evening. And if she didn't we'd spend the evening in silence." Who talks more? . . . At home, in what I call private speaking or rapport talk, that's when women talk a lot. In public . . . then it's the man that talks more. And women think men talk too much because they're thinking of the public situation, when they don't talk. And men think women talk too much because they're thinking of the at-home situation, where they don't think talk is necessary.

Section 2

H.F.: I'm not at all surprised when Deborah said, "Women want to keep talking after the argument because for women, talking is intimacy. I mean, when women get together, they sit face to face and talk. . . . And the reverse for men—I mean, men get intimacy, there's a great many psychological studies that men get intimacy out of side-by-side *doing*—doing things together. . . . But I will tell you one thing, um, back to the basics here. I mean, if men really—if a man really wants to, to please a woman, sit down and *talk* to her. . . . And if a woman wants to get along with a man, she should *do* something with him. Pick one thing that that man does and *do* it with him, uh, because that's intimacy to a man.

(Excerpt from *Modern Times with Larry Josephson*, 2/9/91. D.T. is Deborah Tannen, and H.F. is Helen Fisher.)

The Sound of It, page 119: Understanding Reductions

In normal or fast speech, you will hear reductions of some words. Listen to these examples. Can you hear the difference between the long forms and the short forms? (Note: The short forms are not correct in writing.)

Long form: Get out of here.
Short form: Get outta here.

Long form: Give me that book.
Short form: Gimme that book.

Long form: Let me ask you something.
Short form: Lemme ask you something.

Long form: I don't know.
Short form: I dunno.

Long form: You like it, don't you?
Short form: You like it, doncha?

Long form: You liked it, didn't you?
Short form: You liked it, didncha?

A. Listen to these sentences. Do you hear a reduction? Check *Long Form* or *Short Form* as you listen. You will hear each sentence two times.

Examples:
a. <u>Let me</u> help you.
b. <u>Lemme</u> help you.

1. I <u>don't know</u> him.
2. <u>Gimme</u> a minute, will you?
3. <u>Doncha</u> believe it?
4. I took it <u>out of</u> the closet.
5. We <u>dunno</u> her.
6. <u>Let me</u> talk with him.
7. <u>Gimme</u> your opinion.
8. You believed it, <u>didncha</u>?

B. Listen to these conversations. You'll hear reduced (short) forms. Write the long forms. You will hear each conversation two times.

1. A: <u>Didn't you</u> talk with him about how you feel?
   B: Well, I tried to, but he doesn't like to discuss problems. I <u>don't know</u> why.
2. A: <u>Give me</u> the ball!
   B: No! This is our game. You get <u>out of</u> here!
3. A: <u>Don't you</u> think there's a problem?
   B: Yeah, well, maybe. <u>Let me</u> just think about it for a while.

[Pronounced: didncha, dunno, gimme, outta, doncha, lemme]

Listening 2, page 121: Understanding Intonation

Man 1: (utterly bored) Oh, yeah. Beautiful sunrise, dear.

Man 2: (not at all interested in the swimsuit or the woman) Yeah. That's a very sexy swimsuit.

Man 3: (again, completely bored) This is the happiest day of my life, too, honey.

Man 4: (ecstatic; *wild* with excitement) Tickets for the Olympics?!!!! This is fantastic!!!

Language Learning Strategy, page 121: Expressing Emotion with Intonation

Pay attention to people's intonation—not just their words. In English, people show emotion with intonation. When they are enthusiastic (excited) or very happy, their voices go up on stressed words.

There are more "mountains" and "valleys" in their speech:

It's really wonderful.

When people are *not* very enthusiastic or happy, their voices usually don't go up. In the example below, the person *says* "It's really wonderful," but probably doesn't truly think so.

It's really wonderful.

When a person likes another person and wants to be friendly, the voice usually goes up:

Oh, hi. How are you?

When a person does not feel very friendly toward another person, the voice does not usually go up:

Oh, hi. How are you?

A. Listen to these sentences. Are the speakers enthusiastic or friendly, or not? Check your answers. You will hear each sentence two times.

[Note: ✓ = with enthusiam or warmth]

 1. Good morning.
✓ 2. Good morning.
✓ 3. Yeah, I like it.
 4. Yeah, I like it.
 5. It was a good movie.
✓ 6. It was a good movie.
 7. Is this for me?
✓ 8. Is this for me?
✓ 9. It's good to see you.
 10. It's good to see you.

B. When a person shows quiet sincerity (honest, true feelings) the voice might not go up much, but there is probably a small pause between words or word groups.

Example: He . . . is a great . . . friend.

When the person is not very sincere, there is usually no pause.

Example: He'sagreatfriend.

Listen to these sentences. Are the speakers sincere or not? Check your answers. You will hear each sentence two times.

 1. This is a wonderful meal.
✓ 2. This is a wonderful meal.
 3. I had a good time.
✓ 4. I had a good time.
✓ 5. We're very glad to see you.
 6. We're very glad to see you.

 7. She is a really special person.
✓ 8. She is a really special person.

Listening 3, page 124: Talking About Notices

Conversation 1

Man: Hello?

Woman: Hello. I'm calling about a notice for a piano teacher that was on the board at the college?

Man: Oh, yes. Have you been teaching piano for a long time?

Woman: Well, for over ten years.

Man: Great. Do you have a piano?

Woman: Sure. You don't have one?

Man: No.

Woman: Well, we can use mine. Or maybe there's one at the college.

Conversation 2

Woman: Hello. You've reached 555-1563. I'm sorry we can't answer your call right now. Please leave a message at the beep, and we'll get back to you as soon as possible. (beep)

Man: Hello. My name's Dan. It's Monday at 2:00. I'm calling about your ad for a room for rent. Could you give me a call at 555-1165? Please call between 7:00 and 10:00 in the evening.

Conversation 3

Woman: Good <u>morning</u>. Startime <u>Theater</u> Company.

Man: Hello. I'm <u>calling</u> about your help <u>wanted</u> ad at the <u>college</u>. Uh, what kind of <u>job</u> is it?

Woman: Well, you'd be <u>handing out</u> fliers.

Man: <u>Pardon</u>? Could you <u>explain</u> more about that?

Woman: We're <u>opening</u> a new <u>movie</u> theater. We need you to stand on the <u>sidewalk</u> and give <u>papers</u> to people walking by—you know, to advertise the <u>opening</u>.

Man: Oh, OK. Could I make an <u>appointment</u> for an <u>interview</u>?

Woman: Yes, of <u>course</u>. How's <u>Tuesday</u> morning at <u>10:00</u>?

Man: I'm afraid I have a <u>class</u> at that time. Could we make it in the <u>afternoon</u>?

Woman: Sure. How about <u>3:00</u>?

Man: Great.

**Language Learning Strategy, page 128:
Responding to a Negative Question**

Learn how to respond to a negative question—or,
more specifically, a negative statement with intonation that goes up at the end. People often use statement word order to ask a negative question if they
think the answer will be "no." Their intonation
goes up. Here's an example from Conversation 1:

You don't have one?

In many languages, people answer "yes" because
they're thinking, "Yes, that's right. I don't have
one." But in English the answer is "no."

You don't have one?

No, I don't.

A. With a partner, take turns asking and answering
these questions. In each case, answer "no" and give
the correct answer. Then listen and check your
answers.

Example: a: The main language of Quebec isn't
English?

b: No, it's French.

1. a: It's not strange to experience culture shock?
   b: No, it's normal.
2. a: Osaka isn't the capital of Japan?
   b: No, it's Tokyo.
3. a: Men don't usually talk much at home?
   b: No, they talk more in public.
4. a: Women don't usually talk much in public?
   b: No, they talk more in private.
5. a: English isn't easy?
   b: No, it's hard.
6. a: You're not from Canada?
   b: No, I'm from . . . .
7. a: Today isn't Sunday?
   b: No, it's . . . .
8. a: You haven't been to Antarctica?
   b: No, I've never been there.

9. a: You can't call a teacher by her first name in
   your native country?
   b: No, we call her "Teacher."
10. a: College textbooks aren't free?
    b: No, they're expensive.

B. You show surprise in a negative question if your
intonation goes down low and then up high at the
end.

Example: Question: You don't have one?
Answer: No, I don't.

With a partner, take turns asking and answering
these questions. Person A will show surprise in the
question. Person B will answer "no" and add a short
negative answer. Then listen and check your answers.

Example: a: The main language of Quebec isn't
English?

b: No, it isn't.

[intonation in all questions indicates surprise]

1. a: We don't have class tomorrow?
   b: No, we don't.
2. a: You didn't see it?
   b: No, I didn't.
3. a: He doesn't like it?
   b: No, he doesn't.
4. a: They won't even try it?
   b: No, they won't.
5. a: She hasn't studied English before?
   b: No, she hasn't.
6. a: You're not from around here?
   b: No, I'm not.
7. a: You don't know him?
   b: No, I don't.
8. a: They can't help us?
   b: No, they can't.
9. a: There won't be a problem with that?
   b: No, there won't.
10. a: She doesn't eat meat at all?
    b: No, she doesn't.

CHAPTER 7: MAKING FRIENDS AND FINDING LOVE

**Listening 1, page 139:
A New York Story**

I loved being in New York, and I was walking uptown to go and have lunch with the only person

in New York whom I knew well enough to suggest that we have lunch together, which I wasn't
too sure that he wanted to do. It had been my
idea. But it was a big thing for me, coming from
the Midwest, to have lunch with a New York per-

son in New York—kind of a sign that you belonged.

(It was) a summer day. Walking uptown, when out of a shop and turning towards me came a woman in a black dress and beautiful black hair—a woman so beautiful—a woman such as you see sometimes in New York—makes a man want to do anything to get her attention—even for ten seconds. Do anything: drop your briefcase or ask her for the time or sing a song or do a somersault or anything, just anything, to get her attention.

And what I did—and I'm not sure you'll understand this, but it's true, and it's not untypical of me—what I did as I walked towards her was to reach into my pocket and pull out a dime and stop at a parking meter where there was a white Cadillac convertible and put the dime in. And lean against it, hoping she would notice. And she did. She smiled at me, and she said "thank you" and got in and drove away.

(Used by permission of Garrison Keillor. Copyright © 1984 by Garrison Keillor.)

Listening 2, page 140:
Understanding Invitations

Conversation 1

Woman 1: Hello?

Woman 2: Hi, Laurie. This is Sue.

Woman 1: Oh, hi! How are you?

Woman 2: Fine, thanks. Listen, I'm afraid I can't really talk right now. I'm on my way to an interview. I just wanted to ask if you and Jim can come to dinner next Friday night at our place. About 7:00?

Conversation 2

Man 1: Hey, Yoshi. How ya doin'?

Man 2: Hi, Bob. OK, thanks. What's new?

Man 1: Not much. I'll be glad when final exams are over.

Man 2: Yeah. Me too. In fact, I've got one in about five minutes.

Man 1: Well, good luck. Say, why don't we get together and go to a game or something some day, huh?

Man 2: Yeah. Sounds great. I'll give you a call.

Conversation 3

Woman: (laughing): Well, it's been nice talking with you.

Man: Yeah. I'm glad we finally got a chance to meet. Let's get together sometime.

Woman: Yeah. Good idea.

Man: I'll call you, OK?

Conversation 4

Woman (from Conversation 3) (laughing): Well, it's been nice talking with you.

Man (from Conversation 3) Yeah, I'm glad we finally got a chance to meet. Say, I know this is short notice, but if you're not busy tomorrow night, would you like to go to a movie?

Language Learning Strategy, page 140:
Paying Attention to a Speaker's Choice of Words

Pay attention to a speaker's choice of words when the person is a making an invitation. If you do this, you'll know what to expect. There are two kinds of invitations and suggestions in English: specific and general.

Specific:

Can you come to dinner next Friday at 8:00?

Would you like to go to a movie tomorrow night?

General:

Why don't we get together sometime soon?

Let's have dinner or something in a couple of weeks.

Specific invitation are serious. The speaker really wants to get together and needs an answer. General invitations are friendly expressions but are not very serious. The two people might or might not get together. You need to listen for words or expressions that are specific and words or expressions that are general.

Specific: next Saturday   this evening
on May 24th   tomorrow evening   at 7:30

General: sometime   sometime soon   someday
in a couple of weeks   one of these days

Listen to these sentences. Are they serious invitations? Check *Serious* or *Not very serious*. You will hear each sentence two times.

1. Why don't we get together next Saturday for dinner?
2. Can you come over tomorrow evening?
3. Let's have lunch sometime soon.

4. Would you like to go to a concert on Friday night?
5. We should go to a movie or something one of these days.
6. Why don't we get together sometime soon?
7. Can you go to the game with us on Saturday?
8. Let's go shopping together some day.

Listening 3, page 144:
My Honey

One thing couples often do is call each other by nicknames—Sweetheart, Schnookums, Poopsie-Woopsie—which troubled commentator Robert Rand when he was younger.

[Robert Rand:]

"Babe" and "Honey" are my parents. "Babe" is Florence, my mom. "Honey" is my dad, Al. It wasn't until I was eight years old that I realized that "Babe" and "Honey" were monikers of affection, not birth names. Babe and Honey had some rocky times back then. There wasn't enough money, Dad worked the overnight, he disliked her family, and she suffered the abuse and dysfunction of his. So Babe and Honey fought. A lot. . . . But always, no matter what, to each other they remained "Babe" and "Honey." It was, for them, the bottom line, a constant reminder of the love they shared, pet names that rode out adversity and bound their marriage together. I didn't like "Babe" and "Honey"—the names, that is. To my young ears, they sounded embarrassing and yucky. "Babe" was demeaning and sexist. No clearheaded teenager in the 1960s would dare call a woman *that*. As for "Honey," what a wimpy name for a guy, especially my dad. . . . But we are the product of our parents' loins and idiosyncrasies.

Enter Eriko, my wife. I met her one day on a dance floor, three years ago. Babe and Honey, by the way, don't dance. The nightclub was noisy, so our first salutations were shouted but otherwise unexceptional. "Hi," I yelled. "My name is Robert. What's yours?" "Eriko." "Did you say 'Erica' or 'Eriko'?" "Eriko. It's Japanese." "Oh. Call me Rob." And she did, for many months, and to me she remained "Eriko," at least initially.

Then we fell powerfully in love, and our terms of reference began to change. She became "Erichka" or sometimes "Eri-chan." When she told me that as a child, her father used to call her "Tora," which

means "Little Tiger," Eriko became my "Torichka." For her part, Eriko took to the habit of calling me "Sugar," evidence of her fascination with the American South. And she also fancied the full and formal version of my name and used it so sweetly that "Robert" became, for the first time in my life, a label of enormous distinction, something I was genuinely proud of. We married after a year-long courtship and celebrated our vows by dancing at a place called Slin's. And as we settled into this new phase of our relationship, Eriko startled me one day while discussing the most mundane of affairs. "Honey," she said, "do you think it'll rain this weekend?" I let it pass. But I could not dismiss the fact that Eriko, with one word, had turned my legs into noodles and my heart into chocolate pudding. Eriko persisted in calling me "Honey" with such ease and affection that I quickly adjusted to the habit and to the way it made me feel. When she reverted to "Rob," I actually felt disappointed. I asked her one day whether she ever called any of her former boyfriends "Honey." "No, Honey," she said. "That's just for you." And I grinned the profound grin of a man who loves his wife and who has discovered the wisdom of his parents' ways. And now Eriko has become *my* "Honey," and I use the word often when addressing her. But I vow never, ever to call her "Babe."

Commentator and writer Robert Rand lives in New York City.

Listening 4, page 147:
More Than Pasta

[This "radio drama" is an advertisement for Ronzoni pasta. It is entirely in Italian—more specifically, in Italian words for different kinds of pasta, spoken with feeling! The point of this exercise, of course, is not for students to try to understand these words. Instead, they should be using the intonation and sound effects to figure out—in English—what the characters are saying.]

The Sound of It, page 147:
Listening for Stressed Words

A. Listen to these sentences and repeat them. Notice the stressed words.

1. How ARE you?
2. Let's get TOGETHER sometime.

3. I'll give you a CALL.
4. Let's have LUNCH sometime soon.
5. What do you want to get MARRIED for?
6. I was HOPING she would NOTICE.
7. I'll be GLAD when final EXAMS are over.

B. Listen to the important (stressed) words in these sentences. Underline them. (Some sentences have two stressed words.) You will hear each sentence two times.

1. Who IS that?
2. May I ASK you a QUESTION?
3. I'm BUSY that night.
4. I'll CALL you tomorrow MORNING.

5. I have a QUESTION for you.
6. THAT sounds good.

C.

1. Question: Where does she want to GO?
   Answer: She wants to go to a MOVIE.
2. Question: Where does SHE want to go?
   Answer: SHE wants to go to a movie.
3. Question: What did they DO?
   Answer: They got MARRIED.
4. Question: WHEN did they get married?
   Answer: They got married LAST YEAR.
5. Question: What TIME should we MEET?
   Answer: Let's MEET at about 8:00.

CHAPTER 8: TELL ME WHAT I WANT: ADVERTISING . . . AND SHOPPING

Listening 1, page 157:
Understanding a Radio
Advertisement

Narrator: New Hertz location at 222 East 40th Street, with Doris Cardball of Manhattan.

Doris: Hi.

Narrator: . . . who's volunteered to take the "Do I need to get out of the city?" quiz. Just identify the following four sounds. OK—you ready, Doris?

Doris: Sure.

Narrator: Okay. Sound Number 1.

Doris: That would be the sounds outside my bedroom window.

Narrator: Number 2.

Doris: That's the F train. The conductor says we have a holding light and should be moving shortly.

Narrator: Number 3.

Doris: Central Park.

Narrator: And Number 4.

Narrator: Doris?

Doris: I have no idea.

Narrator: Doris?

Doris: Yeah.

Narrator: Perhaps it's time you got out of the city for the weekend.

Doris: Yeah? How?

Narrator: Uh, simple, Doris. You rent a car from Hertz.

Doris: A car?

Narrator: Uh-huh, like a Thunderbird, for only $46.90 a day at any of the ten Hertz locations in Manhattan. Then you can get back to nature.

Doris: This nature?

Narrator: Yeah?

Doris: Does it have parking?

Voiceover: Limited availability. Rates may change without notice. Mileage limits. Significant restrictions. Advance reservations apply. Optional items extra. So call Hertz.

Listening 2, page 160:
Understanding a Message on a
Business Message Machine

Hi, you've reached the Recyclery. We're open 9:00 a.m. to 6:00 p.m., Monday through Saturday; closed on Sunday. We're at 1955 El Camino, across from the university, at El Camino and Stanford Avenue. Please come in and see us—we have both new and used bikes, and we give free estimates for repairs. Thanks for calling.

Listening 3, page 163:
Buying a Computer

Conversation

Clerk: Can I help you?

Customer: I don't know. I was looking at your computers. . . .

Clerk: Uh-huh.

Customer: You have a lot of different machines here. Which model do you recommend?

Clerk: Uh . . . these two models are the most popular.

Customer: How much are they? . . . Oh, I see the prices. . . . This one's so much less expensive! How come?

Clerk: There's a sale this week on Macintosh equipment.

Customer: Is it hard to use?

Clerk: Oh, no. It's easy. The instruction manual explains everything. And if you don't like it, you can bring it back.

Customer: I can?

Clerk: Yeah. Do you want a printer, too? This one is nice.

Customer: Yes, but I'd rather have a laser printer.

Clerk: No problem . . . we can include it for only $100 more.

Customer: Mmm. . . . Well, OK, I really need a computer, and I'd like to get one now. If I can bring it back . . . I guess I'll take it.

Clerk: How will you be paying for this—cash or charge?

Customer: I guess I'll write a check.

Clerk: Cash, then. Let me write this up, and then you just take it over there to the cashier, and she'll take care of it.

Customer: OK.

Clerk: Thanks.

Customer: Thank *you*.

Ad for Apple Computers

Narrator: Apple Computer presents an offer for the indecisive: If you've been thinking about buying a computer . . .

Buyer 1: Well, I did, but then I thought no, but I'm interested . . .

Narrator: . . . but aren't sure, during the Apple free trial run you can take home any qualifying Apple II or Macintosh system and try it out till the end of the year absolutely free.

Buyer 1: Both? Can I get both?

Narrator: Use your free Apple to do everything from writing letters . . .

Buyer 1: To my sister. No, my mom.

Narrator: . . . to business proposals . . .

Buyer 1: I could start a steel mill . . . or a pet shop or . . .

Narrator: . . . and much more. If you like your computer, you can buy it, and if you don't, you can bring it back.

Buyer 1: It's nice to have the option *to* bring it back if I wanted to.

Narrator: Thank you.

Buyer 1: No, I'd keep it.

Narrator: And now Apple Computer presents an offer for the decisive.

Buyer 2: I know exactly what I want.

Narrator: If you already know all the astounding things an Apple can do . . .

Buyer 2: I do.

Narrator: . . . and you're ready to buy one now . . .

Buyer 2: I am.

Narrator: . . . Apple will give you back up to $300 on printers and other qualifying peripherals.

Buyer 2: I want the laser printer, a scanner, and three reams of paper.

Narrator: Just visit your participating authorized Apple dealer.

Buyer 2: 10:00 a.m. Saturday. Beat the crowd.

Narrator: Choose an Apple system and save from $150 to $300.

Buyer 2: Take the money, buy a sweater—blue— and put the rest in the bank.

Narrator: Thank you.

Voiceover: Certain restrictions and credit requirements apply.

Listening 4, page 165:
Understanding an Advertisement

Boss: So if there's nothing else . . . Yes.

Secretary: Emerson would like to say something, sir.

Boss: Who?

Secretary: Emerson, in accounting.

Boss: Who?

Secretary: Emerson, your son.

Boss: Send him in.

Emerson: Hi, uh, I just wanted to say that I think now's a great time for us to switch to an AT&T communication system.

Boss: Why is that?

Emerson: Well, sir, on top of making sure we get just the right phone system and fax machine, backed up by their reliable service, the AT&T small business division is now offering a money-back guarantee.

(Gasp.)

Boss: A what?

Emerson: A money-back guarantee.

(Gasp.) You practice this?

Boss: So we can get a refund?

Emerson: If we're not completely happy, yes sir. Here's AT&T's number: It's 1-800-247-7000.

Boss: Good work, Emerson.

Emerson: Thank you sir. Oh, one more thing: Money-back guarantee.

(Gasp.)

Emerson: I *love* that!

Narrator: The new AT&T no-risk money-back guarantee is just one more reason to call the AT&T small business division at 1-800-247-7000. 1-800-247-7000. AT&T, the right choice.

Listening 5, page 167:
Expressing Agreement and Disagreement

Woman: Hello, officer.

Officer: Lady, did I or did I not just give you a speeding ticket?

Woman: Uh . . . you didn't?

Officer: Did too.

Woman: Did not.

Officer: Did too.

Woman: Did not.

Officer: I can see it right there on your dashboard.

Woman: Oh, all right, you did. Can I go now?

Officer: Lady, what's your problem?

Woman: My problem is I'm in a hurry and you keep stopping me.

Officer: That's no reason to exceed the speed limit.

Woman: It is so.

Officer: Is not.

Woman: Is so.

Officer: Is not.

Woman: Is. Oh, look. I don't have time to chat. It's Saturday night, and it's almost eight o'clock.

Officer: So?

Woman: Get hip, Maynard.

Officer: Maynard?

Woman: It's time for the Fox weekend line-up on WXIN 59.

Officer: Look, I still have to write you up another ticket.

Woman: Beans!

Officer: Pardon?

Woman: *Beans Baxter*, that's one of my shows.

Officer: Uh-huh.

Woman: And *Boys Will Be Boys, Mr. President*, and *Women in Prison*. (laughs) Bet you'd like that one.

Officer: Uh-huh.

Woman: And more great shows on Sunday night.

Officer: Thanks. I'll be sure to tune in.

Woman: Good, 'cause you need to lighten up.

Officer: Here's your ticket, lady. Now don't let me catch you speeding again.

Woman: Oh, you won't.

Officer: Bet I will.

Woman: Won't.

Officer: Will.

Woman: Won't.

Officer: Will.

Woman: Look, would a sweet little lady like me lie?

Officer: Well, I guess not.

Woman: Well, you guessed wrong! (car roars off)

Officer: Lady!

Narrator: Rev up your weekend with the Fox weekend line-up on WXIN 59. Starting Saturday at eight.

The Sound of It, page 170: Understanding Incomplete Sentences

Language Learning Strategy

Understanding incomplete sentences will help your comprehension. Sometimes people leave out (don't say) certain words, but you can still understand the meaning. People leave out words more often in informal speech than in formal speech or writing. The words that they leave out would not be stressed.

A. Listen to these examples of incomplete sentences from this chapter.

Example: You ready, Doris?
Complete: Are you ready, Doris?

Example: We're open Saturday; closed on Sunday.
Complete: We're open Saturday; we're closed on Sunday.

Example: You practice this?
Complete: Do you practice this?

Example: Bet I will.
Complete: I bet I will.

Example: If you already know what an Apple can do . . . I do.
Complete: If you already know what an Apple can do . . . I do already know what an Apple can do.

Example: . . . and you're ready to buy one now . . . I am.
Complete: . . . and you're ready to buy one now . . . I am ready to buy one now.

Notice the last two examples: *I do. I am.* It is very common to answer a question with a short answer.

B. You will hear eight questions. For each question, circle the correct answer.

Example: Do they have a computer?

1. Are you ready to go now?
2. Is Sue coming with us?
3. Does John want to come too?
4. Are you going to drive?
5. Is there a sale at Sam's Sports Shop?
6. Do we need any tennis balls?
7. Are there any sales on bicycles?
8. Are we going to be home by 12 o'clock?

CHAPTER 9: WHAT'S IN THE NEWS?

Listening 1, page 184: Understanding Weather Reports

Weather Report 1

And now for the weather . . . cool and overcast this morning, with scattered showers. Highs in the fifties, lows in the thirties. Possible thunderstorms this afternoon. Back to you, Jack.

Weather Report 2

It'll be hot today, with a high of nearly 100 degrees. Warm and dry—a good day for the beach. Evening lows will be in the seventies. Now here's Frank, with a special report on the water problems in the West. Keep cool!

Weather Report 3

Unusually low temperatures today, folks. Look for a high of only 28 degrees. It may go all the way down to zero tonight. Gusty winds will be coming our way, and watch for icy snow on the roads. And now for the traffic report, here's Kim.

Weather Report 4

Beautiful day out there—not a cloud in the sky. You can look forward to fair weather and blue skies through tomorrow. Highs in the seventies, lows tonight in the fifties. Have a good one!

The Sound of It, page 186: Understanding Numbers

There are many situations where you will need to understand numbers, such as in prices, telephone numbers, and addresses. Learning to understand numbers will improve your listening comprehension in many circumstances. For example, you heard numbers in the weather reports for temperatures.

A. Practice listening for ordinal numbers, which describe order: *first, second, third, fourth, fifth,* and so on. Circle the number that you hear. You will hear each number two times.

1. 14th
2. 20
3. 21st
4. 32nd
5. 63rd
6. 78

B. Practice listening to numbers that end in *-teen* and numbers that end in *-th*. Circle the number that you hear. You will hear each number two times.

1. 13th
2. 15
3. 16th
4. 18
5. 19th

C. Practice listening to other numbers. Circle the number that you hear. You will hear each number two times.

1. 30
2. 4th
3. 5th
4. 16
5. 50
6. 17th
7. 80
8. 22
9. 70
10. 90th

Listening 2, page 189: Identifying News Stories

News Report 1

Do you know what day it is? November 21st—the Great American Smokeout. Today's the day for all you smokers to quit, according to the American Cancer Society. Every year 1.3 million Americans quit smoking, and the total number of Americans who've quit is over thirty-six million. But there are still fifty million who continue to smoke. Smoking is the main cause of preventable death in the United States. If you need help, call the American Cancer Society at 1-800-227-2345. They can send you information on how to quit.

News Report 2

Families will more than double their spending on entertainment and communications between now and the year 2007 as use of the Internet, wireless phones, and cable TV increases, says a new forecast. A typical household will spend more than $4,200 in 2007 on those and other diversions—including movies, newspapers, and sporting events—compared with about $1,900 in 1997. The Internet will show the fastest growth, soaring about 26 percent a year. The cable and satellite TV businesses will grow more than 10 percent a year.

News Report 3

Experts say we might be able to prevent up to 80 percent of all cancers, according to a report out yesterday. The report says that while genes and heredity are important, lifestyle and environment cause most cancers. There are 1 million new cases of cancer in the United States alone every year. Smoking causes over 300,000 of these; what we eat and drink (like fat and alcohol) cause over 200,000 cases, and chemicals in the workplace and environment cause at least 50,000.

The report, from Columbia University professor Dr. Bernard Weinstein, says that we may be able to prevent some cancers soon. Scientists are developing drugs to turn precancerous cells back to normal cells. Also, the National Cancer Institute is developing special foods that may prevent cells from becoming cancerous.

News Report 4

If you're in your early thirties and have never married, you're part of a growing U.S. population group. University of Texas researcher Norval Glenn said yesterday that in 1970 only 9 percent of men between the ages of 30 and 34 had never married; today it's 25 percent. For women, the numbers went from 6 percent to 16 percent. What's the reason for this large increase? Well, part of it is economic, said Glenn. It's harder for people in their twenties to marry and support a family now because their salaries may not be enough to live on. People are marrying later and having children later than they used to. At the same time, some highly educated women do not marry because they are now able to support themselves without a husband. Also, more single people are having or adopting children than in the past. Most singles who have never married seem to be very happy with their lives, according to Glenn.

News Report 5

In 55 years, we may destroy all of the world's tropical rain forests if the current rate of destruction continues. This according to Dr. Norman Myers, an expert on the environment. In a press conference yesterday, Myers said that people have already destroyed half of the world's rain forests, usually by burning them to open land up for agriculture. According to Myers, rain forests hold 70 to 90 percent of the world's plant and animal species. If we destroy these plants and animals, we will change the world forever and lose possible cures for cancer and other diseases.

Listening 3, page 191:
Understanding an Ad for Eyewitness News

Little Girl: Last night Mommy and Daddy said they aren't going to be married anymore and that Daddy's going to live somewhere else, but not very far. He still wants to see me on my birthday and Christmas. And sometimes we'll go to ball games and play catch, and we'll still be best buddies, just like before. Is Mommy being mean to him? But she was crying, too. Maybe he's leaving (whispers) because I did something very bad. But I'll be good now. So he can stay.

Newscaster: Divorce shatters a child's life. But there are ways to ease the hurt, to help your child understand and cope. Diane Allen reports on children of divorce, a special series tonight at 5:30 on Channel 3 Eyewitness News.

Little Girl: I don't know why they're going to be divorced. I hope my mommy doesn't go away too.

CHAPTER 10: PLANETHOOD

Listening 1, page 201:
Helping the Environment

Interviewer: What do you do to help the environment?

Person 1

Well, three days a week I ride my bicycle to work, so on those days I leave my car at home.

Person 2

At the supermarket, you know, when they say, "Plastic or paper?"—well, I don't use either one. I bring two or three heavy cloth bags with me to the store, and I use those. I've been using these over and over for years. I don't use plastic bags.

Person 3

I bought a car that doesn't have an air conditioner. Pretty soon, I hope, all new cars will have special air conditioners that don't use CFCs. But not now. So I just don't have one.

Person 4

I've planted lots of trees around my house. Uh, I'm a member of this organization—Treepeople—and on weekends we go out and plant trees everywhere. And, of course, I always recycle my newspapers. Also, I save water—I use as little water as possible.

Person 5

I don't use laundry detergent when I wash clothes. I use laundry *soap*. There's a difference, you know. Soap doesn't have phosphates which are really bad for life in lakes, rivers, and the ocean. And I don't use any of those chemical cleaners around the house. For example, you know when you have a problem with your kitchen sink or bathroom sink? When the water doesn't go down? Well, I don't pour any of those dangerous chemicals into the sink. Instead I use one cup of baking soda and one cup of vinegar and then some boiling hot water. It works just fine. Good idea?

Person 6

Well, I stopped eating beef about five years ago. My children don't eat beef either. And I hope my grandchildren won't. I think . . . maybe a hundred years from now nobody will be able to eat beef. It's just too terrible for the environment, especially the rain forests.

Listening 2, page 205:
One Solution to the Problem of Plastic

Robert Siegel: (National Public Radio) A team of university scientists has developed a living plant that makes plastic. Yves Poirier, one of the scientists, says the plastic is made through biogenetic engineering. He says it's the genuine article—real plastic with the same chemical structure as that derived from petroleum.

Yves Poirier: (Scientist) This plastic is—is naturally made by a wide variety of bacteria. And what we've basically done is we've taken these genes and put them into plants so that the plant can now produce the same polymer that is normally produced in bacteria.

Siegel: Well, what does it mean to have a plant grow plastic? Where would the plastic be? . . . If this were done with potatoes, would we have tubers which would look on the outside like a potato, but when you opened it up it would all be plastic?

Poirier: Basically, yes, as far as we know. Probably the potato will look the same on the outside, but when you cut it, inside the cell, instead of being starch granules, you would have small granules of the polymer, the plastic.

Siegel: Mm-hmm. What would be the point—of harvesting plastic from, say, potatoes?

Poirier: First, this is a—a truly biodegradable plastic, so the plastic can be completely degraded in soil by soil bacteria, naturally. The second is that this is a renewable source of plastic. Right now the plastic is produced from petrol, a—a finite, nonrenewable source. If we can produce plastic in plants, then you have a renewable source of plastic. . . .

Siegel: Well, do you think that sometime in the next century there'll be acres and acres of farmland and the owners of that farmland will say, "I'm—I'm growing plastic this year"?

Poirier: Well, we believe it's a very realistic possibility.

(From: NPR's "All Things Considered," April 24, 1992.)

The Sound of It, page 208:
Pronouncing the *t* in the Middle of Words

In some words with a *t* in the middle, followed by the sound *-un*, the *-t* is not usually pronounced as English language learners might expect. Listen to these words.

mountain

bitten

certain

To make this sound, the tongue goes up to the roof of the mouth but doesn't come down before the *-un* sound. Listen again and pronounce the words after the speaker.

mountain

bitten

certain

Listen to these sentences and write the missing words. You'll hear each sentence two times.

1. We spent our vacation in Britain.
2. I haven't written to them for several months.
3. He was concerned that the water in the drinking fountain might not be clean, so he drank only bottled water.
4. She found a tiny lost kitten on the sidewalk. She had no idea where the mother cat was.

Listening 3, page 209:
Finding Solutions to
Environmental Problems

Section 1

. . . In a ramshackle, low-income neighborhood called Vista Alegre, women line up for bags of produce distributed by the municipality in exchange for bags of garbage they've collected from the slum. Distributing food to these needy families costs far less than paying waste collectors, and a local woman says this so-called "green exchange" has transformed the neighborhood. She says Vista Alegre before was sad and filthy, but the change it's gone through with the cleanup program, she says, has been like water changing to wine.

Section 2

In another part of town, a garbage truck alerts residents to put out the non-organic trash that they've separated. The city calls the program "Garbage That Isn't Garbage." Officials say that after much prodding by ads on TV and campaigns in the schools, 70 percent of the homes take part in the project. With the help of machines made locally from scrap metal, the trash gets sorted at a recycling center by a group of men and boys. They're part of a human recycling effort. Many of the men were jobless alcoholics, while the boys had mostly been living on the streets. The municipality has found them and other street children part-time work on the condition that they also attend school every day. . . .

Section 3

Michael Cohen is the head of urban development at the World Bank. He thinks Curitiba is way out ahead of most cities in both the developing and the developed world: "The Curitiba response in terms of sound recycling practice and good transport planning and energy conservation and most of all environmental education for citizens is really something that any North American or European city could, could do."

Mayor Lerner thinks so too. But he believes the greatest thing Curitiba has to offer other cities is simply the example of what it's been able to do through perseverance and creativity: "Sometimes there is a kind of syndrome of the tragedy in our cities. That means, 'Oh the problem is so big,' uh, there is no will to change because it's too big, the problem. It's kind of an excuse for not trying to change. And that happens in every city."

(From: NPR's "All Things Considered," May 24, 1992.)

SKILLS INDEX

TOPICS

advertising and shopping
  advertising and shopping: 154–155 (R)
  bicycle store's answering machine message, a: 159–160 (L)
  computer store, a conversation between a customer and a salesclerk in a: 163 (L)
  models in the media and the effect on the public's self image: 172–173 (V)
  telecommunications company, an advertisement for a: 165 (L)
  television network, an advertisement for a: 167 (L)
communication
  communication in the workplace, seminars for improving: 131–132 (V)
  communication styles of men and women, the differing: 117–118 (R)
  intonation, understanding speakers' level of enthusiasm through: 121 (L)
  language and culture, a talk about: 117 (L)
  socialization of boys and girls, the differing: 115 (R)
culture shock
  adjusting to living abroad, journal entries from two students: 93 (R)
  British culture, changes in: 106–107 (V)
  culture shock, a lecture about: 94 (L)
  culture shock, three people talk about their experience with: 99 (L)
  generalizations about culture, two people discuss their experiences making inaccurate: 102 (L)
environment, the
  biodegradable plastics: 206 (R)
  country borders and the environment, changing: 198–199 (R)
  ecotourism in Brazil: 211 (V)
  environment, six people talk about what they do to help the: 201 (L)
  environmental problems of a Brazilian city, a radio report about the: 209 (L)
  plastic and the environment, a radio report about: 205 (L)
health
  American mentality towards staying young and healthy, the: 70 (R)

exercise, five people talk about what they do to get: 76 (L)
  health, contributing factors to good: 69 (R)
  health expert, an interview with a: 82 (L)
  healthy aging, interviews with people from several different countries discussing: 84–85 (V)
  older people, a television show about: 83 (L)
  stress, four people talk about: 78 (L)
identity
  childhood in Ireland, an author recalls his: 63–64 (V)
  childhood, three famous people speak about their: 47 (R)
  goals, four people talk about their: 58 (L)
  interests and hobbies, six people talk about their: 48 (L)
  job, a woman talks about her: 53 (L)
learning
  language in Singapore, the use of: 19–20 (V)
  learning at the family dinner table, a writer remembers how his father encouraged: 5–6 (R)
  learning English effectively, a teacher lectures about: 8 (L)
love and friendship
  affectionate nicknames, an author talks about: 144 (L)
  get a woman's attention, a man recalls a time he wanted to: 138 (L)
  invitations, four conversations involving: 140 (L)
  "romance level," two surveys about different countries': 149 (V)
moving
  directions, a passenger asks two bus drivers for: 33 (L)
  mobility of Americans, an immigrant to California talks about the: 38 (L)
  moving, advice on: 39–40 (V)
  moving in the United States: 25 (R)
  neighborhood directions, one neighbor gives another: 27 (L)
  tenant and her landlord, a conversation between a: 36 (L)
news, the
  global communication, the development of: 178–180 (R)

news stories, five: 189 (L)

television news show, an advertisement for a: 191 (L)

violence in the media: 193–194 (V)

weather reports from the morning news: 184 (L)

small talk

   making small talk, conversations between people: 11 (L)

   specific situations, small talk between people in: 16 (L)

   R = Reading

   L = Listening

   V = Video

LISTENING & SPEAKING SKILLS

advice, giving: 80–81, 95

apology, giving an: 16–17

appointment, making an: 125–128

cause and effect, understanding: 201–202

clarification, asking for: 49–50, 60, 202–203

comparatives and superlatives, using: 182–183

comparing amounts: 78–79

conversational expressions, using common: 16–17

dialogue, creating and practicing a: 34, 35, 163–164, 195

directions, giving, getting, and understanding: 26–31, 33–34

discussion: 4, 6, 10, 24, 26, 36, 41, 46, 48, 50, 52, 53, 58, 59, 70, 78, 83, 84, 94, 95, 100, 101–102, 105, 114, 119, 121, 136, 137, 139, 143, 156, 167, 198, 203, 210

emphasis and repetition in lectures, paying attention to: 8–9

ending a conversation: 16–17

expressing

   agreement and disagreement: 167–169, 194, 195

   desired actions: 137–138

   encouragement: 54, 60

   thanks: 16–17

future, talking about the: 59–60

gerunds and infinitives, understanding: 48–49

goal setting: 3, 23, 45, 67, 91, 111, 135, 153, 177, 197

group work: 12, 28, 29, 64–65, 79–80, 96, 174, 212–213

incomplete sentences, understanding: 170–171

inferences, making: 53, 58–59, 72, 145, 147

interviewing: 20, 40, 107,

intonation, paying attention to a speaker's: 14, 121–123, 147

introducing people: 16–17

invitations,

   making and responding to: 139–143

   paying attention to word choice when a person makes an: 140–141

knowledge, using your background: 112

main idea and supporting details, learning to distinguish between: 99–100

main ideas, listening for: 38, 82, 117, 124, 138–139, 144, 147, 163, 165, 167, 191, 201, 205

message, taking a: 124

music, improving your English by listening to: 41–42, 92

negative questions, learning how to respond to: 128–130

new words, using: 202

nouns, gerunds, and infinitives, understanding: 49

ordering food in a restaurant: 73–74

organizing your ideas before telling a story: 53–54

pair work: 12, 15, 17, 29–31, 34, 35, 52, 73–74, 80–81, 126–130, 142, 148, 163, 168–169, 186

personal questions, asking: 145–146

poll, getting information by taking a: 32, 40, 77, 116, 166–167

practicing English outside the classroom: 160–161

practicing English with native speakers: 11–12

predictions, making listening: 11, 15, 138, 159, 162–163

present and past participles as adjectives, understanding and using: 100–101

pronunciation

   accents, being aware of the differences in English: 85

   can and *can't*, hearing the difference in stress between: 81

   intonation in questions with *or*, understanding: 50–52

   intonation in tag questions, understanding: 13–14

   numbers, understanding: 186–187, 189, 193

   pronouncing the *t* in the middle of words: 208

   reductions, understanding: 36–37, 61–62, 96–97, 119–120

   short answers to yes/no questions, understanding and using: 169–171

   stressed words, listening for and understanding: 55–57, 125, 147–148

recorded messages, understanding: 160–161, 185

report, giving a: 20, 149–150, 174

returns, making store: 165–166

role playing: 12, 17, 73–74, 126–128, 163–164

small talk, making: 10–17, 20, 186

specific information, listening for: 48–49, 72, 77, 83–84, 124, 209–210

strategies

academic power strategies

dictionary definitions, choosing the right: 207–208

goals, setting realistic: 60

groups, working in: 79–80

journal, keeping a: 41

practicing English outside the classroom: 160–161

practicing English with native speakers: 11–12

sharing ideas with your classmates: 143

stereotypes, avoid making: 102–103

stereotypes, becoming aware of and changing your: 118–119

technology, learning about the news while practicing your English using: 180–181

language learning strategies

accents, being aware of the differences in English: 85

brainstorming to explore your ideas, using: 77

emphasis and repetition in lectures, paying attention to: 8–9

incomplete sentences, understanding: 170–171

inferences, paying attention to context in order to make: 145

intonation, paying attention to a speaker's: 14, 121–122

invitation, paying attention to a speaker's choice of words when the person makes an: 140–141

main idea and supporting details, learning to distinguish between: 99–100

negative questions, learning how to respond to: 128–130

new words, using: 202

organizing your ideas before telling a story: 53–54

poll, getting information by taking a: 32

predicting what people will say: 159

stressed words, listening for: 55–57

summarizing what you hear or read: 189–190

taking notes while listening to a lecture: 94–95

tone of voice, being aware of: 33

watching the news on television, improving your English by: 190–191

word parts, understanding: 204

suggestions, making: 95–96

summarizing what you hear or read: 189–190

tag questions, understanding and using: 13–15

taking notes as you listen: 20, 58–59, 78, 94–95, 132, 160, 190

test-taking tips: 20, 42, 65, 89, 109, 133, 150, 174, 195, 213

tone of voice, being aware of: 33

vocabulary activities, listening

check: 24, 97–98, 143, 205

context, guessing meaning from: 7–8, 52, 82, 98, 116–117, 144, 162, 188, 205, 209

matching

words to definitions/synonyms: 24, 33, 37, 94, 165, 191, 201

words to pictures: 138–139

watching the news on television, improving your English by: 190–191, 192

weather reports, understanding: 184

weather, talking about the: 181, 185–186

VIEWING

viewing highlights: 19–20, 39–40, 63–64, 84–85, 106–107, 131–132, 149, 172–173, 193–194, 211

discussion: 19, 40, 64, 107, 131, 132, 172–173, 211

main ideas, viewing for: 19, 63, 106, 131, 149, 172

predictions, making: 39, 106, 121, 149, 172, 193, 211

specific information, viewing for: 19, 39–40, 63–64, 85, 131–132, 149

vocabulary: 18–19, 39, 62–63, 84, 105–106, 131, 148, 172, 192, 210–211

WRITING AND READING SKILLS

advertisements, reading: 157–158, 159, 164, 173

brainstorming: 77, 146, 150

charts and graphs, understanding: 71, 75–76, 87, 182, 184–185

dialogues, writing: 34, 163–164, 169

headlines, understanding news: 187–188
journal, keeping a: 41
log, keeping a vocabulary: 4
making predictions: 4, 46
maps
  creating: 28
  reading: 26–27, 30–31, 199
notice, writing a: 125
previewing: 154
proverbs, understanding: 24
reading comprehension/discussion questions: 6, 26, 48, 57, 70, 94, 115, 118, 156, 180, 198
readings: 5–6, 25, 47, 57, 69, 70, 93, 115, 117–118, 154–155, 178–180, 198–199, 206

summarizing what you hear or read: 189–190, 191
taking notes as you listen: 20, 58–59, 78, 94–95, 132, 160, 190
vocabulary activities, reading
  choosing the correct word: 69
  filling in the "missing" word: 178
  finding a word for a definition: 46
  guessing meaning from context: 68
  matching words to definitions/synonyms: 4–5, 24, 93, 115, 154
  vocabulary check: 24, 68, 154, 178
word parts, understanding: 204
writings, short: 13, 40, 61, 79, 96, 105, 118, 133, 139, 164, 169, 191, 208

PHOTO CREDITS

• •